A Greater Ireland

History of Ireland and the Irish Diaspora

SERIES EDITORS

James S. Donnelly, Jr.
Thomas Archdeacon

A Greater Ireland

*The Land League and
Transatlantic Nationalism
in Gilded Age America*

Ely M. Janis

The University of Wisconsin Press

Publication of this book has been made possible, in part, through support from the **Massachusetts College of Liberal Arts**.

The University of Wisconsin Press
1930 Monroe Street, 3rd Floor
Madison, Wisconsin 53711-2059
uwpress.wisc.edu

3 Henrietta Street, Covent Garden
London WC2E 8LU, United Kingdom
eurospanbookstore.com

Printed in the United States of America

Library of Congress Cataloging-in-Publication Data
Janis, Ely M., author.
A greater Ireland: the Land League and transatlantic nationalism
in Gilded Age America / Ely M. Janis.
pages   cm — (History of Ireland and the Irish diaspora)
ISBN 978-0-299-30124-8 (pbk.: alk. paper)
ISBN 978-0-299-30123-1 (e-book)
1. Land League (Ireland).   2. Irish Americans—History—19th century.
3. Irish Americans—Ethnic identity—History—19th century.
4. Irish Americans—Political activity—History—19th century.
5. Irish Americans—Societies, etc.—History—19th century.
6. Land tenure—Ireland—History—19th century.
7. Ireland—History—1837-1901.   8. United States—History—1865-1921.
I. Title.   II. Series: History of Ireland and the Irish diaspora.
E184.I6J36   2015
305.8916′207309034—dc23
2014012692

To

Ellen

and to

the memory of my mother

Contents

Illustrations

Figures

Tables

Acknowledgments

I have incurred many debts while working on this book and it is a pleasure to recognize them here. At Boston College, it was my good fortune to have Kevin Kenny as an advisor and he remains today a valued mentor and friend. David Quigley and Lynn Lyerly were unfailingly generous with their time, advice, and guidance while serving on my dissertation committee. The members of my writing group, Mark Doyle, Anthony Daly, Meaghan Dwyer-Ryan, and Adam Chill, read early drafts of every chapter and I thank them for their inspiration, good cheer, and camaraderie. Special thanks as well to Jill Bender, Mimi Cowan, Niamh Lynch, and the rest of my fellow graduate students at BC. Kerby Miller, Timothy Meagher, Alison Kibler, and David Brundage read early versions of the manuscript and I thank them for their sage comments and critiques. I have also benefited from the feedback and questions received at various conferences and I would like to thank the members of the American Conference for Irish Studies, Organization of American Historians, and American Historical Association who discussed this project with me and improved it through their comments and suggestions. Gerol Petruzella's help with digitizing the images found in this book is greatly appreciated. Finally, thank you to my colleagues in the Department of History, Political Science, and Public Policy at the Massachusetts College of Liberal Arts for making it such a welcoming and supportive place to work.

I owe a great deal to the staffs of the many archives and libraries I visited. The Burns Library at Boston College was a home away from home, and the Interlibrary Loan Office at the O'Neill Library also provided invaluable help during this project. My heartfelt thanks also goes out to the staffs of the American Irish Historical Society Library, Kenneth Spencer Library at the University of Kansas, Minnesota Historical Society, Missouri Historical Society, National Archives of Ireland, National Library of Ireland, New York Public

Library, Philadelphia Archdiocesan Historical Research Center, and Trinity College Dublin Manuscripts Division.

Several institutions provided financial support for this research. The Irish Studies program at Boston College awarded me with the Adele Dalsimer Graduate Dissertation Fellowship, which was invaluable in helping me complete the first version of this project. I also received much-appreciated research grants from the University of Kansas Kenneth Spencer Library, the Gilder Lehrman Institute of American History, and the American Historical Association.

Parts of chapter 6 originally appeared as "Petticoat Revolutionaries: Gender, Ethnic Nationalism, and the Irish Ladies' Land League in the United States," *Journal of American Ethnic History* 27 (Winter 2008): 5–27, © 2008 by the Board of Trustees of the University of Illinois. My thanks to the University of Illinois Press for permission to reproduce that material here.

The staff at the University of Wisconsin Press have been a joy to work with. The series editors, James S. Donnelly, Jr., and Thomas Archdeacon, provided excellent advice and guidance in shaping this book. I would also like to thank the two anonymous readers who reviewed the manuscript and the acquisitions and editorial staff at the press who helped me to hone the manuscript into this finished product.

I have also been blessed by the love and support of my friends and family. They have provided much-needed perspective and enjoyment away from this project. Many of them were also gracious enough to open their doors to me while I was doing research away from home. My heartfelt thanks to all of you. My parents, John and Toni, have been a source of inspiration and I cannot convey enough my love and admiration for them both. Clara and Declan grew up with this book and I thank them for putting up with their dad's late night writing sessions and grumpy mornings.

My wife, Ellen, deserves much more recognition than I can possibly give here. Her love, faith, patience, and support has been inextinguishable and has made this book—and so much else—possible. This book is dedicated to her.

Abbreviations

AOH	Ancient Order of Hibernians
BC	John J. Burns Library, Boston College, Chestnut Hill, MA
CTAU	Catholic Total Abstinence Union of America
ICBU	Irish Catholic Benevolent Union
NAI	National Archives of Ireland, Dublin
NLI	National Library of Ireland, Dublin
NYPL	Manuscripts and Archives Division, New York Public Library, New York, NY
PAHRC	Philadelphia Archdiocesan Historical Research Center, Wynnewood, PA
TCD	Manuscripts Division, Trinity College Dublin

A Greater Ireland

Introduction

The cause of the poor in Donegal is the cause of the factory slave in Fall River," proclaimed Patrick Ford, editor of the radical New York newspaper *The Irish World and American Industrial Liberator*.[1] This statement demonstrates the strong transatlantic connections that existed between Irish immigrants in the United States and their countrymen in Ireland in the 1880s. Irish-American nationalism in the Gilded Age was a genuinely transnational movement, with major figures from both sides of the Atlantic, such as Ford, Henry George (the Anglo-American land reformer and author of *Progress and Poverty*), Charles Stewart Parnell (leader of the Irish Parliamentary Party at Westminster), and Michael Davitt (former Fenian and social reformer) participating in Irish and American social and political movements simultaneously.

This book is a study of transatlantic nationalism in the Gilded Age and its impact on Irish immigrants in America. During the early 1880s a continual interplay of events, ideas, and people in Ireland and the United States created a "Greater Ireland" spanning the Atlantic that profoundly impacted both Irish and American society. This "Greater Ireland" presented new opportunities for groups like the working class and women to contribute within Irish-American society. But it also ultimately limited these groups' long-term participation in Irish-American nationalism.

A close examination of the Irish National Land League, a transatlantic organization with strong support in Ireland and the United States in the 1880s, reveals how this "Greater Ireland" worked. Michael Davitt and Charles Stewart Parnell founded the Land League in Ireland in 1879, against the backdrop of crop failure and agrarian unrest. It soon had branches throughout the Irish diaspora, including Canada, Australia, and Britain as well as the United States. The Land League's purpose was to pressure the British government to reform the Irish landholding system and allow Irish political self-rule. In 1880 both

Davitt and Parnell undertook fundraising tours of the United States, and an American Land League quickly spread across America, with hundreds of thousands of Irish Americans participating in branches in their local communities. In Ireland the Land League was suppressed by the British government in 1881, and its efforts left a mixed record, falling short of the sweeping social and economic reforms favored by radicals in the movement but achieving limited land reform and propelling the cause of Irish Home Rule to the forefront of British politics. In the United States participation in the Land League deeply influenced a generation of Irish-American men and women and shaped the future direction of Irish-American nationalism.

Understanding Irish-American Nationalism

Historians have differed over the origins and meanings of Irish-American nationalism. Thomas N. Brown, in his pioneering and enduring work on the Irish in America, argued that Irish-American nationalism was based on American conditions, with its roots found in "the realities of loneliness and alienation, and of poverty and prejudice."[2] The loneliness of life in the United States prompted immigrants to fraternize with other Irish-American men and women from diverse parts of the island, eroding "countyism" and encouraging nationalist sentiments. Irish-American nationalism also served as a response to Protestant American hostility against the Irish. While Brown acknowledged the importance of Irish-American working-class radicalism, he argued that what the Irish in America ultimately hoped to achieve through Irish-American nationalism was to become "middle-class and respectable."[3]

Some scholars have taken issue with Brown's focus on assimilation through respectability. Eric Foner challenged Brown's argument and focused instead on the working-class dimension of Irish-American nationalism. He argued that while nationalism did serve as a vehicle of assimilation for Irish Americans, this assimilation did not have to mean an accommodation with the "dominant culture and its values, but with a strong emergent oppositional working class culture."[4] Foner believed that Irish-American nationalism in the late nineteenth century not only helped to shape the Irish-American working class but also demonstrated "the complex interplay of class, ethnicity, and radicalism in industrializing America."[5]

Victor Walsh and David Emmons criticized Brown and Foner for their emphasis on class and assimilation. In a study of the Irish-American community of Pittsburgh, Pennsylvania, Walsh argued that historians must consider the cultural and geographical antecedents of Irish immigrants and that they have underestimated the "class and cultural diversity of nineteenth-century Irish-American behavior."[6] David Emmons also rejected key tenets of Brown's and Foner's analysis. Basing his argument on his study of Irish workers in Butte, Montana, Emmons posited that the Irish there created "an ethnic-occupational community whose values reflected neither middle-class nor self-consciously oppositional working-class values but rather came from the work most of them did and, quite literally, the company they kept."[7] Within this Irish-American community there was no need to assimilate into American middle-class or working-class culture. Thus, for Walsh and Emmons, Irish-American nationalism involved interplay between the regional, cultural, and economic differences among Irish Americans.

As this book demonstrates, Irish-American nationalism was malleable and flexible enough to exist along a broad spectrum of ideological, political, and social opinion. The various interpretations of the subject therefore need not be mutually exclusive. This study of the Land League in the United States finds much that is still useful in all of them.[8] While Brown and Foner clearly mapped out the ideological divisions among middle-class and working-class Irish-American men, this book expands on their conception of Irish America. In a testament to the strength of his scholarship, much of Brown's analysis of the motivations of middle-class Irish-Americans remains persuasive. But the current study deepens his arguments by incorporating the voices of local Irish-American male and female members and branches of the Land League alongside those of national leaders.[9] It also widens Foner's examination of working-class radicalism, exploring further the links between Irish-American social radicals and broader American reform. The Land League appealed to both working-class and middle-class Irish Americans simultaneously, and both groups waged a fierce ideological struggle over the future direction of Irish America. It is also true that in places like Pittsburgh and Butte, Irish county origin and local economic opportunities were foremost in shaping local Irish-American responses. The present study reflects this diversity of the Irish in America and is the first major synthesis of this period since Brown's book was published in 1966.

The major points of departure for this project from earlier examinations of Irish-American nationalism are twofold. First, events in Ireland were crucial in providing the possibility for previously ignored groups, particularly working-class radicals and Irish-American women, to come forward and attempt to carve out their own space within Irish-American nationalist debate. Yet events in Ireland ultimately curtailed the ability of these groups to continue these efforts. Second, this work demonstrates the vibrant and vital role of Irish-American women within the Land League movement, a role often overlooked by previous scholars. Women were front and center in supporting Irish-American nationalism, and any examination of the Land League must also focus on their important contributions to the movement.

Many Land Leaguers recognized the transatlantic scope of the Land League and talked of a "Greater Ireland" that encompassed all the Irish people in the United States and Ireland. They believed that the support of this meta-nation would ensure the Land League's success. In a letter to British Prime Minister William Gladstone, Patrick Ford, the radical editor of the *Irish World*, warned, "You are now, unlike the past, dealing with two Irelands. The Greater Ireland is on this side of the Atlantic. This is the base of operations. We in America furnish the sinews of war. We in America render moral aid."[10] The New York–based newspaper the *Irish-American* held that there existed a mass of "Irish emigrants and their descendants, who, having been driven out of their native home . . . would eagerly take advantage of any opportunity to retaliate on their hereditary foe, and aid their kindred in shaking off her yoke."[11] With the increased pace of communication through the widespread dissemination of Irish-American ethnic and Catholic newspapers, the laying of the transatlantic cable, and the shortening of travel time between Ireland and America through the use of steamships, Irish Americans were able to keep pace with events in Ireland and with the speeches and statements made by Irish nationalists in Ireland and the United States. Parnell and Davitt exploited this new awareness by framing their appeals to the Irish at home and abroad and, in the process, becoming international celebrities.

The high level of support for the Land League provided by Irish America worried the British government and presented British ministers with a difficult dilemma in dealing with the Irish agitation. British Home Secretary Sir William Harcourt voiced this frustration. "In former Irish rebellions the Irish were *in Ireland*. We could reach their forces, cut off their reserves in men and money and then to subjugate was comparatively easy," he wrote. "Now there is an Irish nation in the United States, equally hostile, with plenty of money, absolutely beyond our reach and yet within ten days sail of our shores."[12] The safe haven created in the United States generated money and rallied public opinion in ways that kept the Land League in Ireland going. But its impact on Irish Americans was also profound.

The "Greater Ireland" created during the Land League era and the transatlantic connections with Ireland that came out of it are central to understanding Irish-American nationalism. Events in Ireland mobilized Irish Americans in unprecedented numbers and had dramatic effects on the Irish-American community.[13] Certainly other examples of transatlantic connections in Irish-American nationalism were found during the nineteenth and early twentieth centuries, such as the Repeal movement of the 1840s, the Fenian movement of the 1860s, and the final push for Irish independence from 1916 to 1921. But the Land League in the United States is different because of its much larger size relative to the Repeal and Fenian efforts, its inclusion of all divergent strands of Irish-American nationalism into one movement, and its attempted linkage of Irish and American social reform together.

Three competing strands of Irish-American nationalism were active in the Land League: physical-force, conservative, and radical nationalism. All three strands sought the independence of Ireland, but each advocated different methods and goals. Physical-force nationalism, espoused by the New York–based political exile John Devoy and his followers, argued that Ireland would be freed only by an armed and violent revolution to permanently remove British influence in Ireland. During the years the Land League existed, American physical-force nationalists were willing to cooperate with Parnell's parliamentary strategy, believing that Ireland was not yet ready for a successful revolution and that a mass movement like the Land League was the necessary first step in creating a nationalist consciousness among the Irish population. Conservative nationalists supported the League's attempts to reform the Irish land system, but they favored only reform, not revolution. Embracing the goal of parliamentary reform personified in Charles Stewart Parnell, they hoped to remove the stain of colonial status cast on them by British control of Ireland and aimed to assert their fitness for full inclusion in middle-class American society. In contrast, radical nationalists pursued a much more sweeping agenda of social and economic change in Ireland. Popular among many Irish-American workers, radical nationalism linked the struggle in Ireland with a similar desire to dramatically alter the economic and political system in the United States.

In their examinations of radicalism and conservatism in Irish-American history, scholars have generally overlooked the role of gender. They have also largely underestimated the participation of Irish-American women in ethnic voluntary associations and benevolent societies linked to Irish nationalism.[14] But in fact large numbers of Irish-American women eagerly forged and participated in a dynamic Ladies' Land League organization in the United States.[15] Fanny Parnell, a sister of Charles Stewart Parnell, founded the first branch of the Ladies' Land League in New York City in October 1880. Women of different social classes and marital states participated together in the movement. As with its male counterpart, branches quickly spread across North America, ranging from Boston to San Francisco. Irish-American women took the opportunity presented by Irish-American nationalism to participate in the public sphere. Using nationalist rhetoric, many Irish-American women challenged traditional gender norms and asserted their fitness for a public role in their communities. As was the case with men, however, class and ideological differences divided the women, and dissensions emerged between Irish-American women over their role in the struggle for Irish liberation. Despite these divisions, however, Irish-American women were active participants in the negotiation of their ethnic identity; their inclusion is crucial to understanding the possibilities and limitations inherent in the transatlantic debate over Irish-American nationalism.

Irish-American nationalism also had significant repercussions outside the Irish-American community. This book shows that Irish Americans used the politics of Irish freedom to shape their own lives while also influencing American society and social reform in the Gilded Age. One area where this was evident was in Irish-American interest in land reform in the United States as well as in Ireland. The Land League served as a bridge between the American agrarian movements of the 1830s and 1840s and the Populist movement of the 1890s. At almost the same time that Irish Americans were active in the Land League, farmers in the Midwest were calling for land reform and African Americans in the South were struggling for access to land in order to provide a firm foundation for their newly won freedom.[16] An understanding of the Land League movement in the United States illustrates the continued significance of landed property as a social and political question in American history up through the late nineteenth century.

Within "Greater Ireland," these conservative, physical-force, and radical Irish-American voices were brought together into one organization. The Land League was like an image seen through a kaleidoscope, with each group and individual seeing the movement through its own preoccupations and concerns. Their cooperation was temporary and the organization shortly began to tear at the seams. Yet this tearing does not diminish the Land League's importance; in fact, despite its short lifespan, through the widespread mobilization of the Irish-American community in the United States in the Land League, it is possible to understand the fluid process inherent in the formation of Irish-American nationalism and, simultaneously, immigrants' influence on and incorporation into mainstream American society. The Land League provided an opportunity for radicals and women in the United States to assert their right to inclusion within the debate, hitherto dominated by middle-class males, about what it meant to be Irish and American in the late nineteenth century.

New Departures

The Land League emerged out of the listless and directionless condition in which Irish nationalism found itself by the early 1870s. Constitutional nationalism had lacked widespread appeal since the fall of Daniel O'Connell's Repeal movement of the 1840s. The Irish parliamentary leader Isaac Butt's labors to achieve limited self-rule, or home rule, for Ireland were ignored in Parliament. It seemed to many of his supporters that his efforts were at a standstill.[17] Supporters of physical-force nationalism were in a similar state of drift. Prior Irish attempts at violent revolt had failed miserably. In 1848 the Young Irelanders, inspired by the revolutionary rhetoric emanating from the European continent, struck against English control, but their efforts were frustrated by British infiltration and the suppression of the movement. Most of the key leaders were arrested and exiled to Australia and other locations, though many eventually settled in the United States. The Fenian movement of the mid-1860s, which mobilized thousands of Irish men in Ireland and the United States in support of the cause of Irish freedom, collapsed amid factionalism and futile gestures of defiance against Great Britain.[18] Irish nationalism in the 1870s needed a new direction in order to be effective and relevant once again.

The solution to this apathy was found not in Ireland but in the United States. The person most important in this reassessment of Irish nationalism was John Devoy, a former Fenian organizer in Great Britain who spent five years in a British jail for his efforts. Released in 1871 on condition that he settle outside the United Kingdom, Devoy made his way to New York City. He quickly began a career as a journalist, working as a reporter for the *New York Herald*.[19] He also joined the hard-line Irish-American secret society Clan na Gael, an organization committed to ending British rule in Ireland, and quickly rose to a leadership position in that organization. Devoy, a dedicated revolutionary (Brown describes him as "the ideologue, the Lenin, of Irish-American nationalism") unhappy with the course of Irish nationalism, began to think about how to reinvigorate the cause.[20]

The American origins of this reconfiguration of Irish nationalism were not accidental. It is estimated that in 1880 there were roughly 1.85 million Irish-born immigrants alongside another 3.24 million American-born Irish Americans in the United States.[21] The Irish were firmly enmeshed in American political, social, and economic life. Nevertheless, the cultural and social status of the Irish in America was far from being fully settled. Protestant reformers and nativists continued to portray the Irish as feckless, lazy, and drunken people who disturbed the peace and attempted illegitimately to usurp electoral power through their close association with urban political machines and bosses.[22]

One response to these challenges and stereotypes was the emergence of a strong Irish-American nationalism dedicated to achieving Irish freedom from British rule while also gaining acceptance and respect for Irish immigrants in the United States. Irish immigrants used nationalism to construct an ethnic identity as "Irish Americans." For the Irish in America, old-world nationalism was pivotal in creating new ethnic identities while simultaneously helping immigrants and their stock to become "Americans." With Devoy's intervention Irish Americans would also help to shape Ireland's response to the shifting social and political conditions facing Ireland in the late 1870s.

Michael Davitt was Devoy's most important Irish ally in this refiguring of Irish nationalism. Born in 1846 in Straide, Co. Mayo, Davitt spent only a brief time in Ireland as his family was evicted from their home when he was four. The eviction had a lasting effect on Davitt's worldview.[23] Like many Irish families, the Davitts immigrated to England, settling in the industrial city of Haslingden. At the age of nine Davitt went to work in the local cotton mills, but two years later his right arm had to be amputated as a result of an industrial accident. After the accident Davitt attended school and received a solid early education. At nineteen he became involved with the Fenians and was arrested and convicted for attempting to smuggle guns into Ireland.[24] After seven years in prison under harsh conditions, Davitt was released on a ticket-of-leave in 1877 and traveled to America to visit his family and give a series of speeches before Irish-American audiences. An idealist and supporter of various causes such as anti-imperialism and labor reform, Davitt had a long career as an advocate of social reform in Ireland and beyond.

In 1878 Devoy and Davitt, both in the United States, began to formulate a strategy for Irish nationalism that soon became known as the "New Departure." The policy that gradually emerged was a desire to link constitutional and physical-force nationalists on both sides of the Atlantic together in one movement. Advocates of physical-force nationalism pledged a temporary alliance with the constitutional efforts of members of the Irish Parliamentary Party to achieve reform in Ireland. Devoy hoped that this strategy would help to create a popular nationalist feeling in Ireland and, if British officials refused to yield reforms, result in a unified nationalist party comprising both parliamentarians and revolutionists. The key to effecting this unification was a commitment by both sides to reforming the Irish landholding system, an issue that appealed strongly to a majority of the Irish population.[25] Davitt and Devoy reached out to Charles Stewart Parnell, a leader of the obstructionist wing of the Irish party in Parliament, who in 1878 was still a relatively unknown figure both at home and abroad. While Parnell continued to maintain his freedom of action and kept his own counsel, in effect a partnership had been formed between the three men to work together to achieve common interests.

The proposed alliance offered by the New Departure was pushed forward by the outbreak of agrarian crisis in the Irish countryside in 1879. A combination of bad weather, poor crop yields, and low agricultural prices sparked widespread unrest among the agrarian population in the west of Ireland. In County Mayo Davitt and a group of activists helped organize a series of mass meetings designed to arouse the local population to resist evictions and to protest agricultural conditions in Ireland. On 16 August 1879 they established the National Land League of Mayo. Two months later, on 21 October, the Irish National Land League was founded in Dublin, with Charles Stewart Parnell as its president. For the next three years the Land League agitation mobilized the Irish Catholic population to reform the Irish land system and to acquire "the land for the people." This popular phrase was sufficiently vague to be acceptable to all shades of nationalist opinion. The founders of the New Departure held differing interpretations over the best way to solve the Irish land question, ranging from peasant proprietorship (the conversion of tenants to owner-occupiers) to more radical solutions to the land problem.[26] An unwieldy coalition of disparate groups, the Land League eventually collapsed under the weight of ideological and class divisions.[27] But during its brief existence from 1880 to 1883 in the United States (the Land League was suppressed in Ireland in 1881), the Land League mobilized hundreds of thousands of men and women, ready to organize for the homeland, and played a large role in determining the future of Irish-American nationalism.

This study is divided into three sections. The first part, comprising chapters 1 and 2, discusses the transatlantic origins of the Land League. Chapter 1 demonstrates the importance of Charles Stewart Parnell's 1880 tour of the United States in making the Land League a transatlantic phenomenon and in assisting Parnell's ascendancy as the preeminent Irish nationalist leader of his era. By combining his appeal for political support with a humanitarian plea for aid to Ireland's struggling agrarian masses, Parnell rallied and mobilized ordinary Irish Americans across class and ideological lines to support the Land League. Besides raising huge sums of money, Parnell's tour catapulted him into the role of the recognized leader of the Irish at home and abroad. Before returning to Ireland, Parnell also helped to facilitate the organization of the Irish National Land League of America. The organization was the most representative Irish-American nationalist movement of the nineteenth century, bringing together under one banner the various elements of Gilded Age Irish-American society.

Michael Davitt's 1880 visit to America is the focus of chapter 2. Davitt applied his brilliant organizational skills to keep the Land League in the United States going during the first few months after its founding, a period marked by poor Irish-American leadership and stagnation. His close relationship with the leaders of the competing factions among Irish-American nationalists helped to prevent the movement from splintering into open conflict. Upon his return to Ireland in late 1880, Davitt was arrested by the British government, and his incarceration sparked a resurgence of the Land League in the United States as Irish Americans rallied to show their support for Davitt and the widening movement in Ireland. The reaction of Irish Americans to Davitt's arrest demonstrates the importance that events in Ireland continually had in helping to shape expressions of Irish-American nationalism in the United States.

Part II details the effects of the Land League in the United States. The third chapter examines the spread of the Land League across the American continent. Land League members resisted attempts to control the movement through a centralized leadership, allowing ideological and regional differences to exist within the movement and helping to spur a healthy rivalry among branches that increased membership and fundraising totals. The organization's growth was also stimulated by the approval given to it by the American Catholic authorities and by already established Irish-American groups like the Ancient Order of Hibernians and Clan na Gael.

The next two chapters discuss the goals and attitudes of Irish-American conservative and radical nationalists active in the Land League. Chapter 4 analyzes the ways in which support of the Land League among conservative nationalists became entwined with their efforts to secure social respectability and inclusion within the broader American society. Helping to free Ireland, they believed, would assist conservative Irish Americans in achieving this goal. Chapter 5 investigates the very different vision of the Land League advocated by Irish-American radical nationalists. The social radicalism of Patrick Ford and the *Irish World* attracted the support of prominent labor leaders and social theorists like Terence V. Powderly of the Knights of Labor and the social reformer Henry George. Irish-American workers and radicals argued for a critique of Irish and American society that rejected a middle-class or bourgeois view of the Land League.

I argue in chapter 6 that the inclusion of Irish-American women's participation in the Land League is necessary to fully understand the effect of Irish-American nationalism on Irish-American identity in the nineteenth century. Underappreciated by most historians, Irish-American women's membership in the Ladies' Land League in the United States was an important first step in Catholic women's participation in the public sphere. Organized by prominent women like Fanny Parnell and Ellen Ford, members of the Ladies' Land League used Irish nationalism to promote a broader and more vocal role for themselves in Irish-American society.

Part III deals with the end of the Land League in Ireland and the United States. In chapter 7 I argue that the No-Rent Manifesto, issued by the imprisoned male Irish Land League leaders in late 1881, sparked a flurry of activity among radical Irish-Americans but fatally exposed the ideological divisions inherent in the American Land League. The Ford wing of the Land League embraced the manifesto, showing their approval with steady donations and expressions of support for this radical document. They were joined by important segments of the American labor movement, which echoed their endorsement of the Land League's policies. Conservative nationalists in Ireland and the United States, however, saw the No-Rent Manifesto as a dangerous slide toward extremism and social disorder. Chapter 8 discusses the conservative backlash within the Land League in the United States and Ireland. While the mass agitation in Ireland during the heyday of the Land League gave Irish-American radicals and women an opportunity to assert their own visions of Irish-American nationalism, the move in Ireland by Charles Stewart Parnell to close down the organization in favor of an alliance with Gladstone's Liberal party and a strictly parliamentary pursuit of home rule seriously weakened these groups' authority.

The Ladies' Land League in Ireland, under attack by conservative nationalists and church authorities, dissolved rather than submit itself to male control, and Irish women found themselves pushed into a subordinate position in Irish nationalist activities for a generation. In the United States there was no explicit ban on women's continued participation in the Land League, but women were thrown on the defensive by attacks from Catholic bishops and received only tepid endorsement from their erstwhile supporters. Irish-American women increasingly retreated from involvement in Irish nationalism; they moved instead to join or back other Catholic and Irish-American benevolent societies and did not mobilize in similar numbers or passion on behalf of nationalist efforts for a generation.

Radical nationalists, their influence limited by conservative resistance, also retreated from the League, spending their energies instead participating in a variety of American reform and labor movements. The dissolution of the Land League in favor of the Irish National League in April 1883 signaled the victory of a conservative Irish nationalism in the United States and Ireland that separated social reform and radicalism from Irish-American nationalism until the early twentieth century.

PART I

THE TRANSATLANTIC ORIGINS OF THE LAND LEAGUE

The "Uncrowned King of Ireland"

Charles Stewart Parnell's 1880 Mission to America

Parnell's Voice
To-day, to-day, there is a voice,
Beyond old ocean's roar,
That bids poor Ireland's heart rejoice,
And bound as proudly as of yore.
A great man fills a great man's place;
His words are full of balm—
The wondering crowds his action trace,
While tyrants dread his calm.
Parnell's Land League Songster

Standing on the deck of the steamship *Baltic*, during its slow retreat from New York harbor, Charles Stewart Parnell, the already famous Irish member of Parliament (MP) and president of the Irish National Land League, took a last look to the shore. Braving a cold and blustery March afternoon, hundreds of supporters, including members of the famous Civil War Irish Sixty-Ninth Regiment, representatives of several Irish-American societies, and local dignitaries, stood at the wharf bidding him farewell. It was an impressive scene. Having arrived in America only three months earlier, Parnell had undertaken a whirlwind cross-country tour in which he traveled over sixteen thousand miles, spoke in sixty-two cities, addressed a joint session of Congress, and raised over $300,000 for famine relief and the Land League.[1] Parnell had pushed the crisis in Ireland to the front pages of American opinion, in the process assuming the undisputed leadership of the Irish at home and abroad. His secretary T. M. Healy, in light of the tour's success, christened Parnell the "Uncrowned King of Ireland."[2]

Parnell's tour of America was enormously successful. Building on the connections made during the late 1870s between Irish and Irish-American nationalists during the "New Departure," Parnell's mission to America was crucial in bringing ordinary Irish Americans into the Land League. Alternatively presenting himself as a moderate reformer and a committed revolutionary, Parnell crafted an image of himself that appealed to both revolutionary Irish-American nationalists and more conservative, affluent Irish Americans. In addition, through the publicity given to his speeches and parliamentary movements in both American and Irish newspapers, his tour helped create a "Greater Ireland," which linked the Irish at home with the Irish abroad. The success of Parnell's tour in achieving this objective helped cultivate Irish-American sympathy and create a reservoir upon which Irish leaders would draw for the next fifty years.

While Parnell's tour played a major role in creating a "Greater Ireland," the Land League in the United States was organized mainly through Irish-American efforts, and Irish Americans resisted dictation from Ireland. Instead, constant negotiations characterized the relationship between nationalists in Ireland and the United States, as Irish Americans used their participation in the movement to push forward their own agendas and ideas.

The Origins of the Land League Movement in Ireland

Before Parnell's tour of the United States is examined, it is necessary to briefly explore the important ideological, economic, and political changes that had begun earlier in the nineteenth century in Ireland and among the Irish in America. The formation of the Land League in 1879 can be understood only as a culmination of these earlier developments.

The origins of nineteenth-century Irish nationalism can be found in the failed United Irish rebellion of 1798. Inspired by the American and French revolutions, the Society of United Irishmen was founded in Belfast and Dublin in 1791 to advocate Irish parliamentary reform and relief for Catholics from the discriminatory Penal Laws.[3] Radicalized by the growing conflict between

France and Britain, the United Irishmen formed an alliance with the widespread Catholic Defender movement to seek Irish independence from Britain. Owing to severe British military repression, however, most of the United Irish leaders and many of their followers had been imprisoned by the time that the rebellion broke out in May 1798, and the French expeditionary force that arrived in the following August was too small and too late. As a result, British troops under Marquis Cornwallis crushed a short but violent revolt. In the aftermath of the failed uprising the Irish Parliament was persuaded in 1800 to accept its own dissolution and to transfer the governance of Ireland to the British Parliament under the Act of Union. Many former United Irishmen made their way to the United States, where they helped preserve and pass on the memory and legacy of Irish republicanism to future generations.[4]

The cause of reform in Ireland was revived in the 1820s under the leadership of Daniel O'Connell, a Catholic barrister and politician. Despite the earlier removal of many anti-Catholic restrictions, the bar against the holding of seats in Parliament by Catholics remained. O'Connell's political genius lay in mobilizing the Irish population to an extent rarely seen before. Unlike almost all earlier movements, O'Connell reached out and obtained support across a broad spectrum of Ireland's Catholic community, including the rural poor and the Catholic clergy. Such was the political strength of O'Connell's mass agitation, with its implicit threat of revolution, that the British government under Sir Robert Peel and the Duke of Wellington acquiesced in the admission of Irish Catholics to Parliament and their eligibility for most high civil and military offices. These concessions, known as "Catholic emancipation," were enacted in April 1829.

Buoyed up by his victory in achieving Catholic emancipation, O'Connell subsequently turned to securing Irish legislative independence by attempting to repeal the Act of Union. Initially, there was widespread popular support for the Repeal movement among the Irish population at home and in the United States. Adopting many of the techniques of mass mobilization perfected during the fight for Catholic emancipation, O'Connell hoped again to pressure the British government into submitting to popular demands.[5] He was also able to draw on the enthusiasm and support of thousands of Irish-American men and women and of Repeal Associations that sprouted up across the United States. But whereas the British had been willing to accede to demands for ending discrimination against Catholics in Ireland, most British politicians saw the abolition of the Irish legislative union with Britain as a step too far; it seemed to risk the unraveling of the whole justification for the British Empire.[6] In a tense showdown between Prime Minister Robert Peel's administration and O'Connell's huge Repeal movement, O'Connell backed down and called off a mass meeting scheduled at Clontarf in October 1843 in the face of threats of a British crackdown. The Repeal movement also suffered when O'Connell alienated Irish-American supporters by advocating the abolition of African-American slavery and by publicly pledging his loyal support for Britain in case war were ever to break out with the United States. Facing a nativist backlash and eager to demonstrate their bona fides as loyal Americans, Irish Americans roundly condemned O'Connell, and the American Repeal movement collapsed.[7]

O'Connell's leadership of the nationalist movement was openly criticized by a group of young nationalist activists known collectively as Young Ireland. Led by Thomas Davis, Charles Gavan Duffy, John Blake Dillon, and John Mitchel, Young Ireland constituted a diverse group inspired by the romantic nationalism spreading across Europe at this time. In their newspaper the *Nation* they attempted to draw on Ireland's Gaelic cultural past to create a new, unified Irish cultural identity. They rejected what they saw as O'Connell's narrow Catholic sectarianism and eventually came to advocate the use of violence to achieve Irish independence. Despite their heady rhetoric, they toiled in O'Connell's shadow (until his death in May 1847) and could not match the mobilizing power of the old Repeal Association. Any chance of a successful rising was undone by lack of enthusiasm among the general population and by poor timing. When the Young Irelanders, under the banner of the Irish Confederation, finally launched an armed rebellion in 1848, they did so in the middle of the Great Famine, when most Irish people were focused on survival rather than insurrection. The Young Ireland revolt ended in a whimper in July 1848, and the leaders were either transported to Australia or allowed to go into exile in the United States or Europe. Despite their lack of success, the rhetoric and example of Young Ireland would continue to inspire later groups of Irish and Irish-American activists to take up arms for Ireland.

The Great Famine of 1845–51 decimated the Irish countryside and transformed Irish society. Prefamine Ireland had been characterized by a rapidly growing population (though the pace slowed after 1815), high levels of rural poverty, unequal access to land, and a dangerous overreliance among the Irish poor on potatoes as their primary food source. Disaster began in Ireland in 1845 with the arrival and spread of the fungal disease *phytophthora infestans*, which turned healthy potatoes into inedible mush. The potato blight, as it was commonly known, destroyed part of the potato crop in 1845 and most of the crop in the years 1846–50.[8] These failures led to widespread suffering exacerbated by the outbreak of epidemic diseases and by the mass evictions of tenants by Irish landlords. Even when the effects of blight were more limited, as in the case of the 1847 harvest, the acreage planted with potatoes was relatively small, and in any case Irish tenants did not have the resources necessary to buy the food being sold. By the end of the famine Ireland's population had been reduced from roughly 8.5 million in 1845 to 6.5 million in 1851, with about one million dead of disease or starvation. Between 1845 and 1855 another 2.1 million emigrated from Ireland (of whom about 1.5 million went to the United States).

The British government's response to the famine was woefully inadequate. Peel's Tory government (in office until June 1846) responded to the crisis in Ireland by providing for the sale at reduced prices of Indian corn imported from America. Peel's successors, the Whigs under Lord John Russell, at first relied on public works of unprecedented scope (but still insufficient to meet needs) and later established public soup kitchens that fed about three million people at their peak in July 1847. But as the famine persisted, many British officials and members of the British public came to embrace a negative view of Irish people, criticizing the Irish poor for being lazy and indolent and condemning the Irish landlords as improvident and incapable of economic improvement.[9] The belief also took hold that the famine was producing unfortunate but necessary consequences (such as rural depopulation and the consolidation of small holdings) that would lead to the modernization of Irish society. Under Lord John Russell's administration (1846–52) relief from Britain was significantly cut back. The expensive public works were eventually closed, the experiment with soup kitchens in 1847 was not repeated, and landlord clearances were allowed to proceed without government intervention. Instead, what relief was provided came under the ungenerous auspices of the Irish Poor Law system, with its infamous workhouses. In the end, it is fair to say that although the British government did not cause the famine, it could have done much more to lessen its effects if it had not been so driven by ideological considerations, especially its adherence to the principles of political economy or laissez-faire. But for the famine Irish who immigrated to the United States and their descendants, the view that the British had schemed to wipe out large numbers of Irish people and to displace the Irish from their homes was widely accepted.

Out of the failure of the Young Ireland rebellion emerged the Fenian movement of the 1860s. Two refugees of the Young Ireland movement, James Stephens and John O'Mahoney, sought refuge in Paris, and alongside other political refugees began to formulate plans to revitalize the Irish nationalist movement. In 1858 Stephens returned to Ireland and organized a new revolutionary organization, the Irish Republican Brotherhood (IRB). Another organization, the Fenian Brotherhood, was organized in 1859 by O'Mahoney in New York City.[10] Collectively, these two organizations became known by the name "Fenians," and their members committed themselves to carrying out a transatlantic program of armed resistance to Britain. In Ireland the movement was most popular among urban artisans and tradesmen—"a fraternity of young, unpropertied, educated urban dwellers," as R. V. Comerford has described them; estimates suggest that there were perhaps as many as sixty thousand members in Ireland.[11] In the United States veterans of the Union and Confederate armies joined the movement in hopes of using their military training in the service of Ireland.

The key to Fenian military planning was the expectation that Britain would soon find itself involved in a war somewhere in the world, opening up the possibility of a successful Fenian military strike in Ireland. These hopes proved fruitless, however, as British disagreements with France and later the United States never escalated to the level of military conflict. Instead, while James Stephens vacillated and refused to give his approval for an uprising, the British authorities infiltrated the movement with spies and informers, shut down the Fenians' newspaper the *Irish People*, and arrested most of the leadership.[12] Impatient for action, Irish-American Fenians launched several sorties into Canada in 1866. No gains were made from these actions, however, as Canadian officials quickly mobilized their military forces against the Irish-American skirmishers while President Andrew Johnson's administration prevented any further Fenian activity by rounding up Fenian troops, confiscating their supplies, and arresting their leaders. When a revolt in Ireland finally occurred in 1867, it was poorly planned and executed, and the British forces easily put it down.

But rather than these events signaling an inglorious end to the Fenian movement, the British response in the aftermath of the rising made Fenianism much more popular in defeat than it had ever been during its heyday. The reason for this shift in Irish public opinion came from British actions after the rescue of two Fenian leaders in British custody in September 1867 led to the killing of an unarmed British police guard. Three Fenians—William Allen, Philip Larkin, and Michael O'Brien—were tried, convicted, and executed for the murder. After their execution, Allen, Larkin, and O'Brien were written into the pantheon of Irish republican martyrs through the ages. "As with the 1916 rising," Alvin Jackson writes, "so in 1867 the execution of Irish rebels created a consensus for support for Fenianism which had hitherto been conspicuously lacking."[13] It must be said that British policy apart from this incident was quite lenient: all other death sentences given to Fenian convicts were commuted, and the sentences of the remaining prisoners ranged from imprisonment for short terms (twelve to eighteen months) to release on promises of good behavior.[14] But the initial damage done by the execution of the "Manchester Martyrs" proved difficult to undo.[15] A core of committed activists reorganized the Irish Republican Brotherhood in Ireland in 1873, though it remained weak and ineffectual throughout the 1870s.

As physical-force nationalists faded into the background after 1867, the momentum shifted to a parliamentary effort to achieve Home Rule for Ireland. The leader of this effort was Isaac Butt, an Irish Protestant barrister and politician. It is important to emphasize the limited nature of the form of Home Rule advocated by Butt and the Home Rule League founded in 1873. Butt argued for an imperial parliament that would contain Irish, English, and Scottish MPs and that would be responsible for military, foreign, and imperial matters. An Irish parliament would have its own 250 members as well as a House of Lords.[16] For any legislation to be enacted, it would have to pass both houses of the Irish parliament and receive royal assent.[17] There were several other particulars that were left intentionally vague by Butt in order to prevent critics from objecting to it over particulars. Compared with the demands of the Repeal movement of the 1840s and the separatist desires of physical-force nationalists, however, Butt's plan would have given Ireland relatively limited political autonomy. Nevertheless, in the absence of a better alternative this remained the Home Rule movement's agenda through 1876.

There were several other problems that hindered the Home Rule movement under Butt's leadership. One issue was Butt's personality and leadership style. Though he was a sincere and kind individual, according to one of his biographers Butt lacked "both the ruthlessness and glamour, the deliberate showmanship of the great demagogue," and "the supreme self-confidence" of great modern Irish leaders like O'Connell, Parnell, and Eamon de Valera.[18] There was also a lack of unity and singularity of purpose among the fifty-nine Irish MPs ostensibly committed to the Irish Home Rule party. Once again, Butt's indecisive personality manifested itself, and he resisted efforts to enforce party unity.[19] He also believed that Home Rule was a long-term objective that would be achieved only through incremental parliamentary persuasion. This stance had the unfortunate effect of simultaneously creating indifference among British officials dismissive of Home Rule and anger among his nationalist supporters, who were naturally eager for some sign of results.[20] By 1876 a new group of younger and impatient Home Rulers such as Joseph G. Biggar, John O'Connor Power, and Charles Stewart Parnell began to push for using the more aggressive tactic of obstructing government business through parliamentary maneuvers, and within two years Butt's strategy was left behind as these new leaders jockeyed for position and control of the Home Rule party. These new leaders were also conscious of recent developments among the Irish in America.

In 1867 a new, revolutionary organization—the Clan na Gael—was formed in New York to overcome the factionalism of the Fenian movement. Within a decade the Clan na Gael had become the dominant Irish-American nationalist organization, with over eleven thousand members.[21] In 1877 a joint Supreme Council of seven members was forged with the Irish Republican Brotherhood. Initially, the Clan na Gael and the IRB were willing to bide their time until Britain became embroiled in a foreign war and they could take advantage of Britain's distraction. But as the years dragged on, some members began to advocate more direct action.

The architect of what would become known as the "New Departure" was John Devoy. Shortly after arriving in the United States, he joined the Clan na Gael, soon becoming one of its chief leaders and organizers. It was under his direction that Fenian prisoners were rescued from imprisonment in Australia aboard the *Catalpa* in 1876. Looking across the Atlantic, Devoy sensed an opportunity to come out of "the rat holes of conspiracy."[22] In July 1878 the newly freed Irish Fenian prisoner Michael Davitt arrived in the United States and spent the next few months developing a new strategy with Devoy. These discussions eventually culminated in the "New Departure" of 1878. The program of the "New Departure" became public when Devoy sent a telegram to Parnell laying out his plans and had it published in the *New York Herald* on 26 October 1878. In this telegram Devoy offered Parnell the support of Irish-American nationalists under the following conditions:

> First—Abandonment of the federal demand and substitution of a general declaration in favour of self-government.
> Second—Vigorous agitation of the land question on the basis of a peasant proprietary, while accepting concessions tending to abolish arbitrary eviction.
> Third—Exclusion of all sectarian issues from the platform.
> Fourth—Irish members to vote together on all imperial and home questions, adopt an aggressive policy, and energetically resist coercive legislation.
> Fifth—Advocacy of all struggling nationalities in the British empire elsewhere.[23]

These conditions show the intention of Devoy and members of the Clan na Gael to link an aggressive policy in Parliament to an abandonment of federalism in favor of Irish self-government. There was also an emphasis on engaging with the land question in order to mobilize rural Irish men and women. Parnell never publicly acknowledged the telegram, but these terms were to form the basis of a series of negotiations among Davitt, Parnell, and Devoy early in 1879. Though this offer was intended originally to cement a political alliance and not to start a social revolution, events in the Irish countryside pushed the land question to the forefront of Irish politics.

The importance of the land question in the founding of the Land League in 1879 cannot be properly understood without some discussion of the widespread economic and demographic changes that occurred in Ireland after 1850. Even after the famine had ended, emigration continued at strikingly high levels in subsequent decades, and the spread of delayed marriage led to substantially lower birth rates. Both factors contributed to a remorseless fall in the Irish population. By 1881 the Irish population was just over five million.[24] Over these decades (until the late 1870s), however, rural living standards improved markedly owing to rising agricultural prices and (to a lesser extent) increased production. Because of much greater demand in Britain for Irish dairy produce and live-stock from the early 1850s through the mid-1870s, Irish tenants turned away from tillage farming and converted their land to pasture and meadow. Because rents remained stable or rose slowly throughout this period, tenant incomes from the land substantially increased. Provincial towns and their shopkeepers reflected this prosperity, and higher spending and expanding credit led to the establishment of more shops, stores, and banks.[25] For the Irish who remained in Ireland, life for many was reasonably prosperous before the late 1870s.

But below the surface of this prosperity lay important structural problems in the Irish agricultural economy. The problem of too many smallholdings persisted in spite of the earlier process of consolidation, and this issue was most acute in the west of Ireland. Insecurity of tenure, at least as measured by the absence of leases, was common. In 1870, 50 percent of all tenants occupied holdings of less than fifteen acres, and 75 percent of all agricultural holdings were subject to yearly tenancies.[26] If poverty had become less widespread, it certainly had not disappeared, least of all in the western province of Connacht. There the expansion of large grazing farms in the hands of wealthy graziers during the postfamine decades only exacerbated the land hunger of those with small holdings and little capital. As the 1870s came to a close, it would be in the west where an Irish agricultural crisis would be felt most.

In the late 1870s these economic vulnerabilities resulted in widespread agri-cultural distress when adverse conditions multiplied. Wet and cold weather and the return of blight led to poor grain and potato harvests in 1877, and this experience was essentially repeated in 1878. But as bad as these two years were, that of 1879 was far worse. "It is almost impossible," Barbara Solow has declared, "for the imagination to devise a worse combination of weather conditions than befell the Irish in 1879."[27] From March to September it rained nearly two days out of three, and the midsummer months of July and August were unusually cold. The result was a series of record-low crop yields.[28] The potato crop suffered particularly, and in 1879 per-acre yields fell by as much as 60 percent below normal.[29] For western farmers still heavily dependent on the potato, fears of another famine began to grow. Conditions were made even worse for all Irish farmers by a general European agricultural depression that drove down prices for Irish farm products. In 1879 butter prices fell by 50 percent, grain crops by 30 percent, and cattle prices by 12 percent from the previous year.[30] The impact of the depression in Britain greatly reduced the demand for Irish seasonal laborers in England and Scotland, thus removing another potential rural safety valve.[31] "The small western farmers," one historian has observed, "had evolved an economy so delicately balanced on the edge of subsistence that the removal of any single prop would have been a serious matter; by 1879 no prop was standing."[32] Faced with this reality, many western farmers fell heavily into arrears. With many landlords unwilling to grant rent abatements, the number of individuals evicted steadily grew—from 4,600 in 1878 to 10,600 in 1880.[33] There were also increases in incidents of agrarian violence as tenants' desperation became all too manifest. Rather than give up their land, tenant farmers in the west of Ireland began to organize.

Prior to the 1870s there had been voices in Ireland who had argued that reforming the Irish land system should take precedence over Irish independence. James Fintan Lalor, the Irish nationalist and agrarian reformer, had attempted in the 1840s to convince his fellow Young Irelanders that repeal of the union should be subordinate to dismantling the current Irish land system by turning Irish peasants into proprietors.[34] For Lalor it was vital "not to repeal the union, but to repeal the conquest, . . . to found a new nation, and raise up a free people . . . based on a peasantry rooted like rocks in the soil."[35] But Lalor's ideas were rejected by most Young Ireland leaders and he died prematurely in 1849. A different kind of agrarian reform was the objective of the Tenant League, which was organized in 1850 and committed to achieving the "three Fs" for Irish tenants: fixity of tenure (to stop unfair evictions); fair rents (to end exorbitant rents); and free sale (to extend to all tenants the "Ulster custom," i.e., the tenant's right to be paid for any improvements made to his holding). Non-Irish outsiders like Karl Marx and Frederick Engels saw revolutionary potential in the abolition of the Irish land system, although they were primarily attracted to Ireland in the hope that an agrarian revolution in Ireland would spark the English working class to overthrow the British bourgeoisie.[36] All these efforts, however, failed to draw widespread popular support, and it would be left to the Land League to take up the agrarian-reform banner.

It was in the context of the worsening conditions of 1879 that Devoy, Davitt, and Parnell resumed their negotiations in Ireland. Devoy later claimed that Parnell had agreed during their meeting on 1 June of that year to the following conditions in exchange for Irish-American support for Parnell as the leader of a national movement: (1) that Irish MPs would not do or say anything that could harm Fenianism or prevent continued preparations for armed rebellion; (2) that the demand for self-government would not be presently defined; (3) that peasant proprietorship established through compulsory land purchase would be the basis for a solution to the land question; and (4) that Irish MPs would form their own independent party.[37] Both Davitt and Parnell later contradicted this account, and scholars continue to debate what exactly was agreed at this meeting. Certainly, it seems unlikely that Parnell, who was known for keeping his own counsel, would have committed himself to such an explicit plan of action, and well after Parnell's death, Davitt continued to deny that agreement on a formal alliance had been reached.[38] The Supreme Council of the IRB also rejected the terms of this second new departure, although it did allow individual members to follow the dictates of their own consciences about whether to join the movement.[39] But events in Ireland would soon supersede these disputes and lead Parnell and Davitt to take up leadership of a national movement to address the land question.

It was in County Mayo that the Land War began. On 20 April 1879 a mass meeting was held in Irishtown at the behest of local activists but with the assistance of Michael Davitt and other Fenians. This meeting brought together a diverse crowd of several thousand supporters, including farmers, townspeople, local activists, and national politicians. A few months later, another mass meeting was held on 8 June at Westport. It was at this meeting that Davitt and Parnell shared a public platform for the first time. More large gatherings continued that summer across the west, and on 16 August the Land League of Mayo was formed.[40] Just two months later, on 21 October, the Irish National League was founded in Dublin with Parnell as president and Davitt as secretary. It was this event that finally brought the parliamentary and agrarian wings of the movement together, giving both a revolutionary edge.[41]

An Appeal to the Irish Race

Facing a protracted struggle at home, the Irish National Land League recognized the potential benefit of appealing for support from the United States. Though he was a landlord himself, Parnell understood the political utility of the growing anti-landlord sentiment in Ireland and crafted his appeal to the Irish abroad within this agrarian context. In his "Appeal to the Irish Race for the Sustainment of the Irish National Land Movement," published in November 1879 in several newspapers across the United States, Parnell called on the Irish people worldwide to lend their energies to the agitation in Ireland. Attacking the Irish land system as the root of all Irish problems, he declared that the removal of this system was necessary for the future prosperity of the Irish people. This was not just a problem for the Irish at home to solve alone. "None of our race have had such bitter experience of the wrongs of landlordism as those who have been compelled to seek abroad the food denied at home," Parnell declared, "and none should more readily and generously sympathize with those who are resolved to retain a firm grip of their Irish homesteads than the exiled who were forced by iniquitous laws to leave them."[42] Parnell argued that Irish Americans, because they had been driven from Ireland by famine and into exile in America, understood the situation Irish tenants faced better than anyone else and should therefore be willing to help their brethren in the homeland.

The Land League was not content simply to issue newspaper appeals for Irish-American support. At its inaugural meeting in 1879 delegates passed a resolution calling on Parnell to visit the United States. In deciding to send Parnell to America, the officers of the Land League had a dual purpose: to solicit money from the Irish in America and to mobilize American public opinion against British rule in Ireland. Michael Davitt sought the aid of John Devoy, the Clan na Gael leader, in organizing this tour, and Devoy helped to lay the groundwork for Parnell's arrival by calling on members of Clan na Gael to help make the Irish agitator's upcoming tour a success.[43] Thus, from its beginning, the Land League attempted to create a viable, transatlantic movement aimed at securing land reform in Ireland.

Money was vital to keeping the Land League agitation in Ireland going. The costs of promoting an agrarian upheaval and protecting its participants were substantial, with funds needed to support evicted tenants. In an interview with an American reporter in Ireland, Parnell explained the necessity of raising funds: "There are computed to be ten millions of Irish in the States and Canada. If they could send us $100,000 a year for five years, it would not be a half dollar a family in all, and it would go a long way in enabling us to win."[44] It made sense for Parnell to appeal to America for money. Irish America had long been a steady source of remittances for Irish relatives and had contributed to various nationalist and cultural movements since the years of the Great Famine.[45] What the Land League desired of the Irish in America, as Michael Davitt not so subtly confided to Irish nationalist and journalist James J. O'Kelly, "is money, money, money. Without it this movement must fail—with it success is almost certain."[46] Earlier Irish movements had been unable to unite all sections of Irish-American opinion into a single organization; wealthy Irish Americans in particular tended to avoid giving money to the Fenians and other nationalist causes.[47] But Davitt believed that "the wealthy Irish-American class who hold aloof from *other* National work" would support the Land League and join in the struggle "to free the land of Ireland from [the] landlords' grasp."[48] Building on the consensus formed during the New Departure of 1878–79 between constitutionalist and physical-force nationalists, Davitt and others believed that the land issue could unite the Irish people at home and abroad, regardless of class distinctions, behind the Land League movement.

Parnell was an excellent choice to deliver the Land League's entreaty to the people of the United States. A key element of Parnell's worthiness as a candidate to head the Land League's American tour was that his grandfather, Charles Stewart, had been an American naval hero.[49] Stewart's daughter, Delia Stewart (Charles Stewart Parnell's mother), married the Anglo-Irish Protestant landowner John Howard Parnell in May 1835 and moved to Ireland with her husband. Charles Stewart Parnell frequently invoked his American heritage during his 1880 tour of the United States. His public identification with his famous grandfather highlighted his connections with America and underlined his credentials as a representative of the Irish at home and abroad. Parnell's ancestry and gentlemanly manner gave him an aura of respectability that appealed to Irish Americans of all classes.

Parnell had also been to the United States twice before—in 1872 and again in 1876—and had some familiarity with American politics and the challenges that he would face on his mission. His first visit in 1872 was in pursuit of an American woman who ultimately turned down his proposal of marriage.[50] He made his second visit when the Irish Home Rule Party sent him as one of the delegates to deliver a congratulatory address to President Ulysses S. Grant during the U.S. centennial celebrations. Unwilling to alienate the British government, President Grant refused to accept the Irish address. Despite his failure to gain an audience with the president, Parnell's experiences in the United States made him cognizant of the political realities there and would serve him well during his 1880 tour.

On 21 December 1879, Parnell and his first secretary John Dillon, son of the convicted 1848 Young Ireland leader John Blake Dillon, left Queenstown aboard the steamship *Scythia* bound for America. As they left Ireland to the cries of a cheering crowd on shore, Parnell promised the crowd that his visit to the United States would "show that the hearts of Americans would beat warmly towards Ireland."[51]

Parnell's Arrival in America

Parnell and Dillon arrived in New York harbor late in the evening of 1 January 1880. Parnell had decided to visit New York first not only because of its status as the preferred port of arrival for Irish immigrants but also because New York was "the overseas capital of Irish nationalist agitation and mobilization."[52] It was the home of such nationally influential Irish-American editors as John Devoy and Patrick Ford. New York was also home to Irish political refugees, like Jeremiah O'Donovan Rossa, exiled from Ireland by the British government.[53] In the late nineteenth century, much of the coverage of Ireland found in American newspapers emanated from New York. This confluence of Irish and American opinion makers made New York a logical first stop for Parnell in America.

Upon his arrival in New York, Parnell discussed his goals for the tour in an interview with a reporter from the *New York Herald*. Declaring himself to be in America as the official representative of the Land League, Parnell explained the need for continued agitation in Ireland. "Ireland never won any great reform except by agitation," he argued, "and this agitation, like obstruction [in the Westminster Parliament in 1877], has been necessary in order to gain the attention of the Government. When a Government or a country totally disregard you, you must use strong and even disagreeable measures to get their attention."[54] While in America, he planned to focus his lectures on the land system in Ireland and the history and goals of the Land League movement. In his interview Parnell went to great lengths to show that agitation was necessary to change the Irish land system. After all, he argued, "it may be accepted as an axiom that you cannot effect a social revolution by dealing with it by kid gloves."[55] While in America, Parnell continued, he and Dillon hoped that cities they visited would form committees of representative supporters and take up collections and make subscriptions to aid the movement at home.[56]

Parnell was at pains to present himself as a respectable and moderate reformer, but he was also careful not to alienate those of his supporters who favored more violent and immediate actions in opposition to landlordism. In the same interview, in reaction to a direct question from the *Herald* reporter on Fenian sympathy with the Land League, Parnell responded, "A true revolutionary movement in Ireland, should, in my opinion, partake of both a constitutional and an illegal character. It should be both an open and a secret organization, using the constitution for its own purposes, but also taking advantage of its secret combination."[57] Parnell, however, quickly qualified his statement, claiming that the "leaders of the Fenian movement do not believe in constitutional action" and assuring the *Herald*'s readers that he "would not belong to any illegal body."[58] Several times during his tour Parnell veered toward violent rhetoric, though he always retreated to more respectable ground when challenged by reporters.

Such ambiguity became a hallmark of Parnell's public persona, and he cultivated this ambiguity throughout his political career.[59] On the surface, Parnell's adherence to the terms of the New Departure remained strong. His goal in

America, however, was to craft a message that would appeal to committed Irish-American nationalists while also inspiring and mobilizing all segments of the Irish-American population. As one contemporary British journalist observed, "It was Mr. Parnell's business to unite all platforms, and to link an errand of charity with the sterner business of Irish politics; to be received by the most respectable and thriving Irishmen in every large city, and yet to become also the very incarnation of the impossible aspirations of the various Irish Nationalist societies."[60] In pursuit of his objectives while in America, Parnell carefully and deliberately attempted to craft an image of himself that would alienate neither Clan na Gael nor more moderate Irish Americans.

To keep the support of radical Irish-American nationalists, Parnell tended to use more violent and forceful language in his speeches in America than he had in Ireland. Parnell, however, was no radical but, rather, a moderate. Though not at bottom a political radical himself, Parnell employed militant language as a tactic to attract radical Irish-American supporters to the Land League cause. He saw the Land League primarily as a vehicle for mobilizing all elements of the Irish and Irish-American communities behind his leadership and toward the political achievement of Irish Home Rule.

Parnell intended his speeches to be heard not just in the United States but also in London. Using strong rhetoric without explicitly advocating violence, he warned that if the Land League were ignored, then the return of "Captain Moonlight"—the most common signature attached to innumerable threatening notices in Ireland—was imminent.[61] Such a tactic had the benefit of situating Parnell as a crucial moderating influence and underlined the necessity for the British government to negotiate with the Land League lest even more radical elements step into the breach.

Parnell gave his first major speech on 4 January 1880 at Madison Square Garden in New York City before an estimated audience of seven to eight thousand. Here he announced a significant departure from his initial intention to canvass the United States for funds only for the Land League's political agitation. Owing to the worsening economic conditions in Ireland and the "fear of wide-spread famine," he proposed to "open two funds, one for the relief of distress, and the other for the purpose of forwarding our political organization. These things will be kept entirely distinct, so that the donors will be afforded the opportunity of doing as they please in the matter."[62] For those that feared their money would be put toward violent ends he vowed, "Not one cent of the money contributed and handed to us will go toward organizing an armed rebellion in Ireland."[63] This was meant to attract wealthy and middle-class Irish Americans who were traditionally apprehensive of contributing to such causes, and during Parnell's tour donations for famine relief and land agitation were kept separate according to donors' directions on how they wished their contributions to be spent.

Parnell made sure to let his audience know that money for relief was not enough. Merely to focus on preventing famine would be "putting the cart before the horse."[64] The current situation in Ireland was not caused by bad harvests or bad luck but stemmed from "the unequal and artificial system of land tenure which prevails in Ireland. To relieve distress, we must also take care that we take advantage of the unexampled opportunity which is now presented to us for the purpose of sweeping away this bad system."[65] Parnell explained to the audience that the Land League meant to put in its place a more just and equitable system. What the Land League proposed was to "make the occupiers of the soil its owners."[66] If Americans truly wanted to help Ireland then they would support the Land League's efforts to destroy the unjust land system in Ireland.

Parnell told the crowd that American public opinion would also be crucial in persuading the British to act appropriately. What was needed, he continued, was to shame the British government into meeting its obligations in Ireland. If the Land League was successful, "one great step towards the freedom of Ireland will have been made that will put a nail in the coffin of the system of British misrule in Ireland."[67] On completing his speech, a collection was taken up for those designated as starving peasants, and Parnell and Dillon were escorted outside the hall through the throng of cheering spectators.

Building on the reception they received in New York, Parnell and Dillon decided to accept invitations to speak from cities across the United States. On 9 January 1880 they issued a declaration to the "People of America" announcing the establishment of an "Irish Relief Fund" for the purpose of collecting money and sending it home to alleviate distress in Ireland.[68] The funds were to be forwarded to the bank Drexel Morgan and Company of New York.[69] Buoyed by their success in New York, Parnell and Dillon made ready to begin their greater tour of the rest of the country.

Parnell and Dillon traveled nearly nonstop to sixty-two towns and localities throughout America. When he had arrived in New York, Parnell's itinerary had been mostly under the direction of Clan na Gael, demonstrating the early importance of physical-force nationalists in promoting Parnell's mission.[70] Parnell and Dillon made the plans for the tour outside of New York and their itinerary was disjointed and chaotic. Rather than mapping out a logical route, they planned their itinerary as invitations arrived. One example of this confusion was their commitment to visit "Springfield" after receiving several telegrams asking them to come as soon as possible. When the date for the meeting was reached, however, at least three different Springfields, spread across thousands of miles of the country, announced that Parnell would be speaking in three different locations on the same day.[71] Parnell had hoped to travel across the entire United States, but he made it only to the East, Midwest, and Upper South, missing the West Coast entirely. The main reason for this failure was Dillon's unsuitableness as a secretary. To address this disorganization, Tim Healy was brought over from Ireland to act as replacement secretary. He met Parnell in Iowa on 24 February 1880. With Healy directing affairs, the tour became more organized, but he had arrived with only two weeks left on the tour.

Two modern developments enabled Parnell to overcome the poor organization of the tour: the extensive railroad network in the United States and the rapid speed of modern communications like the telegraph. During his tour, Parnell traveled almost exclusively by railroad. The pace of travel was grueling, as evidenced by this four-day itinerary:

> We left Davenport, Iowa at 7 o'clock, on Monday morning for Des Moines, at which place we arrived that evening. I [Parnell] addressed the legislature that evening and left for Peoria during the night, sleeping on the cars. Arriving there at 2 o'clock, I spoke that evening and afterward worked late into the night, as I am obliged to do answering a numerous batch of correspondence and arranging my list of future arrangements. We left for Springfield at 6 or 7 o'clock the following morning, arriving there at 2 p.m. That evening I spoke again and at 6 o'clock this morning started for St. Louis.[72]

To cover greater distances, Parnell and Dillon often split up for a few engagements at a time. Parnell also gave several short "whistle-stop" speeches in which he addressed crowds at train depots from the rear platform of the train. In one day in Minnesota, on his way from Winona to Minneapolis, he delivered three such speeches before giving two major addresses in the evening.[73]

The relatively new transatlantic communication network, involving the laying of the first transatlantic telegraph cable in the 1860s, greatly increased the dissemination of news between Ireland and the United States, further aiding Parnell. News of the Land League agitation in Ireland often reached the United States by the next day or, at the latest, within the span of a week. The rise of a strong Irish-American press—almost every major eastern and midwestern city supported a local Irish-American newspaper—facilitated the spread of this information.[74] One historian has called Parnell "Ireland's first modern media politician," arguing that he "advanced himself and the national project principally through indirect means, that is at a physical distance, through the press and often by what would now be called 'sound bytes.'"[75] His speeches in Ireland and America were quickly communicated back and forth across the Atlantic, helping to create a "Greater Ireland" in North America.

Key Themes in Parnell's American Speeches

Parnell's speeches during his tour were part of a carefully calculated campaign to attract financial support and create mass support for the Land League in the United States. The *New York Herald*, a critic of Parnell and the Land League, accused him of making the same speech at all his stops in America, which was true in many respects.[76] He emphasized several key themes in almost all his speeches, deliberately crafting his message to appeal to Irish Americans of all social classes.

The most effective theme presented by Parnell was the humanitarian crisis looming in Ireland. By focusing primarily on famine relief rather than stressing the Land League's political agitation, he achieved a much wider airing and acceptance for this message in America, both within and outside the Irish-American community. But he did not completely ignore the political dimension. Rather, Parnell made explicit that relief of famine conditions was only a temporary remedy and that sustained political agitation in the British Parliament would be needed to effect permanent change.

Also a key theme was Parnell's assertion that the rallying of public opinion against British policy in Ireland was a necessity. In Boston, he declared: "We must continue our agitation; we must continue to tell the truth about the relations between England and Ireland until we force England to do its duty and get some measure for the relief of the distress that has come upon us."[77] In effect, Parnell wanted to both mobilize the American public in service of the Land League and to shame the British government into acknowledging and responding to the crisis in Ireland. To newspaper critics who claimed that he was attempting to draw the United States into conflict with Britain, he responded, "We do not desire to embroil your Government with that of England . . . , but we think that a people like the American people is entitled to express its opinion upon this question."[78] Parnell's harnessing of public opinion in favor of Ireland made the Irish struggle a popular topic of discussion in the United States. New York Mayor William Grace, the city's first Irish-American mayor, later said of Parnell's visit that it "succeeded in creating a public sympathy with the course of Irish leaders, which I deem hardly less valuable than the money, without which the parent organization in Ireland must have signally failed."[79] Michael McCarthy, the Irish lawyer and author, believed that the effects of Parnell's speeches were even more far-reaching. "His visit to America was the beginning of an impeachment of British government in Ireland," McCarthy wrote, "and the court asked to hear evidence and pronounce sentence was no longer the British House of Commons, but the United States of America."[80]

In his speeches, Parnell also attempted to relate the dire situation faced by Irish peasants at that time to the Great Famine of the mid-nineteenth century in order to link Irish-American memory of the famine to the issue of land reform for Ireland. This approach was bound to yield dividends because the "Famine generation brought a common memory . . . to which all Irish-Catholic immigrants could relate."[81] Later in his tour Parnell claimed, "Our Irish famines are caused by man, not by God. . . . We charge that these continually recurring Irish famines, and that the constant of chronic poverty, which always obtains in Ireland, are due to the conditions of land tenure in that country."[82] In Cleveland, Parnell was more explicit and accusatory, declaring that "it must be our duty in this country if England attempts to starve and exterminate our people to see that she does not do so secretly, silently, and by stealth, as she did in the great famine of '45, '46, '47, and '48."[83] These words echoed John Mitchel's famous declaration that "the Almighty sent the potato blight but the English created the famine."[84] Parnell also reminded his audiences that money alone would not prevent future famines. The Irish in America needed to support the Land League and remember the lessons of the Great Famine. If they did so, Parnell argued, the Irish agrarian problem would be solved. For the famine immigrants and their children, such reasoning had a powerful emotive effect since recollections of the famine (real and imagined) had seeped deeply into their collective memory.

For the nationalists and especially the Fenians among his listeners, Parnell argued that the successful resolution of the land issue in Ireland would be the first step toward achieving Irish nationhood. "If you help us to keep our people alive during this winter," he reasoned in Chicago, "we will kill the Irish land system. And when we have killed the Irish land system we shall have plucked out and ground to powder the corner-stone of British misrule in Ireland."[85] The British government saw such assertions of Irish independence in America as treasonous. In Cincinnati, Parnell allegedly declared: "When we have undermined English misgovernment, we [will] have paved the way for Ireland to take her place among the nations of the earth. . . . None of us . . . will be satisfied until we have destroyed the last link which keeps Ireland bound to England."[86] Parnell later claimed that he was misquoted and never used the words "last link;" an examination of Cincinnati newspapers provides strong evidence to support his assertion.[87] Regardless of the accuracy of the reporting, this incident demonstrates the fine line between moderation and revolution that Parnell navigated in his speeches.

During his tour Parnell often denounced the British government in violent language, drawing the support of many members of Clan na Gael in America and of the Irish Republican Brotherhood at home. At his speech in Boston,

Parnell warned: "Although I am not in favor of revolutionary methods, yet . . . I cannot help saying that if things are allowed to continue as they are in Ireland much longer, our people will scarcely be able to contain themselves or to withstand the influence which must drive them towards violent and revolutionary measures."[88] He was even more explicit in Cleveland, describing his feelings about the armed Irish-American regiments that often escorted him in processions: "I thought that each one of them must have wished with Sarsfield of old when dying on a foreign battlefield, 'Oh that I could carry these arms for Ireland!' Well it may come to that some day or other." If Irish landlords and the British government did not negotiate in good faith with the Land League, the time would come when they would "get very much sharper and worse terms from somebody else."[89]

As previously noted, Parnell himself did not believe in the violent overthrow of the British government. Instead, he was engaged in a rhetorical effort to keep American physical-force nationalists on his side. His purpose in coming to America had been to unify Irish America behind the Land League, and in order to do so, it was important to placate those Irishmen committed to violent revolution. Later, when he was called to account for the violent rhetoric that he had used in America after his return to Ireland, Parnell denied that his speeches in America were very radical in nature. "As a matter of fact," Parnell claimed, "it is far more necessary to speak strongly to Irish people in Ireland than it is to speak strongly to them in America. In Ireland they require to be encouraged and lifted up because they are oppressed and beaten down; in America they require to have cold water thrown upon them."[90] If the occasional allusion to violence was necessary to keep physical-force supporters happy, Parnell was willing to engage in rhetorical fireworks.

The pinnacle of Parnell's visit came on 2 February 1880 when he addressed the United States House of Representatives in Washington, DC. Parnell's speech in the nation's capital had been arranged through the efforts of Clan na Gael and select Democratic representatives. In a secret meeting, Clan na Gael leaders had decided to ask the House of Representatives to name a time and place for Parnell to speak before them; a group of Democratic Congressmen arranged for this offer to be accepted by the House. One of them, Samuel Cox of New York, put forward a specific resolution that Parnell be invited to speak to Congress. After a lively discussion the resolution passed.[91] The invitation was quite an honor, as it had previously been given only to two other foreigners: the Marquis de Lafayette of Revolutionary fame in 1825 and Louis Kossuth, the Hungarian patriot, in 1851.

In his address before Congress Parnell emphasized many of the same ideas he had expressed elsewhere. He went to great lengths to present himself as a reasonable and moderate reformer and focused on the inequity of the land system. Moreover, he assured Congress that he did not mean to embroil the United States in a conflict with the British, yet he claimed that in cases of clear injustice such as those events occurring in Ireland, public opinion in a free country like America should be heard. Boasting of his American blood, he also asked America to help Ireland and maintained that a solution to the land question would prevent him and other Irish leaders from having "to appear as beggars and mendicants before the world" any longer; it would "be the last Irish famine."[92] After his speech Parnell was given a short audience with President Rutherford B. Hayes. Though the U.S. government refused to denounce British policy officially, Parnell's trip to Washington was a marked personal triumph, especially compared with the chilly response he had received from the Grant administration only four years earlier.

Through his carefully designed speeches and appeals to Irish America, Parnell attempted to link the Irish at home with those in America. The idea of a "Greater Ireland" spanning the Atlantic was not merely a rhetorical creation but a cultural and political reality. Irish America was coming of age in the 1880s, and Parnell's visit both coincided with and consolidated the growing assertiveness of Irish Americans. When the Land League issued its call for help to its brethren in America, Irish Americans there were ready to listen; they were also prepared to lead.

American Reaction to Parnell's Tour

Discussing Parnell's visit to America, John Boyle O'Reilly marveled that Parnell, a relative unknown just two years earlier, in a few months had "drawn together all the elements of Irish nationality, and induced them to work in a body. For the first time since 1829, there is only one national Irish movement." It was not that Parnell had removed the ideological divisions that existed among Irish Americans but, rather, that under his leadership "the Fenians, Revolutionists, Repealers, Home Rulers, Tenant-righters, Landlord-abolitionists, are all in one army. They may retain their favorite purpose; but they move together for the general good. . . . Without Parnell it would have taken ten years to bring about complete and operative union."[93]

During Parnell's tour, Irish Americans organized elaborate receptions to greet him. Usually a procession, sometimes involving thousands, would lead Parnell to the speaking hall, which was often decorated with green bunting and an American flag alongside an Irish flag with the golden harp. Bands played patriotic tunes, alternating between such American and Irish patriotic airs as

"America," "Wearing of the Green," and "Hail Columbia." Saloons and the meeting halls of Irish-American fraternal and benevolent societies posted fliers advertising Parnell's speeches.[94] Such expressions of support could sometimes get out of hand, as in St. Louis, where members of the crowd, afraid that Parnell would not make an appearance outside, forced their way onto his railcar, with the result that "the occupants were jammed together much after the fashion of sardines in a box."[95]

The turnout and interest Parnell's visits to American cities generated was quite dramatic. Years later, responding to British claims that Parnell's support among Irish Americans was found among the lowest classes, Parnell replied that his meetings in America had been presided "over or attended by Governors of States, bishops of the Catholic Church, clergymen of all denominations, Senators, Congressmen, judges, the most eminent physicians and merchants, of fortune and position" and had "been supported by all that is best socially among the people of Irish origin."[96] Though Parnell was greeted and fawned over by local dignitaries at every stop, large cross sections of local Irish-American communities turned out to hear him speak. Elizabeth Gurley Flynn, the famous labor radical and organizer, recounted that her mother had heard Parnell speak during his time in New England. In her autobiography Flynn related that her mother and father's Irish nationalism had been passed on to the next generation and that "as children, we drew in a burning hatred of British rule with our mother's milk."[97] In each city thousands of citizens of all classes and views on the Irish question turned out to greet Parnell. In New York, for example, seven thousand people turned out to hear him, while in Chicago, at the largest meeting of the tour, an estimated ten to fifteen thousand people listened to his address.

Despite such enthusiasm, several commentators noted Parnell's subdued style in public meetings and believed him unable to stir Irish Americans to action. John Murdoch, the Scottish land reformer who shared some platforms with Parnell, remarked that Parnell had delivered "a disappointing speech to people who are accustomed to real eloquence on every platform," while an observer in St. Paul wondered in his diary that "one would hardly think him . . . to be the man who has so persistently and successfully pursued the obstruction policy in Parliament."[98] William O'Brien, in a humorous anecdote, described the mayor of Jersey City's reaction when introduced to Parnell. Of Parnell, he said he was not impressed a bit: "'When I saw this sleek young dude, as well fed as you or I and a damn sight better groomed, I said to myself: 'The idea of sending out a man like that to tell us they are starving!'" But upon seeing Dillon (sickly looking at the best of times) "with hunger written on every line of his face, I said, 'Ah! that's a different thing. There is the Irish famine right enough.'"[99]

Though not the rhetorical equal of Daniel O'Connell or certain other Irish agitators, Parnell proved increasingly effective in rallying Irish-American support for the Land League as the tour progressed. The *Catholic Union*, a pro-Parnell newspaper in Buffalo, New York, claimed Parnell's soft-spokenness was actually a benefit, as Parnell seemed "to weave a strange charm round the listener, so that he bends eagerly forward, fearing to lose the slightest word."[100] Parnell also improved as an orator during his tour. Alexander Sullivan, one of the leading Irish nationalists in Chicago, described Parnell's transformation: "When he first spoke in my hearing in public . . . , his feeble monotone, and excessive shyness proved seriously disappointing to great gatherings eager to have another O'Connell." Just a few weeks later, however, Sullivan claimed of Parnell that "every sentence he uttered was clear-cut, incisive, apt, and telling. . . . I never heard any human being, whether uncouth or cultivated, doubt his sincerity, or hesitate, after seeing and hearing, to trust and follow him."[101] The rhetorical skills developed by Parnell in America were crucial in making the Land League a transatlantic success and helped in his emergence as the dominant Irish leader of his generation.

Inspired by Parnell's pleas for relief for the suffering Irish, several prominent non-Irish Americans lent their support to the Land League cause. In Boston, Parnell drew praise from the famous orator and reformer Wendell Phillips. Phillips declared that he had come out to "see the man that has forced John Bull to listen."[102] "It took O'Connell a quarter of a century," he maintained, "to gain the ear of the British people and the house of commons. Our guest, more fortunate after a few patient but persistent years, has brought the English nation, if not to terms, at least he has stunned her into sobriety."[103] Phillips recognized the transformative potential impact of the Land League movement on the relationship between England and Ireland. Great changes did not come from statesmen and from on high. Rather, "world history is written in wisdom forced upon statesmen by the necessities of the protests of the masses. . . . I should be ashamed of Ireland if she had been in anything else than perpetual rebellion."[104] Parnell was so impressed with Phillips that in 1881 the Land League attempted to persuade him to visit Ireland and offered to pay all his expenses.[105] Much to his dismay, Phillips's health and that of his wife prevented him from making a visit.

Another supporter was Henry Ward Beecher, the influential Congregationalist preacher and minister of the Plymouth Congregational Church in Brooklyn, New York. A famous abolitionist and temperance and suffrage supporter, Beecher had previously supported Irish-American workers and supported efforts to make public schools nonsectarian. It is possible that Beecher was won over to the Irish cause by reports of the situation in Ireland from his lecture agent, James Redpath.[106] Beecher shared the stage when Parnell visited Brooklyn on 8 January 1880. Addressing the crowd, Beecher stated that while he did not believe Americans should tell Britain how to manage its own affairs, any government that protected a land system that defended the needs of the few over the many should be denounced. Beecher also pronounced himself in favor of the Irish land agitation. The British government, he argued, "is tepid, is slow, and, like many a strong and usable horse upon the road travels better with spurs than without them. . . . I honor citizens that make the government so uncomfortable that at last it consents to make them comfortable."[107] In his opinion, "a government that does not know how to manage this people [the Irish] except by kicking them out of the country is not a government that ought to stand."[108]

Perhaps the most important American advocate of the Irish cause was the journalist and abolitionist James Redpath. Just prior to Parnell's arrival, Redpath accepted a commission to travel to Ireland and report on the situation in the Irish countryside for the *New York Tribune*. According to Redpath, prior to his departure for Ireland he was not sympathetic to the Land League, but he was soon won over to the cause and became one of its most ardent supporters.[109] His friend Walt Whitman, author of *Leaves of Grass*, said of Redpath, "He is a vehement Home Ruler: fiery, flaming: is an Irish sympathizer of the intensest sort."[110] Redpath's "Letters from Ireland" were syndicated and attracted wide attention in the American press. "The underlying cause of the famine is land-lordism," Redpath argued. "The landlords have always exacted as rent every shilling that the poor tenants could pay, over and above the most meager subsistence for their families. In the best of times the peasants can save nothing. Their cabins are meaner than the slave-cabins of the South."[111] In his writings on Ireland Redpath constantly evoked his earlier abolitionist sentiments, linking land reform in Ireland to the successful abolition of slavery in America. Redpath's advocacy of the Land League further helped win support for the movement among American citizens.

Besides eliciting the backing of several American reformers, Parnell's tour raised impressive amounts of money for the Land League, although it is impossible to tabulate the exact amount of money sent from America because of his visit. One journalist claimed the total amount donated for this cause exceeded five million dollars, a figure probably overestimated but not by much.[112] Most of this money came in the form of personal remittances sent to Ireland.[113] Several different groups in Ireland and the United States also set up relief funds for the suffering Irish farmers, the most prominent one being that of the *New York Herald*. Parnell refused to cooperate with these other funds, denouncing their sponsors' motives for seeking money for Irish relief. He explained to a reporter that he was reluctant to associate with the *Herald* fund because it "had been started in order to check our success."[114] Despite these disagreements, the publicity generated by Parnell and the other funds helped to increase the amount of aid sent to Ireland from the United States. Moreover, "famine" relief for Ireland became a popular cause among large numbers of Americans, and not only those of Irish descent. By the end of the tour Parnell had raised $300,000 for the Land League Fund, including nearly $50,000 pledged for the political purposes of the Land League agitation.[115]

During his time in America Parnell was also able to win the blessings of the American Catholic hierarchy. This was no small feat as members of the hierarchy had traditionally looked askance at Irish militant nationalist movements such as the Fenians. With the blessings of their religious leaders the laity of the archdiocese of New York raised $55,000, the diocese of Hartford $23,000, and the archdiocese of Boston contributed $37,000. Individual bishops also praised Parnell's mission and endorsed the Land League. Bishop John Spalding of Peoria, Illinois, said of Parnell, "He is striking at the root of the evil for there will be no permanent relief for Ireland until the system of land tenure is changed."[116] Bishop John Ireland of St. Paul declared, "No fault can be found with the agitation. The means are legal, the demands are reasonable."[117] The Catholic Church's embrace of Parnell and the Land League cause conferred the agitation a respectability lacking in previous Irish movements; many Irish Americans previously resistant to Irish nationalism flocked to support the cause, making the church's support a vital ingredient in Parnell's success.[118]

Criticism of Parnell in the United States

Not everyone welcomed Parnell's activities in America. His tour rankled several important American newspaper editors. The *New York Times* was strongly anti-Irish, and this animus is evident in its coverage of Parnell.[119] Reporting on Parnell's Madison Square Garden speech, the newspaper mocked his call for a new collection for Ireland. The *Times* wondered if Parnell truly believed that the English landlords, hearing of his action in America, would "at once beg pardon of their tenants for having ever insulted them with suggestions of payment of rent, and will implore them to accept their cottages and potato-fields as free gifts."[120] Dismissing Parnell and Dillon's mission as just another attempt by professional agitators to fleece Irish Americans by appealing to their ancestral fealty, the *Times* advised its readers to watch their pocketbooks and send all relief to Ireland to more trustworthy agents.

Parnell's most vocal critic was James Gordon Bennett of the *New York Herald*. Bennett's newspaper opposed the Land League and he himself seems to have developed an almost irrational hatred of Parnell. As early as November 1879 the *Herald* attacked the Land League's plans for changing the land system in Ireland. In an editorial titled "Parnell and His Principles," Bennett discussed the Land League's advocacy of peasant proprietorship. "Does it need, in order to bring about the Parnell era," he asked, "that wealthy Irishmen should be banished in order that the peasant proprietors flourish?"[121] Bennett elaborated on his opposition in another editorial: "To abolish landlordism would be to abolish property, and nobody is fonder of owning a nice bit of property than an Irishman. Pat does not want property abolished, he only wants it to change hands."[122] Rejecting the idea of peasant proprietorship, Bennett and the *Herald* repudiated the Land League's aims in Ireland. According to Bennett, "The relations of the Irish peasantry to the land they cultivate is not an American question." He believed that "Irish discontent and agitation need no fanning from this side of the Atlantic."[123] Instead, the *Herald* argued that "emigration, and not revolution is the cure for the ills of Ireland and for the grievances of the Irish people."[124]

Bennett's sharpest barbs were reserved for Parnell's proposed fundraising in America. His sustained hostility toward Parnell was based on Parnell's refusal to fuse the Land League's efforts with Bennett's fundraising efforts for Ireland in the *Herald*.[125] Though Parnell had postponed his trip for a month to show his support for the imprisoned Land League leaders, Bennett accused Parnell of cowardice. Claiming that Parnell was a demagogue, the *Herald* bitingly declared that the Irish agitators had "come over to the United States with the purpose to set up an agitation here, where they are safe from the police, leaving the more courageous or less intelligent of their fellow demagogues to take the risk of jails and hanging."[126] Bennett believed that such appeals for aid were an attempt to deprive Irish Americans of their hard-earned money for a dubious cause. "Let us have no Fenian nonsense," the *Herald* pleaded, "no proposition to 'free Ireland' by procession three thousand miles off. That does no good; it only fills the pockets of adventurers and demagogues."[127]

Harper's Weekly and *Puck* both published cartoons echoing other newspapers' accusations of manipulation and chicanery in Parnell's fundraising efforts. As L. P. Curtis observes, many New York cartoonists "regarded the politicized Irish Celt as a menace" to society.[128] A *Harper's Weekly* cartoon showed an Irish peasant declaring, "I Asks Ye Fur a Tator, and Ye Gives Me an Agitator," implying that Land League leaders were really concerned only with their political advancement and not with suffering peasants.[129] The 31 December 1879 *Puck* cartoon titled "The Irish Milch Cow—Parnell Next," depicts Parnell holding an empty bucket while attempting to dislodge Cardinal John McCloskey of New York from his exploitation of the mindless financial support offered by

THE IRISH MILCH COW.—PARNELL NEXT!

"Irish Milch Cow." *Puck*, 31 December 1879.

HARPER'S WEEKLY.
JOURNAL OF CIVILIZATION.

Vol. XXIV.—No. 1204.]   NEW YORK, SATURDAY, JANUARY 24, 1880.   [SINGLE COPIES TEN CENTS. $4.00 PER YEAR IN ADVANCE.

Entered according to Act of Congress, in the Year 1880, by Harper & Brothers, in the Office of the Librarian of Congress, at Washington.

BEWARE OF FOREIGN TRAMPS.

PAT RIOT. "Ah' yon Innercent Bridget, darlint, sure it's not a starvation of food that throubles us, but it's money we're afther."

"Beware of Foreign Tramps." *Harper's Weekly*, 24 January 1880.

Irish Americans. To the left of Parnell, in retreat with coffers fully loaded, is another Irish-American bishop along with James Kelly of Tammany Hall. Parnell is thus portrayed as yet another self-serving drain on Irish-American charity and goodwill. The cartoon also placed Parnell within the unholy triptych in which anti-Irish observers claimed Irish Americans were held: an unthinking devotion to the Democratic Party, an unblinking belief in the Catholic Church, and a misguided devotion to a long-departed homeland.

In a similar vein Thomas Nast's cartoon "Beware of Foreign Tramps," in the 24 January 1880 *Harper's Weekly*, depicted a tramplike Parnell going door-to-door, hat in hand, preying on the generosity of Irish-American domestic servants for his own selfish ends. Parnell (identified as "Pat Riot") says, "Ah! you innocent Bridget, darlint, sure it's not a starvation of food that troubles us, *but it's money we're afther*." There is also an implication of illicit seduction in Nast's portrayal, as Parnell is drawn slightly dandified, attempting to charm the hardworking and respectable Irish Americans, personified in the honest and downtrodden Bridget, out of their money. Both cartoons depict Parnell and, by extension, the appeals of the Land League leaders to their Irish kin in America, as merely base attempts to cover the "expenses of some ruffianly Fenian, or unprincipled, though perhaps enthusiastic agitator, whose only object is to aggrandize himself."[130]

Though both magazines disagreed strongly with Parnell's views, neither *Puck* nor *Harper's Weekly*'s depictions of Parnell reduce him to the simianized or apelike stereotype commonly used in this period when illustrating Irish and Irish-American nationalists. In fact, an extensive, though not exhaustive, review of American political cartoons and anti–Land League attacks in this period revealed no simianized images of Parnell. His Irishness is usually signified in the cartoons already mentioned by his wielding of a shillelagh or his wearing an Irish-style cap, usually with a corncob pipe or shamrock sticking out of it. While the caption in Nast's portrayal of Parnell gives him a stage Irish accent, it is certainly much less virulent than many of Nast's numerous depictions of the Irish in America. Other Land League leaders visiting America fell victim to such attacks in the anti-Irish *Puck* and *Harper's Weekly*. During the Irish politician and Land League leader T. P. O'Connor's visit to the United States in late 1881, a front-page *Puck* cartoon completely simianized his features.[131]

Parnell's Protestantism, his half-American and half-Irish descent, and his upper-class background as gentlemanly landowner insulated him from many of the common stereotypes placed on the Irish character by unfriendly American commentators. As the Cleveland-based *Catholic Universe*, which supported Parnell, noted, "He is Protestant, and the cry of 'Papist' can not be invoked to injure his cause. . . . It is almost as if the child of the oppressor were fighting the battle of the oppressed."[132] The *Universe* went so far as to deny that Parnell was subject to the fierce passions of the Irish race. "Pertinacity, self-restraint, no extra sensibilities to play upon—a cool-blooded self-asserting, English way of trying conclusions with the 'Saxon,' these are Mr. Parnell's public peculiarities novel in a Celtic leader."[133] *Harper's Weekly*, despite its staunchly anti-Irish views, concurred with the *Universe*'s description of Parnell: "Mr. Parnell is so unlike the typical Irish agitator that the papers which oppose his agitation find it hard to treat him in the usual way. He is certainly not an adventurer, nor a blatherskite, nor a wild rhetorician. He is a self possessed and dignified gentleman."[134] Newspapers found it difficult to place Parnell within the prism of common American stereotypes of the Irish-American poor. The negative qualities of laziness and carelessness used to describe female Irish-American domestic servants and male Irish-American laborers did not translate easily to Parnell, a renegade member of the Irish landed elite.

Some American newspapers defended Parnell and the Land League's mission. A Boston *Globe* editorial claimed of the League's goal, "It is the social and political liberation of the people of Ireland, not by revolution, not by defiance of law, by murder or riot, but through legal and constitutional means, urging on the reform by organized and united action."[135] Such a view certified the legitimacy of the Land League in attempting to pressure the British government into fundamentally changing the Irish land system. In San Francisco, the *Daily Morning Call* echoed the *Globe*'s support of Parnell: "Let us relieve Irish distress, but let us at the same time exert our moral influence for the repeal of laws which make the distress inevitable."[136] Several other American newspapers voiced similar endorsements of Parnell and Dillon's activities.[137]

Encouraged by his fundraising and overall success, Parnell hoped to stay in America a few months longer to continue his work. Events in Ireland, however, upset these plans. Early in March 1880, Parnell received news that the British Parliament had been dissolved. He and Healy canceled the rest of their engagements and traveled back to New York in order to depart for Ireland and campaign for the Irish Parliamentary Party in the British general election in April—a campaign that would give the followers of Parnell a majority in the party and elevate him to the position of party leader. But first, Parnell attempted to ensure that the reservoir of Irish-American support he had built during his tour would not run dry.

The Creation of the Irish National Land League of America

Before returning to Ireland, Parnell helped to organize the Irish National Land League of America in New York. On their arrival in America Parnell and Dillon had issued an appeal asking Irish Americans to organize relief committees to collect funds for Ireland. Several communities took up Parnell's request and formed local relief committees. In Philadelphia, for example, Martin Griffith, the editor of the *ICBU Journal*, called on local societies to begin raising funds immediately.[138] To receive donations from local committees or organizations, Parnell and Dillon set up an Irish Relief Office in New York. Parnell's sisters, Anna and Fanny, became steady fixtures in the office, working as volunteers and often putting in twelve-hour days.[139]

Many localities went a step further and independently organized local American branches of the Land League. Several branches claimed the honor of being the first branch organized in the United States, but the evidence available makes it impossible to privilege one claim over the others. It is sufficient to say that by February 1880, Land League branches had been founded in several cities, including St. Louis, Louisville, Chicago, New York, Cincinnati, Detroit, Milwaukee, Rochester, and Washington, DC.[140]

The most active early branch of the Land League was found in Rochester, New York (also known as the Monroe County Land League), and under the leadership of William Purcell, editor of the *Rochester Union and Advertiser*. This League branch, according to resolutions passed at the first meeting, was founded because "famine now rages over the fair fields of Ireland, and its inhabitants who are our kindred cry aloud through their national representatives, the Irish Land League, for food to avert starvation, and for our moral support to destroy the accursed system of laws which by the aid of English misrule keeps an entire nation in perpetual poverty." The Monroe County Land League adopted a constitution under which each member committed himself to pay weekly dues of ten cents and to solicit funds from others outside the organization. Further recruitment took place, first on a ward-to-ward basis and then from town to town. The Rochester/Monroe County branch secretary corresponded with societies and individuals throughout the country urging them to form sister local associations.[141]

Parnell, ever the astute politician, recognized the potential of these local branches and attempted to bring the burgeoning Land League movement in America under his control. On 4 March 1880 Parnell sent out a circular to a list of prominent Irish Americans asking them to join him in New York for the formation of a Central Land League. "Branches of the Land League have in many places been spontaneously organized," the circular informed, "and a system of periodical subscriptions [have been] initiated amongst the members for the purpose of enabling Ireland to continue the struggle." What was needed to keep the struggle going was that "some organization of a permanent character should be established in America, in order that the work that is being done here may bear lasting results."[142] Parnell's original intention had been to craft the

Central League into a tool of the movement in Ireland. He proposed that branch leagues be organized by states, with each state independent of the others but in direct communication with the Dublin Executive.[143]

John Devoy and other American nationalists present saw this strategy as a ploy by Parnell to control the movement from Ireland and to divorce Irish Americans from its leadership. Instead, they called for the creation of an American organization with an American executive "that would keep down faction on their side of the Atlantic, and discourage its growth on the other."[144] After a vigorous discussion, this proposal was accepted and plans were made to organize an American Land League under Irish-American leadership. This early defeat of Irish leaders' attempts to control the movement from Ireland foreshadowed the constant and increasingly bitter battles over the direction of the Land League movement in America. Originally intended as a mere auxiliary, the Land League in America refused to accept the role envisioned for it by Parnell and others in Ireland; instead, more often than not, it followed its own distinctly American priorities and concerns.

After agreeing on the shape of the organization, the representatives in New York resolved that "an auxiliary organization of the Irish Land League be formed in America, in harmony with the organization in Ireland, and to assist its objects."[145] The representatives also decided that the Irish Land League in America should be organized by states and territories, with a national executive elected to conduct the day-to-day business of the organization. Parnell deputized a committee to organize the national movement after his departure.[146]

Some Irish-American nationalists did not agree with the decision to set up an American Land League and became vocal critics of Parnell. While Devoy was closely involved in the work of the American Land League, several of his physical-force comrades denounced the new organization. Dr. William Carroll, the influential Philadelphia Clan na Gael leader, had been an early supporter of the New Departure and the Land League. By the end of Parnell's tour, however, he had come to see Clan na Gael's support for the League as dangerous to the militant nationalists' goal of violently overthrowing the British presence in Ireland. In a letter to Devoy in February 1880, Carroll stated that in his own view, "charity should have been kept separate from politics."[147] By collecting relief funds for Irish peasants and by not focusing exclusively on raising money for the political agitation necessary in Ireland, Carroll believed that Parnell was diluting the revolutionary potential of the Land League. In March, Carroll argued with Devoy that continued participation by Clan na Gael in the America Land League under Parnell's leadership would present Parnell with the opportunity "to dispense with or crush the V.C. [Clan na Gael]" as he saw fit.[148] Devoy, and the majority of Clan na Gael leaders and members, disregarded

Carroll's advice and stayed with the Land League, while Carroll and his supporters turned their back on the movement.

Parnell did not regret Carroll's withdrawal from the Land League. The
Irish leader confided to Healy that aside from Devoy's work, "everything Clan
na Gael took in hand they spoiled and it was only by freeing himself from their
control that he had had any success."[149] Parnell by nature was a moderate, and
his main goal was to bring Irish Americans, who hitherto had been wary of
Irish nationalism, into the fold. While Devoy and other Clan na Gael members
stuck with the Land League, the split with Carroll signified the beginning of a
constant struggle for control over the American Land League between moderate
leaders and Clan na Gael. This struggle, discussed in greater detail in chapter
3, would not be resolved until the Clan na Gael takeover of the Land League's
successor organization, the Irish National League, in 1883.

With the building blocks of an American Land League in place, Parnell
and Healy left New York on the morning of 11 March to rejoin the political
campaign in Ireland. Describing their departure, Healy said, "It was a fine
sight to see the 69th [Regiment] salute as we sailed off, and Parnell wave his
hand in response, looking like a king."[150] On his return to Ireland from America, Parnell took up the mantle of Daniel O'Connell as the preeminent Irish
leader of his generation.

His mission to America catapulted him into this position while also crucially
strengthening the links between the Irish at home and in the United States,
helping to create a "Greater Ireland" that straddled the Atlantic. While the
New Departure had led to a new level of cooperation between Irish and Irish-
American nationalist leaders, it was Parnell's tour that excited and inspired
ordinary Irish Americans to espouse the cause of the land struggle in Ireland.
By crafting a message that various segments of the Irish in America could embrace, Parnell was able initially to overcome the dissension and disunity that
had plagued earlier Irish-American nationalist movements. The overwhelming
response to Parnell's visit in Irish communities throughout the United States
pushed the crisis in Ireland onto the front pages of the world's newspapers and
gave succor to the movement at home while propelling Parnell into an altogether
new level of prominence. But despite Parnell's attempts to control the American
Land League, Irish-American nationalists from its beginning asserted their
right to direct the movement in the United States.

2

"An Agitator of the Best Kind"

Michael Davitt and the Rise of the Land League in the United States

When Michael Davitt is at home he is the real chief of the Land League. Michael Davitt is the William Lloyd Garrison of the anti-landlord movement. . . . He is the tribune of the people.

James Redpath to John Boyle O'Reilly

Parnell's tour of America had been vital in generating support for the Land League in the United States, but it left the organization still in its infancy at the time of his departure. For many Irish Americans it was unclear after Parnell's return to Ireland how the new organization should proceed. John Boyle O'Reilly, editor of the Boston *Pilot*, commented archly to John Devoy after the establishment of the New York Land League: "Do not mind about the Land League. . . . It is at most a paper mountain: it will have a certain effect on English opinion, just to show that Parnell has left tracks in America. But there is no more to it."[1] John Dillon remained in the United States to maintain interest in the cause, but he lacked the personal magnetism of Parnell and was ill suited temperamentally as an organizer. The Land League executive in Ireland believed that the success of the Land League in America was crucial to sustaining the movement in Ireland and decided to send Michael Davitt to the United States to strengthen the fledgling organization.[2]

Davitt's six months in the United States were crucial in preventing the Land League agitation in America from disintegrating. Through his efforts as secretary of the newly formed national executive of the Irish National Land and Industrial League of America (the original title of the American Land League), and his countrywide tour, Davitt kept the cause in the public eye. He was also able to shift Irish-American support from supplying "famine" relief to providing the funds necessary for the political agitation in Ireland. A close confidant of the various factions within the League, Davitt helped to hold the disparate elements together and greatly expand the burgeoning movement in the United States. While Davitt's time in America was important for the survival of the movement, ultimately it was Davitt's arrest on his return to Ireland that provided the impetus for the most dramatic growth of the American Land League. Throughout the Land League agitation, events in Ireland spurred Irish Americans to greater efforts on behalf of Ireland, demonstrating the symbiotic relationship between Ireland and the United States in the emerging "Greater Ireland."

Davitt's Conception of the Land League

After his return to Ireland, Parnell launched himself into a vigorous campaign to increase the Irish Parliamentary Party's seats in Parliament. Under Parnell's leadership the party made impressive gains in the 1880 general election. Parnell was returned to Parliament from three constituencies (Meath, Mayo, and Cork), and overall, twenty-four members faithful to the Land League and to Parnell were elected.[3] Securing these gains had been costly, and with the Irish poor still recovering from an economic and agricultural crisis, the Irish Parliamentary Party lacked money for parliamentary and other political expenses. Seeking an alternate source of funding, Parnell wanted to turn to Irish America for money to cover election expenses. Such a course was difficult, however, as the Land League's constitution barred the use of League funds to defray parliamentary expenses. Moreover, the vast bulk of the money raised during Parnell and Dillon's tour was for the relief of distress, not for political purposes.

To meet this difficulty, Parnell issued an appeal asking Irish Americans to provide funds for election expenses. He held that Irish Americans who supported the Land League understood the necessity of supporting Irish Parliamentary Party candidates in favor of land agitation. He asked future donors to indicate with their donations their willingness to have their money used for political purposes.[4] The Land League executive in Dublin also decided to send Michael

Davitt to America to widen the organization of the Land League there and to further develop its capacity for sustaining the movement at home.[5] Davitt was an inspired choice to send as a delegate to the American Land League. During Parnell's tour of America, Davitt had been very active in organizing branches of the Land League in Ireland. Under Davitt's able stewardship, the League's strength had grown tremendously across the Irish countryside.

But Davitt's attempts to shape Land League policy were stymied by disagreement with Parnell over the direction of the movement. Parnell and Davitt's personalities contrasted starkly. While Parnell was the consummate politician, throughout his life Michael Davitt was most comfortable in the role of agitator. As one of the authors of the New Departure and a founder of the Land League, Davitt had unmatched abilities as an organizer and was popular among Irish Americans. It was primarily this popularity that led the Land League executive to send him to the United States. The Boston *Pilot* lauded him as "an agitator of the best kind: dispassionate, bold, taking advantage of existing things, consolidating his own side, and unflinching in his will to succeed."[6] Devoy said that Davitt "was by nature an agitator and a preacher of ideas, rather than a politician."[7] Whereas Parnell and Dillon in America, because of the economic crisis in Ireland, had been forced to focus on the relief of distress, Davitt's goal in America was to encourage Irish Americans to support the Land League's effort to achieve peasant proprietorship in Ireland.[8] In his diary, Davitt admitted the pressure he felt to be successful: "This Land League organization in America may be a big success or a pretty large failure. If a success Parnell will get credit; if a failure I will get credit."[9]

A major cause of Davitt's anxiety was his differing views with Parnell on what the Land League's ultimate goals were. Parnell saw the movement for land reform mainly as a way to politicize the Irish people and to increase support for his leadership and for the Irish Parliamentary Party. In a speech in Westport, Co. Mayo, in June 1879, Parnell argued that a focus on making Irish peasants the owners of the soil they worked would benefit the political effort for Irish self-government. "I have always noticed," he remarked, "that the breaking down of barriers between different classes has increased their self-respect and increased the spirit of nationality amongst our peoples." In fact, Parnell believed that "if we had the farmers the owners of the soil tomorrow, we would not be long without getting an Irish parliament."[10] Thus, despite the public support he gave for changing the Irish land system, the Land League for Parnell was primarily a vehicle for promoting his political goal of Irish self-government.

While Davitt desired the Irish countryside to rally around the Land League, his desire for land reform centered on the establishment of peasant proprietorship for Ireland's tenants and the poorest peasants above all. Davitt's views on the land question were "broad-minded and generous inasmuch as they seemed to promise advantages to the whole community and not merely to those in actual possession of the land."[11] But having experienced his family's eviction as a child, Davitt was determined that the Land League should benefit the poor smallholders of Ireland, who were especially numerous in the west. As he told a crowd of Irish Americans in New York, "We resort to every fair means to pull down and destroy the tyrant landlordism, and to trample it in the dust of its own rottenness. . . . It is an action of no compromise and no man . . . can say that our people will be satisfied with fixity of tenure or other mild reforms."[12] Whereas other Land League leaders advocated a settlement of the land question that would enable tenants to purchase the land they worked and pay back the current landlords over a twenty-year period, Davitt believed that such compensation was too high, especially since many tenants already owed the landlords large arrears of rent.[13]

It was this strident commitment to ensuring the welfare of Ireland's peasantry that differentiated Davitt from Parnell's more narrow focus of using the land agitation to create momentum for Home Rule. As Parnell and the Land League attempted to politicize and mobilize all rural classes under the banner of the Land League, Davitt predicted the dangers inherent in this strategy for the poorer elements within the Land League, and he was more sensitive to the implications of the class or economic differences that existed within the movement. In the public speeches and utterances of the Land League leaders, the phrase "the land for the people" became the catchphrase of the movement. This phrase, however, lacked any fixed or definite meaning; it was its vagueness that made it so appealing to leaders of varying views.[14] But the "land for the people" had a deep significance for the Land League's rural supporters. Small tenants in particular desired a change to a system of owner-occupancy in Ireland, along with the breakup and redistribution of grazing ranches, while large farmers and graziers were more likely to be satisfied by economic relief in the form of large rent reductions.[15]

Davitt supported Home Rule for Ireland but he wanted a political *and* social revolution in Ireland. His support for social change led him to be suspicious of attempts by some Irish nationalist politicians to subvert the Land League. To his fellow Land Leaguer Matt Harris, Davitt confided that Irish politicians who were committed to Home Rule and not land reform would attempt to reshape the Land League in line with their own designs. But he also believed that "with Parnell acting honestly and ourselves as a Vigilance Committee to watch them, I think it would be difficult to turn the land movement from its legitimate purpose."[16] T. P. O'Connor, the Irish Party MP, later recalled in his memoirs that Davitt was deeply suspicious of Parnell owing to Parnell's status as a landlord.[17]

These suspicions, however, did not contribute to an open split until much later, and he remained a steadfast supporter of Parnell's leadership.[18] Davitt was willing to continue to work faithfully for the Land League, while Parnell and other moderates overlooked their ideological differences with Davitt because of the need to send a popular Irish leader to the United States to keep Irish-American money flowing back to Ireland. Thus, when Davitt left for America, the Land League in Ireland remained a united movement, though important ideological and class differences existed just below the surface.

Irish-American Factionalism

Davitt arrived in the United States just as further attempts were being made by Irish Americans to better organize the Land League in America. His ship arrived in New York on 18 May 1880, several hours early, causing his reception committee to be absent, so he made his way to his hotel on his own. His arrival also coincided with the meeting of the first convention of the Central Provisional Council of the American Land League being held in Trenor Hall. John Dillon and Davitt were both invited and attended this convention.

By May 1880 enough Land League branches had been formed across the country for a convention to be held. Land Leagues had been organized in several states, but there was little statewide or national coordination of efforts. The Trenor Hall convention was called in an attempt to centralize the Land League in America and to provide for a national executive. Parnell had nominated most of the fifty convention delegates before his departure.[19] The delegates included many prominent Irish-American men—"many lawyers, priests and other well-known men from various parts of the country."[20] Though East Coast delegates predominated, others from the Midwest and California were also present.[21] Patrick Collins, the Boston-based lawyer and politician, was elected to preside over the gathering.

John Boyle O'Reilly, editor and joint owner of the Boston *Pilot*, was given the honor of delivering the keynote speech, in which he called on Irish Americans to unite around the Land League and to clearly define the principles and goals of the movement. "To-day, with millions in America, Irish nationality was only a sentiment," he told the delegates. "Tomorrow it should be a system."[22] By mobilizing around clear principles, the Irish in America would avoid the trap of former Irish nationalist movements: the blind following of charismatic leaders rather than the pursuit of principles. "When the masses follow men," he declared, "they may be dangerous to their enemy; when they follow principles they become terrible."[23]

For the delegates' consideration O'Reilly presented a letter from Robert Ellis Thompson, a professor of social science at the University of Pennsylvania, who urged the convention to denounce the allegedly destructive effects of England's policies on Irish agriculture as well as Irish industry. Yet Professor Thompson believed that the Land League's exclusive focus on agrarian reform would prevent Ireland from achieving economic prosperity. "If all that Mr. Parnell seems to desire were accomplished to the letter," Professor Thompson argued, "Ireland would still remain an impoverished and unhappy country."[24] According to Thompson, England's restrictive legislation and unfair suppression of Irish industry and manufactures were the real causes of Ireland's distress. Citing several economic theorists, Thompson urged that rather than have Ireland's population place "all their eggs in one basket" and perpetuate the marginal existence of so many people on the land, the Land League should encourage the development of an indigenous Irish manufacturing base.[25] If the Land League leadership in Ireland refused to recognize this necessity, Thompson warned, Irish Americans should be cautious in their support of the movement.

The convention delegates quickly adopted Professor Thompson's recommendation. A resolution was passed by the convention stating that while the Irish in America were solidly behind the Land League, "we desire to place on record our conviction that the kindred interests of manufacturing, mining, fisheries, and commerce are also being protected by deliberate and wickedly selfish restrictive legislation, and that poverty must remain the normal condition of the Irish people until they regain the power to regulate and protect these interests."[26] It was also decided to rename the organization the Irish National Land and Industrial League, and resolutions were passed denouncing the current land system as one of the chief causes of the widespread distress and pledging to advance the Land League struggle in Ireland.

Davitt welcomed these resolutions in his speech before the convention. He congratulated the delegates on their work, boasting that "the movement extends from Dublin to San Francisco."[27] Noting the resolution concerning Irish industry and manufacturing, Davitt expressed his belief that this addition was a wise step and his conviction that the Land League in Ireland would adopt the delegates' suggestion. In recognition of the Land League's transatlantic origins, Davitt observed, "As the movement for the abolition of the Irish landlord system was first started here, I am glad that this later addition to it is made here also."[28] Davitt's belief, however, was mistaken. The Land League leaders in Dublin rejected this change in the League's platform, and in the United States the word "Industrial" was dropped from the Land League's title at the next convention, foreshadowing the increasing ideological disagreement that would undermine the League's united front.[29]

The one serious area of disagreement at the Trenor Hall convention was over the appointment of a national treasurer. Conservative delegates opposed the appointment of a national treasurer to forward funds to Ireland and proposed instead that local branches send their money directly to Ireland.[30] They feared that the appointment of a national treasurer would leave the league open to being hijacked by extremists and that League funds would be used for violent action against Britain. John Boyle O'Reilly and others countered this argument by contending that the unity and sense of purpose created in the wake of Parnell's tour would dissipate without a strong central executive.[31] Aligning themselves with O'Reilly, Clan na Gael leaders secretly hoped that a central treasurer would allow Clan na Gael to eventually take over the national treasurer position and the League itself.[32] Another faction supported the transmission of funds through the *Irish World*, which had begun unofficially taking donations for the Land League in January 1880. This disagreement also highlighted the tension between localism and centralism that plagued the American organization throughout its existence. A compromise was eventually reached, with the election of a prominent conservative, Father Lawrence Walsh of Waterbury, Connecticut, as national treasurer.

The convention also filled the other national officers of the American Land League. For president the delegates originally nominated John Boyle O'Reilly, who declined owing to his other commitments. They next turned to Patrick Collins, who also declined because of the section of the League constitution requiring general officers to be from different parts of the country.[33] The delegates then unanimously elected James J. McCafferty, a young lawyer from Lowell, Massachusetts, as president, though his only prior notable achievement before his election was the title of "the third handsomest man in New England."[34] William Purcell of Rochester, New York, and editor of the *Union and Advertiser* there, was elected vice president. Michael Davitt agreed to serve as temporary secretary, making him secretary of both the American and the Irish Land League simultaneously. The initiation fee for membership in the Land League was fixed at one dollar, and it was decided that the annual fees were not to exceed that amount. The convention then adjourned.

Shortly after the convention the new officers of the League issued an appeal to Irish Americans to raise funds for the movement. While Parnell and Dillon's mission had sought primarily to raise funds to help those suffering from bad weather, poor harvests, and low prices in Ireland, this new appeal was explicitly political. "Our appeal is not for charity," the address began. "In conjunction with the Land League in Ireland, we desire that our kindred in the parent land should henceforth be free from the humiliation of a beggar's position among nations, and that the liberal charity of this and other civilized countries should be taxed no more in their behalf."[35] What the Land League desired in place of relief of distress was money to fund its political activities. The Irish in America were considered by Irish leaders to be crucial for the Land League's success in Ireland. The appeal laid out exactly what the movement in Ireland desired from Irish America: first, to enlighten American public opinion on the injustice of the landlord system and to make Ireland's case in the American press; second, to furnish moral support to the Irish people, encouraging them to remain steadfast in their struggle; and third, to provide the funds needed to sustain the movement in Ireland and ensure the achievement of its goals.[36] With the Irish people in America and Ireland united behind the Land League, the appeal argued that success was inevitable.

Davitt quickly assumed his responsibilities as the new secretary of the American Land League. For the Land League's offices he engaged rooms at 40 University Building on Washington Square in New York City for an annual rent of $300 and began work responding to queries from Irish Americans across the country interested in forming local branches of the Land League.[37] He drafted and sent a letter to several Irish-American newspapers detailing the procedure for forming a Land League branch and enclosed a copy of the organization's constitution for printing and distribution.[38]

Davitt endeavored to establish an orderly and regularized system of organization for the Land League in America. He advised communities wishing to form a Land League to first acquire the signatures of five or six prominent and influential local men for a resolution calling on Irish Americans to meet and form a branch. At this first meeting the constitution of the Land League of America should be read, together with the objects of the Land League of Ireland, and, if those assembled were then willing to follow the terms of the constitution, a new branch should be formed. For larger cities, Davitt suggested that an Executive Committee be formed to coordinate action among various branches and that branches be organized along ward lines. Branch leagues should contribute to the cause by holding lectures, picnics, and demonstrations in order to "keep the aims and objects of that body fresh in the minds of Irishmen, and influence powerfully the public sentiment of the American people."[39] Once a branch was formed, Davitt requested that the name of the branch and a list of officers be forwarded to him for recording. Despite Davitt's earnest entreaties, most branches ignored his advice and sent their information directly to newspapers to be published rather than to the central office in New York. Such fragmentation continued to be a problem throughout the Land League's existence in the United States.

The decision of the Trenor Hall convention to require officers to be from different states left Davitt isolated and estranged from the other national officers scattered across the country. Shortly after the convention, James McCafferty suffered a nervous breakdown and disappeared while William Purcell was active only around Rochester, leaving Davitt and Lawrence Walsh as the only effective national leaders.[40] Anna Parnell and John Devoy occasionally visited the Land League office and helped Davitt in fulfilling his onerous secretarial duties. Anna Parnell was especially useful in assisting Davitt. She believed that it was essential to promptly address requests from local branches to "keep them in good humor with the Land League" and that "the presidential election and the large sums subscribed for the famine render it necessary to nurse our people here a good deal."[41] Davitt welcomed such advice and appreciated her energy and organizational acumen. He remained in New York for the next thirteen weeks attending to the duties attached to operating the League's central office.[42]

Davitt's efforts were also stymied by the growing factionalism within the American League. During his time in the United States, Davitt recognized that while the Land League in America seemed to be united behind a common cause, important disagreements among different factions threatened to undermine the League's success. Davitt identified three distinct factions within the League. The first faction was the conservative one led by John Boyle O'Reilly and Patrick Collins of Boston, along with most of the clergy; it supported a limited land settlement in Ireland and was strongly in favor of Parnell's Home Rule ambitions. Patrick Ford and the readers of the *Irish World* constituted the second, or radical, faction. Ford and his supporters believed that the land agitation should move beyond simply achieving peasant proprietorship and push for the nationalization of the land in Ireland.[43] They also believed that the principles advocated by the Land League should not be confined to Ireland alone but should serve as a guide to similar movements in America and the rest of the industrialized world. The third and final faction were the Clan na Gael physical-force advocates, led by John Devoy, who believed that the Land League's primary purpose lay in mobilizing and politicizing the Irish peasantry. Devoy hoped that the British government's suppression of the League would then push Irish tenant farmers toward supporting an armed rebellion against England.[44] While these groups were able to coexist in the beginning of the Land League, their disagreements over policy and personal animosities would eventually tear the movement apart.

Though at times he was tempted, as he confessed to Devoy, "to fling the 'I.N.L.I.L.U.S.A.' to the limbo of partisanship and sail away where more solid and satisfactory work can be performed," Davitt was able to keep these various factions together because of the unmatched confidence that all these groups had in him.[45] In fact, Davitt initially saw such divisions as healthy. Rather than harming the Land League in America, he believed that as long as these divisions did not break out into open conflict, "only good to an honestly governed movement can result from the friction of fair criticism and of sane inquiry."[46] During his time in America Davitt carefully cultivated friendly relations with all three groups.

For Irish Americans like Patrick Collins much of the impetus of their support for Irish nationalism could be found in their quest for middle-class status and respectability in American society.[47] Though the Irish were beginning to achieve greater levels of economic and political power in the 1880s, the fact that their homeland was still under England's yoke led many status-conscious Irish Americans to see Ireland's continued subjugation as a stain on the character of their race. If Irish freedom could be obtained, they believed, the standing of the Irish in the United States would improve. Michael Davitt focused on this concern in his speeches before American Land Leaguers. He declared that if they wanted to be honored in America, if "you want to be regarded with the respect due you; that you may thus be looked on, aid us in Ireland to remove the stain of degradation from your birth . . . and [you] will get the respect you deserve."[48] While Davitt was on close terms with Patrick Collins and John Boyle O'Reilly, his political opinions were much more firmly aligned with the radical faction of the American Land League.

While in New York acting as Land League secretary, Davitt renewed his friendship with Patrick Ford. Ford and Davitt were well matched temperamentally and intellectually. Unlike most of the other Land League leaders, Ford's belief in Irish independence went hand in hand with his struggle for social reform in America. For Ford, the overthrow of the Irish land system, and not Irish independence, should be the Land League's primary goal. If the Irish people were successful in this endeavor, Ireland would be a beacon for the rest of the world to follow. As Ford declared, "Every sledge-hammer blow they have dealt at Landlordism in Ireland has been serviceable also against Landlordism here in America, away in Australia and South America, in England itself, and, in fact, wherever the gigantic wrong of Land Monopoly exists."[49] Though Davitt at this time had not yet been converted to Ford's belief in land nationalization, he shared Ford's expansive view of the Land League's purpose. "If an unjust and immoral power such as landlordism is to be allowed the right of plundering an industrious people, and driving them like dumb animals from the land of Ireland," Davitt asked a Boston audience, "what encouragement would this not be to aid monopoly here in America and elsewhere?"[50] Ford respected Davitt's opinions and hired him to be a correspondent for the *Irish World* when Davitt eventually returned to Ireland.

Another important friendship that Davitt made at this time was with the American economist and social reformer Henry George. Davitt was introduced to George at Patrick Ford's home in Brooklyn during his last few months in America.[51] George had already written and published *Progress and Poverty*, a biting critique of the rising inequality present in the United States during a time of unprecedented industrial expansion. It went on to become the best-selling work of political economy in all of the nineteenth century.[52] Ford later employed George as a traveling correspondent in Ireland. Davitt and George quickly became friends and George gave Davitt a copy of *Progress and Poverty*, which Davitt promised to promote in Ireland and Britain.[53]

Davitt's Western Tour

After a short burst of activity following the Land League convention, popular enthusiasm for the Land League in America waned. Davitt was impatient with the slow pace of Land League activity in the United States, confiding to John Devoy that he wished he could leave, as he was "heartily sick of this damned country already."[54] Soon afterward, however, he resolved to undertake a tour of the United States to invigorate and extend Land League activity among the Irish in America. In late July 1880 Davitt began his tour, which would take him from New York to San Francisco as he attempted to revive the flagging fortunes of the Land League in America.

Davitt's tour covered much more territory than Parnell's, and his message was delivered to many different audiences. Davitt planned the tour himself, using his position as league secretary and his numerous Clan na Gael contacts to correspond with various Irish Americans across the United States. Unlike Parnell's tour, Davitt's had less the form of a tour of a conquering hero than that of a humble worker for Ireland.[55] His tour began with a visit to Pennsylvania, continued with stops in various towns and cities in the Midwest and Rocky Mountain states, and culminated in a visit to California. All told, Davitt's tour lasted nearly three months.[56]

Davitt began his tour in August 1880 in Scranton before moving on to Pittsburgh. He was no newcomer to this area, having given various lectures in the region in 1878. His mother (who had passed away only a few weeks before) and sister also lived there. At a stop in Wilkes-Barre, Davitt noted in his diary the economic woes of the coal miners, remarking that "men [were] but working three days a week."[57] In Scranton, Davitt resumed his friendship with Terence Powderly, the mayor of Scranton and Grandmaster Workman of the Knights of Labor. The national convention of the Catholic Total Abstinence Union was then being held in Scranton, and Davitt was invited to address the assembly. He thanked the delegates for the honor, telling them that he believed that "when Irishmen learned the virtues of temperance, they would be better Irishmen at home and abroad."[58] At the convention Davitt also met Martin Griffin of Philadelphia, the editor of the *ICBU Journal*. Griffin was so impressed with Davitt that he became the major organizing force behind the Land League in Philadelphia.[59] After a brief stop in Washington, DC, Davitt proceeded west through Ohio, Indiana, and Illinois, reaching Chicago on 14 August, where he addressed eight thousand members of the combined Irish-American organizations of the city.

In the early speeches on his tour, Davitt told audiences that the movement in Ireland had shifted from seeking charity to prevent famine to teaching Irish men and women to assert their native right to the soil. With Irish-American help Ireland would no longer be forced to seek charity from across the sea. The Land League, Davitt argued, was "teaching peasants and all people that the land was made for them and not for 10,000 lazy Englishmen . . . and that they are to rely upon themselves alone and not upon foreign or hostile legislators."[60] The struggle in Ireland was now about removing the root cause of the people's problems—the lack of land ownership among the great majority of the rural population. Irish Americans' continued support of the Land League was crucial, Davitt argued, as Irishmen and women learned to assert their collective power against landlordism. If the Land League agitation were successful, they would never "see the inhabitants of our fertile country again become a nation of beggars."[61]

In many of the cities Davitt visited, Land Leagues had not yet been founded, and he was welcomed by members of various Irish-American organizations, such as Clan na Gael and the Ancient Order of Hibernians (AOH).[62] He continued his tour from Chicago, stopping briefly to address picnics in Joliet and Braidwood, Illinois, and lecturing in Terre Haute, Indiana. Everywhere he stopped, Davitt encouraged the local inhabitants to organize a Land League. In his speeches before Clan na Gael branches, Davitt told audiences that while he was not opposed in principle to an armed revolution against English authority in Ireland, he thought that to pursue such a path would be suicide as there was no chance of military success. In Braidwood, Illinois, he declared, "Experience has taught us that our worshiping of idols like O'Connell and others, that our appeals to arms, that our desires to gratify revenge, and exciting of the impulses and sentiments were vain and useless."[63] What the Land League proposed instead was to unite the people of Ireland in a peaceful mass agitation for their right to the land. In the face of such a peaceful but militant national movement, he believed, the English government would have no answer and certain victory would be assured.

On 19 August Davitt arrived in St. Louis, and before an assembly of over 10,000 persons, he attempted to answer various critics (including some members of the American press) who claimed that the Land League in Ireland was just an excuse for a vicious attack on the property rights of Irish landlords. In his speech, he used an American example to defend the Land League's policy. "Twenty-five years ago, all would recollect that the papers were defending the rights of property in human beings," he said. "Was it Communism to attack that principle then? Is there anyone now who does not honor Abraham Lincoln and Wendell Philips?"[64] In an earlier speech in Scranton, Pennsylvania, he had also addressed the charges of communism and nihilism emanating from the English press. To these charges he replied that he was not either, "but if it was Communism to desire the destruction of landlordism, and nihilism to pray for the banishment of its blighting influence from Ireland, then he *was* a Communist and nihilist."[65] During his tour of America Davitt was eager to not just simply influence Irish-American opinion but to also educate the American and English press on the Land League's principles.

He also argued that solving the Irish land question was necessary to ensure the future happiness of ordinary Americans. In Leadville, Colorado, Davitt told the assembled crowd, "You have no aristocracy yet," but he warned that "rich Americans may desire to perpetuate their families" and introduce "the doctrine of primogeniture . . . on American soil."[66] By framing the struggle in Ireland in this manner, Davitt sought to appeal not only to Irish Americans' charity but also to their self-interest. His words seem to have been effective, as a branch of the "Irish National and Industrial League No. 1 of Leadville, Colorado" was formed a week later.[67]

Davitt traveled through Missouri and into Nebraska before he was stricken with illness in Omaha on 28 August. He had been diagnosed with malaria in St. Louis but had continued on against doctor's orders. His illness reached a crisis in Omaha, and he was confined to bed for almost a fortnight.[68] Davitt gradually regained his strength, and by 12 September he was able to continue on to California, though he was forced to cancel most of his return engagements.

Davitt's time in California was the climax of his tour. Parnell had been unable to proceed further west than Chicago, so Irish Americans in California were eager to hear Davitt's discussion of the Land League's principles and activities. On 18 September he arrived in Oakland, where he was greeted by a torchlight procession. While there, he also met Mary Yore, whom he eventually married in 1886.[69] The next day, he was ferried across the bay to San Francisco.

Upon his arrival in San Francisco, a massive crowd greeted Davitt with unbridled enthusiasm. He was escorted from the wharf in a carriage in the company of the Civil War General William S. Rosecrans. His carriage then took part in an enormous parade, which included mounted police, several bands, various Irish-American benevolent societies, eight divisions of the AOH, and the Father Mathew Temperance and Benevolent Society. The San Francisco *Monitor* estimated the parade participants to be close to four thousand and noted approvingly that it "even outranks the monster anti-Chinese demonstration held last Saturday."[70] The platform of the lecture hall was decorated with the Stars and Stripes and the golden-harp flag of Erin, along with banners celebrating the four provinces of Ireland.[71]

In his lecture before the meeting Davitt again stressed the importance of the movement and its commitment to nonviolent action. He thanked those in attendance for their support over the last six months when Ireland faced the danger of famine. Luckily, the time of crisis had passed, and now the Land League could attack the root of the problem: landlordism. "A people or a system must perish in this struggle," he declared, "and guided by such motto no people have ever yet perished, but accursed systems have gone down before their anger."[72] The Irish people were asserting their rights to the land, and with the support of the Irish in America they would be successful. But he warned the crowd that the path to success lay through peaceful agitation and not through violent methods. In 1880, unlike 1867, the Irish people would not make the mistake of turning to violence and giving the British government an excuse to harshly suppress the movement.[73] "We mean no harm to the landlords," he declared. "We want to kill Irish landlordism and not Irish landlords."[74] With landlordism defeated, the foundations of Irish independence would be laid.

Davitt spent the next few days in San Francisco as the guest of the local Irish-American community. The day after his lecture, Davitt was greeted by a delegation headed by Denis Kearney, the leader of the California Workingmen's Party and a vehement opponent of Chinese immigration. The delegation's address to Davitt hailed him as "an apostle of a New Civilization" and announced sympathy with Ireland because "the same system that has brought such misery to Ireland is being fastened upon us. . . . We speak the welcome of labor—impoverished labor of every kind and everywhere."[75] Davitt responded with a warm gratitude. "If the overthrow of land monopoly in Ireland and the establishment of the tiller of the soil as the owner is to create . . . a 'new civilization,'" he observed, "then I am satisfied to be known as its advocate, not only in Ireland but in every country afflicted with the same or a similar unrighteous system."[76] But Davitt soon developed a personal dislike of Kearney, whom he found to have a "low type of face and character."[77] Davitt's position on the Chinese question is unknown, but he did end his personal tour of San Francisco's Chinatown prematurely and remarked, "I've got enough of this; this is worse than Ireland."[78] On 26 September he left San Francisco and began his return trip eastward, stopping in various cities in California, Nevada, Colorado, Illinois, and Ohio. He arrived in New York on 18 October.

During his tour, Davitt attempted to mediate the conflict between the conservative and radical factions of the American Land League. In late 1880 the main area of contention was still over the means of transmitting funds to

Ireland. During Parnell's visit, Ford, sensing an opportunity, had placed a small ad in January 1880 in the *Irish World* telling readers that he would accept contributions to the Land League and would forward them to Ireland. Soon afterward the *Irish World* began acknowledging donations and tabulating the amounts weekly under the heading "Land League Fund." By March collections already averaged more than $1,000 per week and were up to $2,500 per week within another month.[79] Ford had refused to participate in the Trenor Hall convention, choosing instead to follow his own independent course. This decision angered conservatives, since in their mind the only legitimate vehicle for donations to the Land League was the League treasurer Father Lawrence Walsh. To alleviate the tensions between the two groups, Walsh and Davitt came to an informal agreement designed to avoid conflict and advised branches to send their money through a variety of sources. In his correspondence with Land League branches and in his public speeches, Davitt suggested that donations be sent direct to Ireland or through Walsh, the Boston *Pilot*, or the *Irish World*.[80] This policy did not solve the disagreements within the League, but it did allow for a temporary truce between the competing factions.

This arrangement also led to a falling out between Davitt and John Devoy. When he first arrived in America, Davitt had been closest with Devoy and the Clan na Gael, but by the end of his time in the United States this relationship had become increasingly frayed. Davitt was a modest and humble man, but he could also engage in petty conflicts and squabbles. Devoy described Davitt as possessing a "warm, impetuous temperament and impatience of difference of opinion."[81] Shortly before his arrival in America, Davitt had been expelled from the executive committee of the Irish Republican Brotherhood (IRB) for his support of the Land League.[82] Davitt's relations with Devoy became strained during this period. Devoy was angry that Davitt had encouraged that funds for the League be sent through different channels.[83] The lack of centralized control of funds hindered Clan na Gael's efforts to infiltrate and take over the Land League for its own purposes. He was also worried by Davitt's increasing focus on social reform in Ireland over the struggle for Irish independence. In a speech before miners in Virginia City, Nevada, Davitt had said, "We can afford to put away the harp until we have abolished poverty, mud cabins, and social degradation from Ireland. Then it will be time enough to think of the best means of achieving independence for Ireland."[84] In Devoy's mind such statements were a diversion from the real ultimate goal of the Land League: the freedom of Ireland. Over time Devoy and Davitt's friendship dissolved in the face of their political disagreements.[85]

Davitt ended his tour in New York in early November, eager to return home and concerned about the Land League campaign occurring in Ireland.

As he told a reporter for the Boston *Globe*, because of the threat of coercive measures by the British government, he felt "that whatever danger the people have to face I should be there to share it with them."[86] He also believed that he had done all he could in America. In the same interview, Davitt boasted, "The work done in establishing Land League cooperative societies in America has been very satisfactory. A continuous line of them exists between New York and San Francisco which will rally at every cry of distress from Ireland."[87] Davitt's last speech of his tour took place before a mass meeting in New York at Cooper Union on 7 November, under the auspices of the newly formed Ladies' Land League.[88] The meeting raised $1,000, and Davitt was given a floral arrangement of a ship named "Agitator."[89] Three days later, he sailed for Ireland.

British Coercion and Davitt's Arrest

While Davitt's tour had helped to sustain the Land League during a period of slow growth and disagreement, two events in Ireland after his return were ultimately crucial in sparking the startling growth of the Land League in America: Davitt's arrest on a revocation of his ticket-of-leave in February 1881 and the adoption of coercion in Ireland by the British government in the next month. Throughout the history of the Land League in the United States, events in Ireland and the reaction they sparked in America often propelled the League forward. This dynamic interplay between events on the ground in Ireland and the corresponding responses in Irish America further demonstrates the transnational nature of the movement.

During Davitt's time in America, the Land League in Ireland remained very active. Branches had been founded throughout the country and agitation was being carried out on a large scale. Now that the threat of famine had passed, the Land League urged tenants to hold onto their crops and refuse to turn them over to landlords if the latter pressed for the payment of arrears of rent. John Dillon, who had returned to Ireland in August 1880, warned Irish tenants that if they turned their harvests over to rack-renting landlords rather than keeping them to feed themselves, the Irish in America would turn their backs on the movement and Irish tenants would deserve no more help from the rest of the world.[90] The methods promoted by the Land League to achieve the aim of keeping the harvest out of the hands of landlords were to urge tenants not to pay unfair rents, to resist the collection of arrears and oppose eviction, and to "boycott" anyone who took over an evicted family's holding.[91] But as the amount of resistance among Irish tenants grew, incidents of agrarian violence dramatically increased. While not all these cases of rural violence can be blamed on the Land League, as the movement spread, relations between land-lords and tenants became increasingly volatile.

In response to the growing scale of the land agitation, the British govern-ment, under the Liberal prime minister William Gladstone, attempted to halt the momentum of the movement by accusing Parnell and thirteen other Land League leaders of criminal conspiracy. The trial took place in January 1881 and ended with the leaders being discharged after the jury was unable to reach a decision.[92] With the acquittal of the Land League leaders, it seemed to members of the Gladstone administration that without extraordinary legislation events in Ireland would move beyond the control of the government. The British gov-ernment responded to the intractable resistance in Ireland with the Protection of Persons and Property Bill in January 1881, which suspended habeas corpus in Ireland and allowed for the prolonged imprisonment without trial of pris-oners suspected of agrarian offenses.[93] The Irish MPs attempted to prevent the enactment of this bill through obstruction, but their efforts were defeated in Parliament.

Davitt arrived in Ireland on 20 November 1880 and immediately restarted his organizing efforts for the Land League, but his status as a parolee released on a ticket-of-leave left him in a vulnerable legal position.[94] Despite this handi-cap, in December and January he addressed a number of land meetings and denounced Britain's Irish policy. On 3 February 1881 Davitt was arrested in Dublin and accused of giving seditious speeches; he was taken to London, where his ticket-of-leave was revoked, and he was committed to Millbank prison. In the House of Commons members of the Irish Parliamentary Party denounced Davitt's arrest, and thirty-six Irish MPs were suspended and ejected from the House of Commons for their angry protests.[95] Patrick Egan, the treasurer of the Land League, crossed over to Paris to secure the Land League's funds from the threat of British seizure.

Several members of the Land League executive, including Davitt, wanted the Home Rulers to withdraw from the British Parliament and begin a no-rent campaign. Supporters of this policy believed that such a step would push the Land League, at the height of its popularity and power in Ireland, into a suc-cessful confrontation with British rule in Ireland. Parnell feared that this strategy would in effect throw the Irish countryside into uncontrolled violence and push the agitation in a more radical and uncertain direction.[96] Instead, Parnell, who was more inclined than Davitt to see the Land League movement as needing the hand of strong central leadership, persuaded his political colleagues to return to Parliament to resist the government's coercion bill and to continue the agrarian agitation, but without a no-rent campaign. Despite the Parnellites' best efforts, Gladstone's administration carried the day on coercion. Once the

Protection of Person and Property Act was implemented in Ireland, the hammer fell on agrarian agitators: over nine hundred members of the Land League were arrested and held without trial.[97] But any hope that the British government had of ending the crisis in Ireland soon withered, as agrarian violence increased and the Land League campaign accelerated.

Since Davitt's departure the Land League movement in the United States had largely stagnated. A Land League convention was held in Buffalo, New York, in January 1881, when Patrick Collins was elected president. Despite this attempt to push the League forward, by the end of January only 292 branches had been formed nationwide, and the treasurer Lawrence Walsh had forwarded only $5,000 to Dublin.[98] Patrick Ford had been more successful, but even the *Irish World* had sent only about $44,000 to Ireland at that point.[99]

Davitt's arrest and the parliamentary battle over the Irish coercion bill early in 1881 galvanized Irish-American opinion and resulted in dramatic growth for the Land League. By the end of February, the *Irish World* reported that 687 American branches had been formed in the last eleven weeks alone.[100] The amount of money forwarded by the newspaper to Dublin also increased significantly. Numerous American cities exhibited massive increases in local activity. In Philadelphia the Land League presence went from one branch to twenty-two in just over a month.[101] A large meeting held there on 21 February to "protest against coercion" was attended by several thousand persons, with the numbers outside the hall equaling those within.[102] The British consul general in New York confirmed the Land League's increased activity in America. "The unlooked for arrest of Michael Davitt has given a fresh impulse to the Land League throughout this country and many more clubs have started into existence," the consul reported in a confidential memo sent back to London.[103] While Parnell's and Davitt's tours played important roles in laying a foundation for the Land League in the United States, Davitt's arrest and British coercion (both the threat of it and then the harsh reality) were the catalysts in the rapid spread of the influence and strength of the Land League movement in the United States. But now that there was a mass movement in the United States, the question was whether it could withstand the internal pressures brought about by the conflicting class and ideological tensions between its members.

PART II

THE EFFECT
OF THE LAND LEAGUE
IN THE UNITED STATES

3

From Plymouth Rock
to the Golden Gate

The Growth and Spread
of the Land League in the United States

What a sublime spectacle, is it not, Mr. Editor, in this age of greed and gain, to behold the noble, the magnificent manner in which America is answering the cry of Irish distress. In nearly all our populous towns, from Plymouth Rock westward to the Golden Gate, from the pine of Maine to the magnolia groves of the South, everywhere throughout our beautiful country immense relief meetings have been held and relief funds established in aid of the struggling tenants of Ireland.

Letter to the Editor of the *Western Watchman*, May 1880

Without the publicity and energy provided earlier by the tours of Parnell and Davitt, the Land League in the United States in the last months of 1880 lingered on life support. Events in Ireland and at Westminster, as we have seen, spurred the movement forward, as Irish Americans responded to the British arrest of Davitt and the introduction of British coercion in Ireland with an explosion of new branches and money.

Land League branches spread rapidly across the United States. From the beginning, the decentralized nature of the movement prevented attempts by conservative and radical nationalists to gain control of the Land League.

Important differences based on local and regional circumstances added further to disagreements within the Land League and shaped its character in America. The Land League's widespread popularity in the United States also cast a wide shadow over Irish-American associational, religious, and political life. The League intersected with and influenced three key social foundations of the Gilded Age Irish-American community—the Catholic Church, Irish benevolent and fraternal organizations, and American electoral politics. These interactions had important consequences not just for the Land League but also for Irish-American identity in the Gilded Age.

The Reconfiguration and Reinvigoration of the Land League in the United States

After Davitt's return to Ireland in November 1880, the Land League in the United States still remained weak in several respects. Many local branches had been organized in the wake of Parnell's and Davitt's tours, but a vacuum remained among the national leadership. Davitt's departure and the resignation of the president of the American Land League, James J. McCafferty, left the treasurer, Father Lawrence Walsh, as the only remaining active official for the national organization. After consulting with other prominent members of the Land League, Walsh decided to hold a national convention in Buffalo, a city with strong Land League activity, in early January 1881. He hoped that the convention would reinvigorate the movement in the United States.

Conservative delegates dominated the national Land League Convention held in Buffalo on 12–13 January and moved to assert control over the movement. Patrick Collins of Boston was elected president, Father Patrick Cronin of Buffalo was elected first vice president, and Father Walsh was reelected as treasurer. After Collins refused to accept the presidency unless the secretary was also located in Boston, Patrick Flatley of that city was elected secretary by a narrow margin. Resolutions were passed declaring the American Land League to be auxiliary to the Irish Land League and focused primarily on contributing moral and financial support to the movement in Ireland. The convention delegates also thanked the U.S. Congress for the sympathy that it had extended toward the Irish people.[1] Finally, in a shot aimed at the growing popular identification of the *Irish World* as the tribune of the movement in the United States, the delegates declared that the League "has never recognized, and does not recognize, any paper as an authorized organ to speak in its name."[2] Ford's response to the convention was an uncharacteristic but very effective silence. He did not publish any of the proceedings of the Buffalo convention. The delegates to the convention returned home confident that their work would reignite the enthusiasm of the Irish in America and set the movement on a constructive conservative course.

But despite the efforts of the Buffalo convention, the Land League in the United States grew slowly until events in Ireland sparked widespread popularity and enthusiasm for the League among Irish Americans. The arrest of Michael Davitt in February 1881 and the imposition of coercion in the Irish countryside, described in the previous chapter, outraged many of the Irish in America. As Devoy vividly recalled in 1882, Davitt's arrest was met in America with "angry speeches and resolutions, and the increased interest in the movement swelled the numbers at the meetings and the amounts sent to sustain the agitation at home."[3] The state legislatures of Iowa, Maine, New Jersey, and Texas all adopted resolutions declaring sympathy for Davitt.[4] President Collins called on Irish Americans to increase their activity. "As the Bael-fires flamed upon all the hills in the olden time when the edict went forth," Collins declared, "so now in every American city, let the fire of your indignation blaze. Call public meetings everywhere at once."[5]

The American Land League grew rapidly throughout 1881. On the eve of the Buffalo convention in early January 1881, the national organization reported that a total of 292 branches had been in contact with Father Walsh. By 10 July 1881 the number of branches had reached 792.[6] In large cities like New York and Chicago, branches were organized by ward, while Milwaukee was divided into east, south, and west districts.[7] As enthusiasm for the League grew, so too did financial receipts. Several cities decided to forgo their traditional Saint Patrick's Day parade and contribute the money instead to the Land League.[8] As of January 1881 the League treasurer had forwarded only $5,000 to Ireland. By the following July, Father Walsh had sent over $69,000 to Dublin.[9] The Buffalo Convention now looked to have been a great success. Despite the growth and increasing power of the American Land League, however, it faced stiff competition from Patrick Ford and the *Irish World*.

Ford began his own branch of the Land League in competition with the official American Land League. In a small advertisement in January 1880 the *Irish World* offered to accept money for transmission to Ireland and the Land League there.[10] Unlike other prominent Irish-American leaders, Ford refrained from attending the Trenor Hall convention in New York during Davitt's visit. As we have seen, he also turned a cold shoulder to the Buffalo convention, refusing to publish any accounts of the meeting, and began to urge his readers to form *Irish World*-affiliated branches.[11] From the beginning of the Land League movement in the United States, the official Land League and the *Irish World* regarded each other warily.

The simmering tensions between these two factions came to the fore in March 1881. Ford published an editorial in the *Irish World* laying out his objections to the Buffalo convention. He opposed it on four main grounds: (1) that it was irregularly called; (2) that territorially and numerically it was unrepresentative; (3) that the selection of officers had been "hatched in a corner" in New England; and (4) that Patrick Collins was a machine politician who should be shunned.[12] Ford's criticisms for the most part were overblown. The next Land League convention had originally been scheduled for Saint Patrick's Day in 1881, but because of the lagging activity of American branches and the need to elect new executive officers after the departures of Davitt and McCafferty, Father Walsh had issued the call for the Buffalo convention to be held in the previous January.[13] On the question of whether the Buffalo convention was unrepresentative, Ford had a much stronger case. The presence of representatives from only thirteen states, overwhelmingly from the East Coast, and the New England–dominated executive officers did not represent the full diversity of the Land League in the United States. The *Weekly Visitor* noted this fact: "It was plain to see that the Land League has not obtained its full growth in this country. Two or three of the Eastern states, it is true, showed in good proportions, but west of the Hudson River the organization is yet in embryo."[14] The newspaper blamed much of this state of affairs on the ineffectual national leadership prior to the Buffalo convention.[15] It was also true that many branches in the Midwest and on the West Coast, rather than selecting delegates to travel the long and expensive journey to Buffalo, decided to save their money and forward it instead to Ireland.[16] But after Davitt's arrest and the raging controversy over British coercion in Ireland, Irish Americans supported the Land League nationwide.

Ford's complaints against the New England–dominated leadership of the executive offices and against Collins's political activities contain a grain of truth but are overly harsh. Father Walsh proved a tireless worker for the Land League and was well liked, while Collins and Father Patrick Cronin were nationally prominent Irish-American nationalist leaders. Collins was active in the Democratic Party, winning election to Congress in 1882, but during his tenure as president of the Land League he was careful to keep the Land League out of American politics, mindful of the partisan passions that such politics could arouse. As president of the local Boston branch, he passed a resolution forbidding the discussion of American politics at meetings.[17] Collins responded to Ford's criticisms of the Buffalo convention by accusing Ford of a "purely selfish desire to make the *Irish World* the executive head of the League in the United States."[18]

In the end much of the conflict between these two factions was based on mutual dislike and distrust of each other's motives, heightened by a fear that the dominance of the opposite bloc would lead the movement to ruin. In the short term the animosity between Ford and Collins did not have a negative impact on the Land League but instead created a healthy rivalry between conservative and radical nationalists, which translated into increased activity on both sides. In the long term, however, the seeds of discord planted after the Buffalo convention would eventually come to fruition and divide the Land League movement into hostile and warring camps.

The quarrel between the *Irish World* and the official Land League highlights the local nature of the movement and the difficulties in creating a centralized leadership. Despite the best efforts of Collins and other members of the Land League executive, their attempts at centralization failed. Resistance to centralization did not come from the *Irish World* and its supporters alone. The Central Council of the New York Land League, angered by the domination of New Englanders among the executive officers, split off to form its own New York Land League — one that would be "second to none."[19] It had over ten thousand members and sent its money directly to Ireland through its own treasurer.[20] In Chicago the Clan-dominated Land Leagues were estranged from both the American Land League and Ford and appointed Dennis O'Connor as treasurer, calling their financial repository the Anti-Coercion Fund.[21] California too appointed its own treasurer, but this was primarily because of its distance from the New England–based Land League executive. Thus, while the Land League movement mobilized all elements of the Irish-American community under its banner, it never became a truly unified national body. Instead, the day-to-day direction and actions of individual branches were decided on a local level, and the reactions of individual Irish Americans to the League were based on their own class, gender, and ideological perspectives.

The evidence available makes it difficult to determine the exact number of Irish Americans who joined the Land League. No central membership records have survived for the organization, and even if they did, it would be impossible to assemble an accurate count of the various manifestations of the League in the United States. There are, however, enough clues among various sources to make an educated estimate. Patrick Collins, in an interview with the *Pall Mall Gazette* in April 1881, expressed the belief that the membership of the American Land League exceeded 300,000.[22] Margaret F. Sullivan, the prominent Irish-American journalist and member of the Ladies' Land League, gave the same approximate number.[23] Some estimates are higher, with Kerby Miller suggesting that the total may have been over half a million.[24] The real extent of the Land League's membership at its peak probably lies somewhere between 300,000 and 500,000. Whatever the actual total, the Land League was undoubtedly the largest Irish-American nationalist organization in American history to that point.

The Land League was active not just in the East Coast and Midwest but also nationwide, with significant regional variations. Southern cities had many League branches, even if they were fewer than in the East. It took far longer for the Land League to become popular in the South than elsewhere. Of course, there were far fewer Irish Americans in the South, but that is only part of the story.[25] Yellow-fever epidemics in 1878 devastated Irish-American communities in major southern cities such as Memphis and New Orleans, and they were still recovering when the Land League agitation began in the United States. In addition, neither Parnell nor Davitt spoke in any states south of Virginia. Nevertheless, as in the rest of the country, the movement in the South grew dramatically after Michael Davitt's arrest. The *Irish World* announced early in February 1881 that "the South, which has been the most backward of sections, is pulling up very fast, as is shown by the fact in New Orleans, where the movement was started but a few weeks ago, and whose first subscription we acknowledge this week, has now eight branches."[26] Branches were formed in almost every major southern city. Parnell's brother, Alabama peach farmer John Howard Parnell, was a member of the Atlanta Land League.[27] Congressman M. P. O'Connor of South Carolina was an early supporter of Parnell and gave several talks along the Eastern Seaboard on behalf of the Land League.[28]

One significant difference between the Land League in the South and elsewhere in the country was that many southern Irish Americans shaped their perceptions of the Irish question through the prism of recent southern history. This was reflected in a variety of ways. At a League meeting in Savannah, Georgia, for which thousands turned out, after the invited speaker finished his comments the band "played 'Wearing of the Green,' merging it into 'Dixie,' and the applause from the orchestra, galleries, and stage almost drowned the music."[29] Conversely, despite their seeming nostalgia for the Confederacy, some southern Land Leagues also attempted to place the conflict between the British and the Irish into a narrative of slave and slavemaster, with the Irish symbolizing the slave suffering under bondage and desiring freedom. A San Antonio branch resolution stated: "The colored people of the South have but recently celebrated the anniversary of their emancipation. God grant that that day may not be far distant when our countrymen [in Ireland] may be able to follow their example."[30] John Ellis made a much less benign comparison to African slavery in a speech before the 6th District New Orleans Land League: "I declare before God and the civilized world that the institution [of African slavery], as practiced in the Southern states of the Union, was humane and Christian and merciful and provident when compared with Mr. Gladstone's system of white slavery as practiced and enforced against the tenant farmers of Ireland." Ellis continued his analogy by asserting that the South had taken an inferior race, allegedly without God or civilization, and in the "school of slavery . . . prepared it for the exalted sphere and privileges of American citizenship," whereas the British had conquered a race of poets, orators, philosophers, and statesmen.[31] In this formulation southern slaveholders were the paternalistic teachers of civilization, and the British, a nation of cruel and demanding taskmasters.

Negative southern attitudes toward Reconstruction were also applied to the Irish struggles back home. In the minds of some southern commentators the Irish people were counterparts to the Confederacy, with the British and Irish landlords being representative of the North. Father Abram J. Ryan, an Irish-American Catholic priest famous for his pro-Confederacy poetry, argued in a speech before the Baltimore Land League that "unreconstructed English landlords are to Ireland what carpetbaggers were to the South. We suffered and were patient and now the carpetbaggers are not there, and we have the power in our hand. So will Ireland one day get rid of landlords."[32] In a similar vein a pamphlet titled *English Tyranny and Irish Suffering* and dedicated to the Memphis Irish Land League declared that "a people must have the right to rule themselves as they wish—it matters not whether that people live in a country called Ireland, or Poland, or the Southern States of America."[33] The southern experience of the Civil War shaped southerners' views of American government as well as their perspective on events in Ireland. In some sense sympathy for the Irish people served as another ideological tool for southerners in their attempts to create a narrative of the South as the victim of aggressive and continued northern oppression.

Irish-American participation in the Land League was also impressively strong in the West. San Francisco, the center of the movement in California, boasted several large and active branches of the Land League. Both men and women of Irish origins or descent worked for the cause, and Branch No. 1 in that city alone had 511 members.[34] Branches of the Land League were founded throughout California. By July 1881 there existed forty-nine branches in the state, and together they had raised $13,420 to send to Ireland.[35] According to David Emmons, the combined 85,000 Irish born in California and Colorado gave as much to the Ford Land League fund as the 400,000 Irish-born found in Massachusetts and Connecticut.[36] In Oregon there was a strong Portland Land League. Several mining communities in California, Colorado, the Dakota Territory, Nevada, and Montana also supported the Land League.[37] Together, these numerous branches clearly demonstrate the popularity of the Land League among western Irish Americans.

It may at first seem surprising that in the West, unlike the South where the racial politics of Reconstruction were grafted onto southern Irish-Americans' interpretation of the Land League, there was almost no mention in Land League circles in 1880 or 1881 of the dominant political issue in California, even though the anti-Chinese immigrant movement was taking place simultaneously with the emergence of the Land League. Henry George, for example, had achieved local fame in California during the 1870s for his anti-Chinese newspaper writings. But there are several possible explanations for the absence of anti-Chinese rhetoric within the Land League. Much of the anti-Chinese agitation had been centered in San Francisco during the second half of 1877 (and more sporadically in 1878 and 1879), and much of this agitation had revolved around the California Constitutional Convention, which took place in 1878–79.[38] During this period the Denis Kearney–led California Workingmen's Party held violent street protests and physically attacked Chinese immigrants. While the anti-Chinese movement persisted until the passage of the Exclusion Act in 1882, "Kearneyism" had all but disappeared by 1880. Among white Californians, regardless of class or ethnic background, anti-Chinese sentiment had become ingrained by the time of the Land League agitation. But middle-class and "respectable" Irish-American Californians wished to distance themselves from Kearney, who was often regarded suspiciously by Catholics owing to his socialist leanings and anti-Catholic-Church rhetoric.[39] San Francisco Land League branches, which were largely led by middle-class Irish Americans and Catholic priests, may have shared this anti-Kearneyism. In addition, Irish Americans in California, unlike their brethren in the South, would have been hard pressed to place themselves in the role of the oppressed since they were the leaders of the anti-Chinese movement. They were also unwilling to speak of themselves as oppressors. In California, for whatever reason, Irish Americans sought to keep the issues of Irish freedom and Chinese exclusion separate from each other.

It should also be noted that the Irish regional origins of Irish Americans could play a role in their level of participation in the Land League. In an important sense, no one simply emigrated from Ireland. Rather, they emigrated from home counties, parishes, and townlands.[40] Victor Walsh's research on the Irish in Pittsburgh, Pennsylvania, demonstrates how Irish regional origins, settlement patterns, and work in the United States combined to shape local Land League activity. The "Point" Irish, occupying one of the poorest and most isolated neighborhoods in Pittsburgh, hailed primarily from the western province of Connaught, a region grounded in "a communal and tradition-bound Gaelic culture." Gaelic speaking and socially isolated, the Point Irish retained "loyalties to the ancestral land of Connemara" rather than organizations like the Land League that promoted a united Irish nationhood.[41] In contrast, the Irish inhabitants of the Wood Run neighborhood, coming from the more modernized province of Munster and working in the Pittsburgh steel mills, possessed a more "well-developed sense of nationalism" and joined the Land League in large numbers.[42] A more extensive analysis of the regional origins of Land League members is beyond the purview of this study, but Walsh's research illustrates the potential interplay between regional, cultural, and economic differences in determining Irish-American responses to organizations like the Land League.

By the end of February 1881 the Land League cast a wide shadow over the Irish-American landscape. In all regions of the country men and women joined the League in large numbers and provided much-needed financial and moral support to the movement back in Ireland. But underneath the organization's surface unity, strong class, regional, and ideological divisions were ever present and profoundly shaped the nature of the Land League in the United States.

The Land League and the Broader Irish-American Community

The widespread membership and popularity of the Land League pushed it to the forefront of Irish-American life. It even moved beyond nationalist activity into other areas of Irish community life. The League's influence is most clearly seen in its impact on three key institutions of the Irish-American community—the Catholic Church, ethnic electoral politics, and previously established Irish-American groups and societies. This interaction was a dynamic process, as the League exerted an impact on these outside elements, and these elements in turn affected the structure and direction of the Land League movement in America.

The participation of Catholic clergymen in the movement greatly increased the ability of the Land League to mobilize all elements of the Irish-American community. The prominent role of the Catholic clergy was evident at the Buffalo convention, which twenty-six priests attended as delegates. This helped to give the convention a strongly ecclesiastical character. Bishop Hendricken of Providence, Rhode Island, beseeched the delegates to send plenty of money and encouraging words to the suffering Irish at home.[43] The Detroit-based *Western Home Journal* lauded the priests present at the Buffalo convention as "active, watchful, vigorous, and effective" and as proof that the "land agitation is not anti-Catholic."[44] Several members of the American Catholic hierarchy also came out publicly in favor of the Land League: Archbishop John Williams of Boston; Bishop Augustus Toebbe of Covington, Kentucky; Bishop John Ambrose Waterson of Columbus, Ohio; and Bishop John Hogan of St. Joseph, Missouri, all endorsed the American Land League.[45] The archdiocese of Boston issued an address of support to the "clergy and people of Ireland." Priests in the diocese of Newark echoed these sentiments, granting the Land League their full approval and promising "to aid it . . . by the voice, by the pen, and by the purse."[46] This involvement in Irish-American nationalism by Catholic authorities was unprecedented, as the church had denounced earlier groups like the Fenian Brotherhood, going so far as to sometimes refuse Catholic burials for Fenians.

The Land League was also popular among parish priests, multitudes of whom were active workers in local branches, and many Catholic priests were popular speakers at Land League meetings. Father Thomas J. Conaty of Worcester was active in New England, and Father Maurice F. Dorney stumped the broader Chicago area.[47] It was his participation in the Land League that first brought the Reverend Edward McGlynn of St. Stephen's in New York City to national notice.[48] Father Abram J. Ryan, the popular poet-priest and Confederate apologist, canvassed the southern states. On the West Coast the Reverend J. A. Rooney was one of the leaders of the League in San Francisco. The Buffalo *Catholic Union* hailed priests as "among the chief speakers wherever those [League] meetings are held throughout the United States."[49] Land League meetings were often held on Sunday afternoons after church services, and the local Catholic clergy regularly provided facilities for meetings and lectures.

The Land League cause was also given valuable publicity by various Catholic newspapers. They covered local League meetings as well as important happenings in Ireland. John Dillon believed that the American Catholic press had not only supported the movement but "had gone quite as far in the movement as the most advanced man in the Land League has gone."[50] But there were instances when the League's secular values clashed with church edicts. In several localities local bishops and priests issued edicts to their parishioners forbidding them from attending League-organized Sunday picnics and entertainments. They argued that the Sabbath was not a time for dancing, drinking, and playing games.[51] Such disagreements, however, were usually resolved quickly.

Unlike the close links sought by Land League leaders with the Catholic Church, a guiding principle of the League from its beginning was to keep it removed from any connection with American partisan politics. Previous Irish-American nationalist movements had been badly weakened by the entanglement of Irish nationalism with American politics. Daniel O'Connell's attempt in the 1840s to enlist Irish Americans in support of repeal of the Act of Union had crashed on the rocks of O'Connell's strident abolitionist views.[52] Perhaps with this example still in their minds, League leaders stressed the need for a politically neutral platform in order to appeal to all supporters of the Irish cause. The New York League branch declared: "There are men of all shades of political opinion among us, but they are not questioned as to their opinions. All we want to know of them is, 'Are they friends of Ireland?'"[53] Article XIII of the constitution of the Land League, adopted at Buffalo, also reflected this concern and banned "the introduction and discussion of American politics."[54] The Land League in America was meant to be a nonpolitical entity as far as American politics were concerned.

Despite this stance, some American politicians, particularly Democrats, attempted to marshal their support for the Land League into electoral votes. Tammany Hall, the New York Democratic political machine, endorsed the Land League during Parnell's tour and appointed a general committee for raising money for Ireland. The Tammany leader "Honest John" Kelly presided over a meeting held in New York City in hopes of winning Irish-American votes.[55] The *New York Tablet* encouraged its readers to combine their votes so as to elect Irish-American representatives to Congress and state legislatures who would be sympathetic to Ireland's cause.[56] Such attempts by politicians to curry favor through association with Ireland's struggle did not always work out as intended. Mayor Carter H. Harrison of Chicago drew the ire of the local Irish-American community when he refused to preside in his official capacity at a mass meeting to denounce British policy in Ireland.[57] In Pennsylvania there was an attempt to direct local Land League members' votes behind a particular gubernatorial candidate, which led to a scandal when the plot came to light.[58]

Land League leaders loudly rebuffed these attempts to politicize the movement and promote the political advancement of certain individuals. Martin Griffin, the editor of the *ICBU Journal*, called on members to spurn "young lawyers" who were attempting to "use this Land League agitation as a stepping stone to notoriety," while Patrick Ford warned that "we can use the Land League organization in American politics only to drag it down from its noble mission to an ignoble destruction . . . , no matter what the complexion desired to be given—Greenback, Democratic, or Republican." Ford insisted that "the Irish National Land and Industrial League must be kept free of American politics."[59] Such statements reflected the nonpolitical nature of the movement in the United States and the general determination to keep it that way. The Land League was not interested in effecting change through the means of U.S. electoral politics. Rather, like the abolitionist movement of the antebellum period, members of the Land League wanted to effect change through moral suasion and financial support.

Two notable exceptions to the League's aversion to the politics of personal advancement were the campaigns of Patrick Collins and John F. Finerty for election to the U.S. House of Representatives in 1882. Both men benefited from their leadership roles in the movement, as they were well known in the

Irish-American press for their Land League activities. Their association with the Land League, however, does not fully explain their electoral victories, and their elections did not undermine the nonpartisan nature of the Land League. Collins had a long history as a Democratic operative in Massachusetts, having served several years in the state legislature. The seat for which he ran in Boston—the Fourth District—was newly created, consisting of the overwhelmingly Democratic wards of the North and South Ends of Boston, as well as East and South Boston.[60] In his own self-image Collins considered himself an American politician, not an Irish-American one. "I kneel at the altar of my fathers, and I love the land of my birth," Collins declared, "but in American politics I know neither race, color, nor creed."[61]

Finerty, the editor of the *Chicago Citizen*, ran in Chicago as an independent. During his campaign he proclaimed that "he would be an Irish rebel whether he was fighting the English or corrupt machine politicians."[62] In contrast to New York, politics in Chicago were far less centralized, with modest interest groups such as Clan na Gael influencing political decisions by acting as "mini-machines" that were able to deliver solid voting blocs to aspiring politicians in exchange for political favors and patronage.[63] During Finerty's run for Congress internal divisions among these various "mini-machines" allowed him to emerge victorious by a substantial margin. Thus, while both men benefited from their association with the Land League, it was primarily a combination of local causes that led to their election to Congress.

Nevertheless, the actions of both men in Congress were shaped by their nationalist feelings against Britain. Almost all of Finerty's Congressional activities were linked to his concern for Ireland and his distrust of Britain. He favored building up the American navy so that the United States could resist British control of the seas, and he believed that a strong navy was necessary as America began to assert its power overseas. Finerty also favored a high tariff in order to protect American manufacturing from cheap British goods.[64] In his own mind such views were also pro-American, as they protected the United States from British economic and military domination. Finerty's Anglophobic views inspired the editor of the *New York Tribune* to mockingly call him the "member from Illinois elected to represent Ireland in the Congress of the United States."[65] Collins was generally frustrated during his time in Congress owing to the glacial pace of change in the House of Representatives.[66] But his most significant actions in Congress were based on supporting and protecting the rights of naturalized citizens and preventing any changes to the existing naturalization laws. Thus, both men's policies were shaped in many ways by their Irish nationalist convictions. Despite the elections of Collins and Finerty to Congress, however, the Land League was very successful in avoiding the dangerous introduction of American politics into the movement, and this achievement helped the Land League avoid one of the major pitfalls of previous Irish-American organizations.

After Parnell's tour the principles of the Land League began to win enthusiastic support from other Irish-American organizations. "By 1880 Irish America boasted a rich and expressive associational life," Victor Walsh has noted, "which included parish and parochial school systems and a whole constellation of Catholic temperance, beneficial, literary, and fraternal-aid societies."[67] The effectiveness of the Land League greatly benefited from the infusion of support that it received from various Irish ethnic associations. Many Land League branches were originally organized as offshoots of other societies, and some of the most energetic and useful leaders of the League in America were drawn from the ranks of other groups. In effect, the Land League was able to graft itself onto these other societies and profited enormously in popularity and numbers from these close relationships.

Many of the most active and effective leaders in the Land League were also members of other Irish societies. The national treasurer, Father Lawrence Walsh, had been president of the Connecticut branch of the Catholic Total Abstinence Union of America (CTAU). Martin Griffin, one of the League's best organizers, was secretary of the Irish Catholic Benevolent Union (ICBU) and used his position as editor of the society's journal to promote the Land League cause. On the West Coast Thaddeus Flanagan served as the national secretary of the AOH and was instrumental in the growth of the League in California.[68] By drawing on the organizational acumen and enthusiasm of these leaders, the League was able to establish itself quickly in the constellation of Irish-American associational groups.

The growth of the Land League in Philadelphia provides a local example of the interconnected relationship of the League and other Irish-American societies. The first local branch of the Land League, the Parnell Branch, was organized in the offices of the ICBU on 25 November 1880. By April 1881, Philadelphia had thirty-four branches with a total membership of over 3,500.[69] These League branches were overwhelmingly middle class and closely linked with the ICBU. The president of the Parnell Branch, Charles Fay, was also president of the ICBU, and all the executive officers of the branch were ICBU members.[70] Martin Griffin used the pages of the *ICBU Journal* to report on local and national Land League meetings and frequently editorialized on the movement. The bourgeois nature of the Philadelphia branches is also evidenced by the support that they received from Archbishop Wood and the local clergy.[71] Philadelphia's financial contributions to Ireland totaled over $10,000.[72] By merging with already established local patterns of Irish-American fraternal and benevolent life, the Land League was able to grow and spread much more quickly than earlier Irish nationalist organizations.

The esteem for the Land League among other Irish associations was national in scope. Favorable resolutions in support of the League were made at the national conventions of several organizations, and positive editorials appeared in their journals. The AOH expressed fervent support for the League's principles. Their national journal called on Hibernians to involve themselves in the League, while their 1880 national convention in Philadelphia pledged the group's fidelity to Parnell. The AOH Grand Lodge went so far as to declare that the "Ancient Order of Hibernians is the bone and sinew of this body [the Land League] in America."[73] In 1881 in Boston the CTAU announced that its members "heartily sympathize[d]" with the Irish people and with the Land League in America.[74] The ICBU convention held at Wilmington, Delaware, hailed "the efforts of the Irish people at home and abroad to disestablish land-lordism and regain their national rights."[75] The assistance given to the League by these organizations was not confined to forming new branches and offering kind words. Irish-American societies were also important conduits for financial funding for the movement in Ireland. The AOH called on its divisions to con-tribute 5 percent of their overall funds to the Land League. The Massachusetts AOH branches alone sent almost $11,000 to Ireland.[76] Across the country as a whole a host of Irish societies and associations provided valuable financial con-tributions to the Land League cause.

The leaders of these societies did not always welcome the attention given by their members to the Land League. Clan na Gael had been instrumental in providing early support for the movement, and its members played highly sig-nificant roles in the success of both Parnell's and Davitt's tours. Clan leaders like John Devoy believed that these efforts entitled Clan na Gael to control the direction and finances of the movement in America. The executive board of the Clan secretly instructed its members to spare no pains to "secure control of these movements or organizations."[77] But Clan na Gael's efforts to gain control over the Land League were soon defeated; the League's funds were placed be-yond its reach, and the League gained in popularity among non-revolutionary-minded Irish Americans, effectively pushing the Clan into a subordinate posi-tion. In fact, the Clan soon found that its members were getting caught up in the constitutional methods of the League, to the detriment of preparing for revolutionary action in Ireland. One local organizer complained to Devoy: "I find it difficult to get men in the V.C. [Clan na Gael] owing to the League. Good Irishmen believe they are performing their duty to their native land by paying money to the League and will not at present recognize anything else."[78] The Clan na Gael national executive was forced to issue a circular calling on its members to remember that their first allegiance was to the agenda of the Clan rather than to that of the League. Fortunately for the Clan, it was strong enough to endure the centrifugal pull of the Land League on its members. Other Irish-American organizations were not so lucky.

At almost the same time that the Land League was growing in the United States, another Irish-American movement with significant backing from the Irish-dominated Catholic Church was founded to remove poor Irish from the cities of the eastern United States and reestablish them as self-sufficient yeoman farmers in the American heartland. In 1879 Bishops John Ireland and John Lancaster Spalding founded the Irish Catholic Colonization Association of the United States. Their plan was to establish a joint-stock corporation to raise the money needed to move poor Catholics from eastern cities and poor immigrants from Ireland to newly established colonies in Nebraska, Minnesota, and Arkansas.[79] The ICBU also formed a Colonization Committee in 1875 to pursue its own efforts for rural resettlement. That these efforts were occurring at the same time that an agricultural crisis was emerging in Ireland was coincidental, but the coincidence had a huge impact on Irish-American perceptions of colonization.

Across the Atlantic the poor harvests, bad weather, and low agricultural prices in Ireland in the late 1870s led some British and Irish philanthropists to believe that the assisted emigration of poor peasants to the United States and elsewhere was a necessary remedy to relieve Irish distress. There were several groups involved in this enterprise. One major advocate was John Sweetman, a wealthy Irishman, philanthropist, and friend of Parnell. In 1879 Sweetman visited a successful colony in Minnesota; he returned to Ireland to organize a joint-stock company along with an Irish emigrant society, purchasing with his own money ten thousand acres in Minnesota for settlers.[80] Another source of assisted emigration was the Tuke Committee, an organization of influential British politicians and businessmen. Emigrants were provided under its scheme with clothing and transport to North America and were handled on arrival by emigration agents who directed them to their ultimate destinations.[81] The British government partially funded this scheme, though the control and implementation of the program remained in private hands. The Irish Land League denounced the Tuke Committee and warned its members to "beware of 'philanthropic' emigration agents doing the work of the British government."[82]

American proponents of planned settlement tried to persuade members of the Land League to help, or at least not to hinder, their actions. The Reverend John F. Fanning, a member of the ICBU committee, denounced the fact that "in the name of patriotism . . . men would keep their countrymen at home and feed them a scant allowance of Indian meal flavored with seaweed" and "deprive them of the opportunity of eating meat three times a day, as every American citizen can do, if he so pleases."[83] The secretary of the Irish Catholic Colonization Association, William J. Onahan, decried the hypocrisy of helping the suffering tenant in Ireland but turning a blind eye to the needs of newly arrived Irish immigrants. "Surely the Irish peasant farmer, when he lands in America, perhaps friendless and helpless," he argued, "is no less an object of our sympathy and appeals no less strongly to our friendly aid than his struggling countryman at home."[84] But these appeals met with little approval from Land Leaguers.

The American Land League joined its Irish counterpart in rejecting efforts to aid and promote assisted immigration to the United States. The negative response to these movements toward Catholic colonization provides clear insights into many contemporary Irish-American views of emigration from Ireland. Members of the Land League remained dedicated to improving the lives of poor tenants in Ireland, but their reactions to poor immigrants coming to America reveals the kinds of class and ideological tensions that existed within the Land League.

Substantial sections of the native-born American population resented and disapproved of poor and unskilled Irish immigrants settling in the United States. An article in August 1882 in the *Pittsburgh Dispatch* complained of the increase of immigrant paupers in Pittsburgh and attributed this "undesirable and remarkable immigration" to the Land League agitation in Ireland.[85] Governor Benjamin F. Butler of Massachusetts commented in April 1883 that in spite of his sympathy for the suffering Irish peasants, he would stop assisted emigrants from landing at Boston if he had the authority to do so. A few months later, the New York superintendents of the poor pushed for the enactment of legislation that would change the immigration system to prevent European paupers from freely entering the United States.[86] In both Boston and New York officials feared that these poor Irish men and women would fall onto city relief rolls and become a long-term drain on municipal resources. The anti-Irish newspaper *Harper's Weekly* published a cartoon denouncing assisted emigration from Ireland. In this cartoon an overloaded and careening British steamship filled with Irish paupers and malcontents makes its way toward America, while a small dinghy with Irish-American-bought dynamite heads toward Ireland; its title declares the balance of trade with Britain to be against the United States. In an editorial the same magazine complained: "Honest, intelligent, and industrious immigrants from all parts of the globe are always welcome, but this country should not be made the dumping ground of European crime, pauperism, and idleness."[87]

Rather than countering these objections to incoming Irish emigrants, Irish-American leaders joined in the chorus of denunciation. In 1883 the Irish

THE BALANCE OF TRADE WITH GREAT BRITAIN SEEMS TO BE STILL AGAINST US.

650 Paupers arrived at Boston in the Steamship *Nestoria*, April 15th, from Galway, Ireland, shipped by the British Government.

"Poor House from Galway." *Harper's Weekly*, 28 April 1883.

National League sent resolutions to President Chester A. Arthur asking him to limit the number of poor immigrants entering the United States.[88] They told the president that it was "the duty of the United States to decline to support paupers whose pauperism began under and is the result of English misgovernment, and to demand of England that she send no more of her paupers to this shore to become a burden upon the American people."[89] This strategy toward Irish immigration left incoming Irish immigrants in the double bind of having to face fierce resistance not just from native-born Americans but also from their own kinsmen as well.

There were several reasons why members of the Land League rejected widespread immigration to the United States as a solution to the crisis in Ireland.

The most prevalent argument made by members of the Land League was that assisted emigration was unpatriotic. Even though he was a member of the board of directors of the Irish Catholic Colonization Association, John Boyle O'Reilly denounced assisted emigration on patriotic grounds and compared it to English settlement hundreds of years earlier in Ulster. "The people are to be 'transplanted,'" he noted, "and if they are not ordered out of their homes by placard and sound of trumpet at the cross-roads, there is much cruelty and more hypocrisy in the tyranny that compels them." He added sharply, "Cromwell banished them west of the Shannon; to-day they are to be banished west of the Atlantic Ocean."[90] The belief among many Land Leaguers was that assisted emigrants were being forced off their Irish holdings and compelled to undergo involuntary exile, not because there was not enough land in Ireland but because landownership there was monopolized by avaricious and often absentee landlords. Land Leaguers completely overlooked the fact that many poor tenants in Ireland welcomed opportunities to emigrate and free themselves from their terrible and unhappy living conditions.

Economic arguments were also marshaled to denounce assisted immigration. According to one historian, the arrival of poor immigrants was particularly unwelcome among those elements of the Irish-American population striving for respectability in bourgeois America.[91] Critics also asserted that these immigrants were a drain on precious American resources. The Reverend C. F. X. Goldsmith argued before the Land League branch in Chippewa Falls, Wisconsin, that "the Irish land system is a tax upon the American people for the benefit of the Irish landlords and English manufacturers and tradesmen," and that this indirect taxation helped England to "maintain its mastery in Ireland."[92] James Redpath seconded this comment and warned that Americans would soon be called upon to support these poor immigrants in American workhouses.[93] On the local level, Irish Americans in some cities feared that new immigrants would compete for scarce jobs and drive down wages. In Rochester, New York, newly arrived immigrants were asked to move on to other areas.[94] Critics ignored the fact that many Irish immigrants during the Great Famine had arrived in the United States in an even more dire economic condition.

The unpopularity of assisted emigration among members of the Land League and others helped to sabotage colonization schemes in the United States. Proponents of colonization came increasingly under fire as critics often lumped assisted emigration and colonization schemes together. Within the ICBU such opposition led to a gradual decline in support for colonization. Father Thomas Ambrose Butler, a member of the ICBU Colonization Committee, withdrew his backing and resigned from the board. At the 1882 national convention of the ICBU, delegates agreed with his sentiments and closed down the colonization activities of the organization.[95] The Irish Catholic Colonization Association continued its work but suffered from diminishing effectiveness and interest.

In addition to the negative impact of Land League opposition, the failure of Catholic colonization schemes in the United States is also attributable to misunderstanding and conflict between the leaders of the movement and the immigrants they sought to help. Advocates often found that the goals of colonizers and newly arrived settlers were not the same. At the Graceville colony in Minnesota, for example, settlers favored taking jobs as day laborers working for wages rather than farming their own lands. In the end most settlers surrendered their farms, and most of the men found work laboring for the railroads.[96] The attempts of colonizers to raise funds for settlers also fell considerably short of their goals. The money raised for colonization paled in comparison with the funds gathered by the Land League, and as one historian has aptly remarked, Irish Americans "were never convinced that [colonization] was a more deserving charity than the resettlement of cottiers in Ireland."[97]

The embrace of the Land League by other Irish-American societies was crucial in making it a success. Leaders of these groups gave the movement invaluable expertise and experience, while also encouraging rank-and-file members to lend their support as well. But the wide shadow cast by the League was not always beneficial to less popular groups or to efforts like those of Clan na Gael and the Catholic colonization societies. On both of these latter movements the popularity of the League exerted a damaging influence, and in the case of Catholic colonization, it constituted a fatal distraction from the promoters' agenda. Whether positively or negatively, the close connections of the Land League with other elements of Irish-American life profoundly affected and shaped the broader Irish-American community in the late nineteenth century.

4

"Ireland to Us Is Father and Mother and America Is the Wife"

Conservative Irish-American Nationalism, the Land League, and the Quest for Respectability

The indirect influence of Irish want and misery debases the standing and hurts the prospects of every man of Irish blood or birth throughout the world. Their entrance to every path of honor is challenged. They are weighted in the race of life, the disgrace and reproach of national poverty and degradation rests upon them and is not to be lightly shaken off. So for their own sake it behooves Irishmen everywhere to put an end to this condition of things; it is to their interest that Ireland shall cease to come before the world periodically as a beggar.

Joseph O'Connor before the Monroe County Land League

As the Land League agitation spread in the United States, diverse groups with very different views about the purpose of the Land League struggled over control of the movement. The meaning of the Land League in the United

90

States was far from stable, changing and responding to the competing claims of the various elements that created it.

Conservative nationalists in the American Land League held their own ideological conception of the movement. They believed that the American Land League should follow the lead of Parnell and his party colleagues in Ireland and confine their own activities to fundraising and providing moral support. Much of the backing for this faction came from a coalition of the newly emerging Irish-American middle class, better-off workers, and the Catholic Church. Such leaders as John Boyle O'Reilly and Patrick Collins attempted to centralize the movement and ensure that it remained under conservative control. For conservative Irish nationalists the movement to free Ireland also became intertwined with their struggle to prove their fitness for social advancement and participation in American republican political institutions.[1]

The Conservative Wing of the American Land League

After the founding of the Land League in the United States, conservative nationalists attempted to control the movement. In the beginning they were fairly successful in their efforts. Conservative nationalists were predominant at the Land League Convention held in Buffalo in early 1881. Father Patrick Cronin, editor of the Buffalo *Catholic Union and Times*, hosted the convention and Father Daniel O'Connell of Oswego, New York, was elected chairman. Twenty-four other priests were present. Overall, 129 delegates represented 292 branches in thirteen states. Of these delegates, 124 came from New England or one of the Middle Atlantic states, and conservatives dominated these branches.[2] Clan na Gael, which was strongest in the Midwest, essentially ignored the convention and had little representation among the delegates. The conservative makeup of the delegates limited the influence of radical and physical-force nationalists in attendance.

The election of officers and the bylaws and resolutions approved by the delegates further cemented conservative control of the organization. Patrick Collins of Boston was elected president, Father Cronin was elected first vice president, and Father Walsh was reelected as treasurer. All these men were conservatives who believed that the Land League was an auxiliary movement and must defer to the Irish leadership in Dublin. The only radical delegate elected to an official position was Terence V. Powderly, mayor of Scranton, Pennsylvania, and Grand Master Workman of the Knights of Labor, but the triumvirate of Collins, Flatley, and Walsh directed the official work of the

American Land League.[3] The bylaws and resolutions adopted by the convention reflected the moderate proclivities of the delegates. The organization changed its name to the "Irish National Land League of the United States," dropping "Industrial" from its title and thus further signaling the delegates' hostility toward social radicalism. The stated objects of the League were "to furnish moral and financial aid to the National Land League in Ireland in its efforts to obtain such changes in the system of Irish land laws as will make those who cultivate the soil of Ireland its owners."[4] The movement in America was to be "auxiliary to that in Ireland" and to have "no part in shaping the policy of the Irish body."[5] The delegates repudiated the revolutionary ideals of the Clan and joined "the Irish National Land League of Ireland in deprecating all forms of violence and earnestly urge the Irish people to continued patience under all provocation."[6]

Who supported this conservatism, and what did it entail in the United States? The conservative faction of the American Land League was a loose amalgam of three elements within the Irish-American community—the emerging Irish-American middle class, members of the comfortable working class, and the American Catholic Church. We must be careful not to simply ascribe ideological convictions to class status, as there were important exceptions, but generally members of the these groups made up the majority of supporters of conservative Irish-American nationalism.

The Buffalo branch of the Land League provides a clear snapshot of this conservative coalition. Just prior to the national convention held there in early 1881, the Buffalo Irish met to establish their own branch of the Land League. The branch was headed by Father Cronin and over the next two years remained a bastion of conservative nationalism. The branch sent its money to Ireland through the Land League treasurer Father Walsh and denounced the *Irish World*'s attempts to make itself the organ of the movement.[7] An examination of the branch's membership list through use of the 1880 census yielded data for 90 of the 183 members.[8] While these results cannot give us an exact account of the League's social composition, they do provide enough information to make some plausible claims. Given the occupations most prevalent in the branch—12.2 percent from professional and merchant categories, 20.0 percent white-collar workers, and 47.8 percent skilled workers—it is clear that the vast majority of the Buffalo League were members of the comfortable working class (see table 1).

This result corresponds with William Jenkins's findings that the Buffalo West Side "lace-curtain Irish" were a "mix of comfortable working class and the emerging middle class."[9] The small proportion of manual laborers in the branch also corresponds with his data showing low numbers of unskilled laborers

Table 1. Buffalo, New York, Land League occupations

Occupation	Numbers of members	Percentage of total
Skilled workers	43	47.8%
White-collar workers	18	20.0%
Professional/Merchant	11	12.2%
Other	10	11.1%
Manual workers	8	8.9%
Total	**90**	**100.0%**

Source: Membership list with members' street addresses found in *Catholic Union*, December 30, 1880, 3. Demographic information found via United States Census (1880), Schedule 1 (Population) via ancestry.com.

within households in the area.[10] It is necessary to note that within the broader Land League movement, not all skilled workers agreed with conservatives. Some of them were drawn to the social radicalism advocated by Patrick Ford and the radical nationalist wing of the League.[11] The Buffalo branch also gives us a glimpse at the generational diversity within the movement. Roughly 68 percent of the members were born in Ireland, 28 percent in North America, and 3 percent elsewhere in Europe. Thus, while the Irish-born element predominated in the branch, a significant number of its members were American born. Although we should not extend these results too far outside of Buffalo, these data do provide a welcome insight into the demographic makeup of supporters of the conservative faction of the Land League.

Members of the Irish-American middle class constituted the dominant bloc among conservative nationalists. The rise of Irish Americans into the middle class in the United States was a relatively new development. What exactly it meant to be a middle-class Irish American in the late nineteenth century is not always easy to measure or define. Members of this bourgeoning class included clerks, teachers, and sales personnel who, though they often earned less than highly skilled workers, maintained a higher social status reflected in their leadership positions in their local communities.[12] Also included were lawyers, other professionals, and politicians. We should note, however, that the majority of Irish Americans remained working class in this era. In his examination of Irish Americans in Newburyport, Massachusetts, Stephan Thernstrom has noted the modest gains made by Irish workers. "Through toil and sacrifice," Thernstrom observes, "they had been able to buy homes, build their church, and obtain a slender margin of economic security."[13] Conditions were improving, but it was a gradual process. Instead of the "rags to riches" stories so popular in Horatio Alger's novels of this period, social advancement was usually achieved not by reaching the upper echelons of American wealth and status beyond expectation but by obtaining a better position within the working class.[14] Social advancement was also achieved by women. Irish-American women, according to Hasia Diner, "experienced a steady movement out of the ranks of domestic service into white-collar and semiprofessional positions."[15] Together, these developments helped to create a small but significant Irish-American middle class.

Patrick Collins and John Boyle O'Reilly are good examples of this emerging Irish-American middle class. Born in Ireland in 1844, Collins and his family immigrated to Boston when he was four. Thus his formative years were spent in the United States and not in Ireland. He was raised in South Boston, where he experienced firsthand the anti-Catholic nativism of the Know Nothing movement while attending public school.[16] In the face of this discrimination, as Collins later recalled, he "had to fight to get to school, at recess, to get home; in fact, to go anywhere."[17] Leaving school at the age of twelve, he received training as an upholsterer and helped organize the Upholsterers' Union in Boston.[18] Collins studied and taught himself law at the Boston Public Library before attending Harvard Law School. His efforts soon paid off with his election to the Massachusetts state legislature in 1867 and his receipt of a law degree in 1871.[19] By 1880, Collins was one of the leading Irish Americans in Boston. Self-made and prosperous, he represented a "respectable" middle-class version of Irish-American identity in the United States.

Collins was also heavily involved in Irish-American nationalism. In 1864 he joined the South Boston Circle of the Fenian Brotherhood. During the next few years Collins organized fourteen new branches in western Massachusetts and was active in the issuance of Fenian bonds in New York.[20] But by 1867 he had left the Fenian movement and repudiated violent methods to free Ireland. Instead, he became heavily involved in Massachusetts Democratic politics.

His conservatism emerged from his experience with the Fenians and from his views of American society. Having witnessed the internecine fighting between Fenian factions in the United States and Ireland, Collins keenly wanted the Land League to be united and to follow the direction of political leaders in Ireland.[21] He also dismissed the social radicalism of Patrick Ford and his attempts to link land reform in Ireland with social change in the United States. According to his biographer, Collins held a "fixed and immutable conviction" in American democracy.[22] Unlike Patrick Ford, he believed that social reform could be achieved through the American electoral process. A self-made man, Collins believed that others could likewise improve themselves and achieve success. His personal experience in the United States led him to favor a constitutional and nonviolent solution to the Irish crisis.

Collins's good friend John Boyle O'Reilly, the Irish-born poet and editor of the Boston *Pilot*, provided further proof of the heights achieved by some Irish Americans in the late nineteenth century. A former Fenian, O'Reilly had been convicted and transported to Australia by the British government before escaping to the United States in 1870.[23] Sometimes described as "the most distinguished" Irishman in America, O'Reilly was popular among both Irish Americans and Boston's Brahmin elite. As a result of his wide popularity, he was given the honor in 1889 of delivering the main address at the dedication ceremony for the monument to the Pilgrims at Plymouth Rock. O'Reilly, like Collins, believed that much could be achieved by hard work and determination. According to one historian, he "was, if nothing else, a true believer in the concept of the self-made man."[24] He espoused African-American rights, denounced anti-Semitism, and supported strikes by American workers.[25] But O'Reilly did not favor the form of social radicalism promoted by Patrick Ford. Instead, O'Reilly tempered his ideas so as not to alienate other Irish Americans, and he too believed that unity was crucial among Irish Americans.[26] He also shared Collins's faith in the egalitarian nature of American society and supported nonviolent constitutional Irish nationalism. Despite his reformist tendencies and his support for the Irish cause, O'Reilly was "moderate with respect to the United States" and did not support social radicalism in the movement.[27] Many other middle-class activists in the Land League shared the moderation of Collins and O'Reilly.

Any consideration of the class status of Irish Americans has to take account of geographical location and its effect on the Irish-American experience. As many historians have noted, the experience of Irish Americans in New England was not typical of the majority of Irish Americans.[28] For a variety of reasons the Irish in America generally did better the further west they went. Irish settlers in the urban centers of the Midwest and West were often among the first waves of pioneers in these regions. These new cities did not have the entrenched Anglo-American elites hostile to new immigrants that could be found in Boston or in well-organized anti-Catholic movements along the Eastern Seaboard. In addition, because of the fluid and dynamic economies of these new cities, social mobility was much easier and occurred more quickly than in the East. According to one historian, in these cities "the progress of recent Irish immigrants often surpassed that of third- and fourth-generation New England Irish Americans."[29] In the mining city of Butte, Montana, for example, Irish-American settlers dominated local politics and the local economy owing to their early arrival in the area.[30] In the urban setting of San Francisco, Irish Americans as early as the 1870s had achieved levels of political, economic, and social success that dwarfed their eastern counterparts.[31] As David Emmons has noted, the Irish in America were at the forefront of "America's western advance," serving in large numbers in the western army as well as settling the cities of the Bonanza West.[32] Depending on location and time of arrival, rates of social advancement varied greatly among the Irish Americans.

Perhaps the best definition of middle-class Irish Americans is that they had achieved a modicum of economic security and rising prominence in their local communities but were still insecure and striving for greater standing within the broader American society. This insecurity will be discussed shortly, but evidence for the rising prominence of members of the Irish-American middle class in their communities is found in the prevalence of their leadership in many Land League branches. In some areas this was the result of working-class indifference to the official League. For example, in Denver, David Brundage has found that the Irish Americans who formed the active core of the local branch were lawyers, judges, politicians, newspaper editors, and building contractors.[33] The middle-class leadership of the Denver branch was able to dampen intraethnic class conflict for a time. Similarly, Kerby Miller has established that "leadership cadres, citywide membership lists, and delegations to national conventions were disproportionately dominated by men of white-collar status, including affluent businessmen and professionals as well as small proprietors and clerks."[34] Their disproportionate presence is not that surprising. Such individuals had the time to devote themselves to meetings and administration. Shopkeepers and saloon owners, moreover, had a customer base that was predominantly working class, and their positions of local prominence made them natural community leaders. This, of course, does not mean that only middle-class and upper-class individuals held leadership positions in the Land League, but middle-class Irish Americans were clearly involved deeply in the movement.

While many Land League supporters like Collins and O'Reilly had been born in Ireland, there were also significant numbers of second-generation Irish Americans who participated in the Land League. Unfortunately, a lack of data prevents us from measuring the exact proportion of Land Leaguers who were American born, but contemporaries believed that the figure was sizeable. "The whole Irish-American element, the second-generation as strongly as the first," an editorial in the Richmond *AOH Journal* claimed, "thoroughly approve of the Land Agitation and are in perfect accord with its action."[35] A more concrete example of second-generation participation in the movement was Martin J. Griffin, the Philadelphia-based editor of the *ICBU Journal*. Born in Philadelphia in 1842, the son of Irish parents from County Wicklow, Griffin worked as a correspondent for a variety of Catholic newspapers.[36] He also joined several Catholic societies, becoming the national secretary of the ICBU in 1872. After hearing a speech given by Michael Davitt in late 1880, Griffin became an avid supporter of the Land League. In Philadelphia alone he helped organize more than twenty-five branches of the American Land League and nine branches of the Ladies' Land League.[37] Thomas N. Brown also found that second-generation nationalists were prevalent in the Land League.[38]

The middle class rather than wealthier Irish Americans dominated the conservative wing of the movement. Land League leaders often noted the lack of wealthy Irish Americans in the movement. "They [wealthy Irish Americans] made a little money accidentally during the war," Father Daniel O'Connell declared in his report on the success of the Oswego, New York, branch, "and don't think it is just genteel to mix with such fellows as the Land Leaguers."[39] Martin Griffith questioned the patriotism of rich Irish Americans. "If all Irishmen were rich," he tartly remarked, "Ireland would have few friends."[40] Further evidence of wealthier Irish Americans' aversion to the Land League can be found in their response to Parnell's tour. Rather than donating to Parnell's relief efforts, they gave most of their money (when they gave at all) to James Gordon Bennett's Irish Relief Fund.[41] During his tour out west in 1880, Michael Davitt encountered J. W. Mackay, "the bonanza king," one of the country's wealthiest Irish Americans, who had made his fortune in the Comstock Lode silver find outside Virginia City, Nevada. Mackay attended Davitt's lecture but in a meeting afterward informed the Irish leader that he thought the land movement was a complete waste of effort.[42] It was only after the demise of the Land League and the emergence of its successor, the Irish National League, that rich Irish Americans overcame their resistance and pledged their support to Parnell's Home Rule strategy. Within the Land League it was middle-class rather than wealthy Irish Americans who steered the movement in a conservative direction.

The other strong element within the conservative wing of the Land League was the American Catholic Church. Ecclesiastical hostility had damaged or weakened earlier nineteenth-century Irish-American nationalist and labor organizations, but from its inception the Land League in America drew strong backing from many church officials.[43] One early supporter was Richard Gilmour, the Scottish-born bishop of Cleveland. On 6 November 1879, two months before Parnell's visit to America, Gilmour issued an appeal to his diocese to send whatever money people could spare to Ireland for alleviating distress. Dismissing anti-Irish critics who claimed that Irish laziness, drunkenness, and disorder explained the distress in Ireland, Bishop Gilmour pointed to the success and decency of the Irish in America. What was happening in Ireland, according to Gilmour, was the result of a combination of poor harvests and British misrule. He called upon all Catholics to lend their aid. "Hunger is a cry that appeals to no nationality," Gilmour told his flock, "hence also, those congregations not Irish will lend a helping hand to their brethren of a common faith, who by oppression and persecution have been reduced to their present state of suffering."[44] Bishop Gilmour ordered that collections be taken up in Cleveland churches until Christmas and that the proceeds be forwarded to the Irish hierarchy. His efforts were mirrored in several other Catholic dioceses across the United States.[45]

This early support for the Land League by Catholic Church authorities was not unanimous. Bishop Bernard J. McQuaid of Rochester was distrustful of the Land League; he believed that the League was linked to secret societies previously outlawed by the church, particularly the Fenian Brotherhood.[46] He was also suspicious of leaders like Parnell. "It will surprise me to learn," McQuaid confided in a letter, "that Parnell is not working designedly in the interest of the worst section of the *Fenian* party."[47] Manny Tello, editor of the Cleveland-based *Catholic Universe*, expressed similar concerns. In an editorial on the Land League Tello maintained that "there were many who dreaded lest the movement would be captured by socialistic agitations . . . [that] under the pretext of nationality . . . have vilified the Catholic Church, led men into forbidden societies, and reflected generally what discredit they could on a cause which of itself is worthy of the highest devotion."[48] Yet he ended his editorial by stating that he was worried more about his followers than Parnell himself.[49] Despite their early misgivings, both McQuaid and Tello later became enthusiastic supporters of the Land League, having been encouraged by the leadership of such men as Collins and O'Reilly.

The vast majority of Catholic clergymen associated with the Land League, with a few notable exceptions like Father Edward McGlynn, were staunch supporters of the conservative faction of the Land League. In Worcester, Massachusetts, Father Thomas J. Conaty dominated the local male Land League branch and guided it along a conservative path.[50] The United Catholic clergy of the Archdiocese of Boston, with Archbishop John Williams's approval, published a letter of support for the Land League's efforts in Ireland, as did clergy in New Jersey.[51] Twenty-six Catholic priests attended as Buffalo Convention delegates, with Father Patrick Cronin of Buffalo delivering the opening address and Father Daniel O'Connell of Lake Oswego, New York, elected temporary chairman.[52] The identification of the Land League with the church provided useful protection against critics' claims that its goals were too radical or even "communistic." External opponents of the League often argued that its purpose was to expropriate Irish landlords and to trample on the rights of property. Father Conaty denied these claims. "Must a whole nation live in poverty," he asked, "to preserve the rights of a few men who have little interest in the land except for the revenue which the industry of the tenants draws from it?"[53] By giving their support to the Land League, church officials bestowed on the agitation a respectability lacking in the Young Ireland movement of 1847–48 or the Fenian movement of the 1860s.

The involvement of churchmen also allowed them to exert a moderating influence on the League. They shared a deep distrust of the revolutionary aims of Clan na Gael, and they worked to keep such groups under control. A notable exception to the hostility generally shown to militant nationalists was Archbishop Patrick Feehan of Chicago, who was on good terms with local Clan na Gael leaders.[54] But Feehan's attitude toward the Clan was highly unusual. Church officials also sought to temper Land League support for the social radicalism of Patrick Ford and his followers. Implicit in the support given by members of the church was a warning that the League would continue to receive such backing only as long as its goals and methods remained morally correct in the eyes of the church. In Chicago one historian has found that the church "used its influence to make Irish labor politics more conservative" and to restrict their aims.[55] Archbishop John Williams of Boston praised the principles endorsed at the Buffalo convention, saying they were "justified by religion and morality," and he extended his "sympathy and cooperation to all those who are laboring in such a just and righteous cause as long as they are guided by these principles."[56] As this statement reveals, the help given by church leaders was conditional. Later, when the movement in the United States assumed a more radical character, some of its prominent former supporters in the Catholic Church became vocal critics. Despite these defections, however, the threat posed by the bid of radical nationalists to take over the Land League helped to keep the conservative alliance together.

Conservative Irish-American Nationalists' Conception of the Land League

Conservative nationalists shared certain core beliefs. They believed in the necessity for change in Ireland but did not favor the radical social reform advocated by Patrick Ford or the revolutionary methods encouraged by members of Clan na Gael like John Devoy.[57] They also backed Parnell's leadership of the movement, seeing in him a symbol of respectable and moderate political agitation, and advocated a measured solution to the Irish land problem. What conservatives desired was gradual reform, not drastic social change.

Conservatives rejected the economic radicalism of Patrick Ford and the violent dynamite tactics of Jeremiah O'Donovan Rossa. They bristled at what they believed were attempts by Ford and members of Clan na Gael to subordinate the Land League to their own special agendas. They also believed that this subversion opened the Land League and themselves to criticism from outsiders. As Thomas N. Brown argues, conservatives "wanted to aid the Irish farmer but not at the expense of doing an injury to their standing in America."[58] Throughout the years of the Land League in the United States conservatives fought a two-front battle within the Irish-American community against both the supporters of economic radicalism and those favoring armed revolution in Ireland.

Among middle-class Irish Americans ethnic nationalism served several purposes in their attempt to win acceptance and success in the United States. According to Thomas N. Brown, Irish-American nationalism had its sources in immigrants' lives in America, where they developed "a pervasive sense of inferiority, intense longing for acceptance and respectability, and an acute sensitivity to criticism."[59] Middle-class participation in the Land League certainly reflected many of these concerns, but among the immigrant middle class a new assertiveness was developing as well. While middle-class members of the Land League were concerned with improving the conditions of the Irish people in Ireland, they were also working to improve their status in the United States. They responded quickly to nativist attacks and increasingly protested negative portrayals of Irish Americans in American society. Around the same time as the Land League, Irish-American theatergoers mobbed several performances of Dion Boucicault's *The Shaughraun* because they were angered by the play's depiction of Irish drunkenness.[60] In the Land League and other organizations, many middle-class members desired a chance to show their fitness for social ascension and equal membership in the wider American republican community.

For many conservative members of the "Greater Ireland" created by the Land League, the effort to free Ireland from British oppression went hand in hand with the push by Irish Americans to rise to positions of prominence in the United States. This perspective was based on the belief that Ireland's continued existence under British rule left the Irish "race," including the Irish in America, as a colonized people.[61] John Boyle O'Reilly saw participation in the Land League as an obligation owed beyond simply the Irish at home but also by Irish Americans to themselves. "Irishmen in America have a duty to perform to Ireland out of self-respect to themselves," he declared. "They must elevate the old country in elevating the race, and thus so live as to hasten forward the time when the Celtic names—McCarthy, Murphy, and O'Donnell—will stand as high in eyes of the world as are the names of Hayes or Grant."[62] Patrick Collins echoed O'Reilly's call for Irish Americans to feel ethnic pride. "We meet here in America and as American citizens, loyal, devoted, and true as the best," he told a Boston audience, "but also as men in whose veins run the blood of the race who kept the book of knowledge open wide and the torches of civilization and religion flaming in ages when all was dark elsewhere."[63] In freeing Ireland, Irish Americans would be liberating themselves from nativist insults against their heritage and from challenges to their fitness for American society.

At stake were both a more positive self-image and Irish-American manhood. One member of the Land League warned that if Irish Americans could not "secure the just claims of Ireland, you are neither Americans nor Irishmen, nor true men of any kind whatsoever."[64] Individual exertion was not enough. A concerted effort by all Irish Americans was needed to ensure the success of the movement. "If they did not want to see the begging box going around again," Michael Davitt declared in a speech in St. Louis, "to the humiliation and disgrace of their race, they would aid in abolishing the landlords [and] in doing away with the cause of Irish distress."[65] The linkage made between freedom in Ireland and advancement in the United States helps to explain some of the allure of the Land League among conservative Irish Americans.

Supporters of the Land League often had to fend off accusations that their actions were unpatriotic and un-American. Critics like *Harper's Weekly* claimed that assertions of ethnic nationalism were dangerous to the well-being of the American republic and would create "a nation within a nation, a separate population among the people."[66] Patrick Collins responded to these claims by stressing that he was both an "American citizen and an Irish nationalist."[67] Furthermore, Collins likened his continued interest in Ireland to a familial obligation. "Ireland to us is father and mother," he explained, "and America is the wife."[68] To turn their backs on Ireland was thus not an act of loyalty to the United States but a betrayal of one's duties and obligations. Instead, Irish Americans argued that the Land League shared the best characteristics of Americanism. James Mooney, a member of the Buffalo Land League, maintained that as the "fundamental principles" of the movement included a hatred of tyranny, resistance to oppression, and the espousal of "charity, enlightenment, and humanity," the Land League was in full accord with the spirit of American republican institutions.[69] According to Mooney, the oppression and suffering faced by the Irish in Ireland made their arrival in the United States and the "transition from oppression to freedom so great a boon that we become more ardently attached to republican institutions than the native born themselves."[70] Seen in this way, Irish Americans agitating for land reform and Home Rule in Ireland were simply bestowing the gift of the best of America's republican traditions.

The struggle for freedom in Ireland also became wrapped up in the history of race in America. The Irish had been subject to caricature in both Ireland and America during the antebellum era, and as the racial taxonomy of Social

Darwinism and imperialism gained currency in the mid and late nineteenth century in the United States and Europe, Ireland's domination by Britain left Irish Americans' racial status vulnerable to questioning.[71] It is important not to overstate the effect of this prejudice on Irish Americans' daily lives. Unlike African Americans or Chinese immigrants, Irish Americans faced cultural prejudice but not any major discrimination, as they were always able to vote, serve on juries, sue and be sued, and become naturalized citizens of the United States.[72] But such magazines as *Puck* and *Harper's Weekly* often depicted Irish Americans as uneducated, simianized brutes, unfit for American republican responsibilities.[73]

Irish Americans were quick to refute any negative aspersions. "No man here will ever return to live in Ireland," John Boyle O'Reilly claimed of the Irish in America. "We and our children belong to this Republic. We shall never leave it. We are not Chinese."[74] While O'Reilly merely argued that Irish immigrants were different from Chinese immigrants owing to their unwillingness to return to their original homeland, other Irish-American voices made much harsher distinctions. "The Asiatic is not of our race," insisted the Irish-American newspaper the *Brooklyn Daily Eagle*. "He would constantly be a turbid, concentrated, and unmixable sediment in the national crucible. . . . Whatever may be the hope of future developments, Chinese immigration in the past has been anything but a blessing."[75] By implicitly juxtaposing Chinese immigrants' negative attributes in opposition to the positive ones of European immigrants, this editorialist further asserted Irish-American fitness for inclusion in American society. Other examples demonstrate the use of race within Land League rhetoric and the importance of race in Irish-Americans' self-image. A flyer for a Philadelphia Ladies' Land League meeting asked if Irish Americans were prepared to allow their countrymen to continue as the "white slaves of England's tyrannic rulers."[76] T. P. O'Connor further illustrated that race was a powerful tool in the creation of the Irish-American self-image by his use of America's racial hierarchy to spur Land League activity in the United States. O'Connor, one of the leaders of the Irish Land League, warned the Irish in America: "If Ireland is defeated, you are defeated; if Ireland is degraded, you are degraded. Blush when the emancipated negro passes you."[77] According to O'Connor, the failure of the Land League would mean not just the further subjugation of the Irish people but also the racial diminution of Irish Americans. Thus, conservatives believed that ending Ireland's dependent status was key to changing their status in the eyes of native-born Americans.

In their desire to achieve freedom for Ireland, conservatives eschewed violent methods in favor of constitutional agitation. Their distance from the frontlines in Ireland and their memories of the Fenian debacles pushed conservatives well away from embracing revolutionary schemes. The San Francisco *Monitor* denounced men who made violent speeches at American Land League meetings, claiming that "not one of this class would dare speak in this style if in Ireland, but here, five or six thousand miles away from the reach of the British lion's claws, it is the very essence of Falstaffian bravado to bluster about 'dynamite' and 'blowing up Windsor Castle.'"[78] Instead, the movement in the United States should restrict itself to furnishing moral and financial succor to political leaders in Ireland. "No man in America," C. M. McCarthy of the Land League branch in St. Paul, Minnesota, declared, "can have the right to dictate to the men at home."[79]

Despite their strong beliefs and their hold on the executive leadership of the Land League after the Buffalo convention, conservatives' control over the movement proved far from absolute. As discussed in the previous chapter, attempts to centralize control of the movement at the national level failed; Land League branches made important decisions locally and enjoyed a very wide measure of autonomy. Many branches did pledge their fidelity to the leadership of Collins and other nationally prominent conservatives, but serious personal and ideological disagreements continued to linger in the Land League. Leading the charge against conservative control of the movement would be the radical faction of the Land League led by Patrick Ford, which rejected conservatives' goals, arguing instead for the need for wide-ranging social change in both the United States and Ireland.

CHARLES S. PARNELL, M. P.,
IRELAND.

Copyrighted 1881, by L. C. Dillon, 1227 Penn. Avenue, Washington, D. C.

Charles Stewart Parnell. Parnell's 1880 tour of the United States spurred Irish Americans to turn their attention to Ireland and support the Land League. Courtesy of the Library of Congress.

Michael Davitt. Davitt's time in the United States was crucial in helping the American Land League movement continue to grow. Courtesy of the Library of Congress.

Patrick Collins. Collins was president of the Irish National Land League of the United States and leader of the conservative faction of the movement. Courtesy of the John J. Burns Library, Boston College.

Patrick Ford. Ford was editor of the *Irish World* newspaper and leader of the radical faction of the American Land League. Courtesy of the New York Public Library.

Delia Tudor Stewart Parnell. Along with Ellen Ford, Parnell traveled extensively, helping to organize Irish-American women in the Ladies' Land League. Image from Emily Monroe Dickinson, *A Patriot's Mistake: Being Personal Recollections of the Parnell Family by a Daughter of the House* (Dublin: Hodges Figgis & Co., 1905), 212.

Fanny Parnell. Parnell inspired Irish-American women to join the Ladies' Land League until her death in 1882. Image from Robert F. Walsh, *A Memorial Volume to Ireland's Incorruptible Son, Patriot and Statesman, Charles Stewart Parnell* (New York: Gay Brothers & Co., 1892), 3.

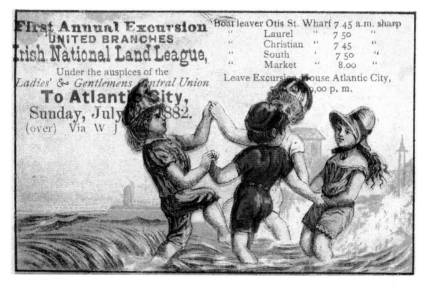

This is to Certify that *Stephen Talbot* is a member of the QUINCY BRANCH I. N. L. LEAGUE, and has paid the following assessments to date:

George Cahill Secretary.

MONTHLY DUES AND LEVIES.					MONTHLY DUES AND LEVIES.				
Date.	Paid.	Extra Sub.	Arrears	Secretary's Signature.	Date.	Paid.	Extra Sub.	Arrears	Secretary's Signature.
Jan. 188 1	25				Jan. 188 2	25			
Feb. 188 1	25			*George Cahill*	Feb. 188 2	25			
Mar. 188 1	25				Mar. 188 2	25			*N McCarthy*
April 188 1	25				April 188 2	25			
May, 188 1	25			*Geo Cahill*	May, 188				
June, 188 1	25				June, 188				
July, 188 1	25			*Geo Cahill*	July, 188				
Aug. 188 1	25				Aug. 188				
Sept. 188 1	25			*Geo Cahill*	Sept. 188				
Oct. 188 1	25				Oct. 188				
Nov. 188 1	25				Nov. 188				
Dec. 188 1	25				Dec. 188				

Land League membership card. Irish Americans joined the Land League in larger numbers than any other nineteenth-century nationalist organization. Courtesy of the John J. Burns Library, Boston College.

Land League excursion card. In the author's possession.

No Rent Fund card. The No-Rent Manifesto exposed the ideological divisions in the Land League and helped lead to its collapse. Courtesy of the John J. Burns Library, Boston College.

"Spreading the Light"

Patrick Ford,
Irish-American Radical Nationalism,
and the Land League

We in this country are beginning to see the dark shadow of land monopoly creeping over the Republic, and we know that if that shadow be not lifted, it will only be a question of time when we shall have here an Ireland on a gigantic scale. It is not, therefore, a mere sentiment that makes us extend a helping hand to Ireland. In helping the Irish people to continue their fight against landlordism, we have been consulting our own interests; for let the principle that the land belongs to the people be once established in Ireland, and it will find its way into England, and from that country it is sure to cross the Atlantic.

Patrick Ford, 1881 editorial

The cover of the 13 March 1880 issue of the *Irish World* displayed a solitary, robed, torch-bearing female standing atop a pillar rising from the soil of Ireland, serving as a beacon to the outside world, reminiscent of the Statue of Liberty being built for New York harbor. The statue featured in Patrick Ford's newspaper, holding a placard inscribed with the words "Free Soil" in her left hand and an Irish harp slung over her shoulder, has rays radiating from her torch, symbolically spreading the gospel of land reform across the seas to America and beyond. This cartoon, titled "Ireland Enlightening the World," illustrates clearly the "Greater Ireland" created by the Land League and presents a

IRELAND ENLIGHTENING THE WORLD!

"Ireland Enlightening the World." *Irish World and American Industrial Liberator*, 13 March 1880.

radical vision of the agitation occurring in Ireland as the precursor of a trans-atlantic movement for reform.

Alongside the conservative faction of the Land League in America there existed a radical element that argued for a wide-ranging view of social reform encompassing both Ireland and the United States. Any examination of the Land League in the United States has to account for this strong strand of radicalism in the movement. Such an assessment is also important for a broad understanding of the Irish in America during the Gilded Age. Sean Wilentz and Eric Foner have warned against "the dangers of assuming that the Irish were monolithically 'conservative'" in this period.[1] While middle-class figures like Patrick Collins and John Boyle O'Reilly tended to dominate Irish-American public discourse, the majority of Irish Americans remained workers and working class.[2] The Land League agitation provided radical and working-class Irish Americans with a rare opportunity to assert their own priorities and beliefs concerning what it meant to be Irish American in the United States in the late nineteenth century. Although short lived, this radical dimension of the Land League challenged conservative Irish-American ideological dominance and demonstrates the substantial element of social radicalism within the Irish-American community in the 1880s.

There was no fixed radical ideology among Land Leaguers but rather a combination and adaptation of several strands of American political thought. Whereas conservatives tended to favor the social status quo and sought to achieve inclusion within it, nationalists enthused about social reform pushed for a profound reshaping of American society. Radicals in the Land League commonly expressed a set of beliefs that argued that workers the world over were under attack from the forces of unchecked capitalism and monopoly. Subscribing to a "labor theory of value" that all wealth derived from labor, reform-minded nationalists argued that workers should not see the bulk of the profits produced by their toil go to employers.[3] Changing economic conditions and economic exploitation by employers threatened workers with a state of dependency that would render them unable to break free from the repression of wage labor and the factory system. This vision of society appealed to a host of American workers and mobilized many of them in support of the Land League. But the organization also had important limitations in this respect. By focusing exclusively on white, skilled male workers, the movement almost entirely ignored unskilled workers, women, Chinese Americans, and African Americans.[4]

Radical nationalists believed that the key to relieving workers from economic and social oppression was the abolition of land monopoly. Patrick Ford, Michael Davitt, and Henry George advocated various schemes for land

nationalization, but most radicals in the Land League did not favor the abolition of private property. Instead, they pushed for the more equitable distribution of land. The hoarding of land, whether in the form of classic landlordism in
Ireland or speculative land buying in the United States, undermined workers'
ability to be virtuous and productive citizens. In many ways radical nationalists
carried forward an earlier tradition of agrarian reform first advocated in the
United States and the United Kingdom in the 1840s and 1850s.[5] Radicals in the
Land League argued that by giving workers access to land, society would be
strengthened and protected from predatory market forces and nonproducers.
Radicals did not want to destroy capitalism but rather to redeem it from the
excesses of the Gilded Age.

Patrick Ford laid out in the pages of the *Irish World* a comprehensive critique
of the situation in Ireland that called not only for fundamental change in the
Irish land system but also for a transformation of social conditions in the towns
and villages of the United States. Responding with tens of thousands of dollars
in donations, working-class and radical Irish Americans embraced Ford's arguments linking Ireland's problems with those faced in America as a result of
rapid industrialization. They used the rhetoric of the Land League to critique
their own position in American society, offering a much different perspective of
the United States than their conservative Irish-American counterparts. "Radical Irish Americans," Eric Foner rightly observes, "wished to transform their
society even as they became a more integral part of it."[6] Members of broader
American working-class and radical movements, like Henry George and his
followers and the Knights of Labor, soon found themselves engaged in the
Land League cause. George used the opportunity provided by the Land
League to stimulate discussion of his economic theories among Irish Americans, while in many areas the League and the Knights of Labor were almost
synonymous with each other. Together, various radical nationalists in the Land
League helped to fashion a critique of the United States that connected it to the
Irish crisis and challenged the bourgeois vision of the League held by conserva-
tive members.

Patrick Ford and the *Irish World*

Patrick Ford, editor of the *Irish World and American Industrial Liberator* published
in New York City, was the most influential spokesman of Irish-American social
radicalism. Born in Galway in 1837, Ford immigrated with his family to the
United States in 1845 and settled in Boston. Interested in learning the printing
trade, he became a printer's devil at the age of fifteen, working for the radical

abolitionist William Lloyd Garrison's *The Liberator* for nine years. His experiences with Garrison were formative in shaping his political and social opinions and set him on the path to becoming a committed advocate of radical social reform.[7] Serving on the Union side during the American Civil War, Ford spent a few years in South Carolina editing a Republican newspaper before moving to New York. In 1870, now settled in Brooklyn, Ford founded his own newspaper, the *Irish World*.

In the *Irish World* Ford advocated a variety of late nineteenth-century radical causes. He supported women's rights, African-American rights, and temperance, and he railed against British and American imperialism. The economic depression that struck the United States beginning in 1873 led Ford to become a strong backer of labor and industrial movements. The origins of the exploitation of the laboring poor, he believed, lay in the monopolistic control of land and other forms of wealth by the privileged and nonproducing class of speculators and monopolists.[8] He favored the eight-hour workday, trade-union organization, and land nationalization, and he supported Greenback-Labor candidates in American politics. Ford's commitment to labor issues was further demonstrated when he added to the title of the *Irish World* the words *and American Industrial Liberator* in 1878. Though a quiet and shy man in person, Ford argued passionately for his beliefs in his newspaper editorials. William O'Brien, the Irish journalist and agrarian activist, memorably described him as "one of those types of solemn, self-immolating, remorseless, yet intensely religious natures to be found more frequently among the revolutionists of Russia than of Ireland, whom you might expect to see either recommended for beatification as a saint or blown up by an infernal machine fired by his own hand in a cause which for him has the sacredness of a religion."[9]

The *Irish World* was the preeminent Irish and Irish-American newspaper during the Land League era. With a weekly circulation of over sixty thousand copies, the *Irish World* was one of the largest Irish-American newspapers of its time.[10] While the paper had a New York–based focus, it also had subscribers throughout the United States, including the urban areas of the West, and at only five cents an issue, or $2.50 for one year's subscription, purchasing the paper was well within the reach of ordinary workers.[11] Outside of America, the *Irish World* was sold in London, Manchester, Liverpool, Sheffield, Preston, and Dublin.[12] Alongside his paper's print circulation, Ford's skill as a fundraiser and the thousands of dollars flowing through the offices of the *Irish World* every week allowed him to greatly increase his influence within the Land League.

Like many of his Irish-American contemporaries, Ford shared a hatred of Britain. Ford was a vehement anti-imperialist and argued that support for the Land League should be part of a wide-ranging critique of British imperialism.

In his view many of Ireland's problems stemmed from its being a part of the British Empire. "Heartless landlords, extortionate rents, despotic agents, and barbarous evictions" were all caused by British colonialism in Ireland.[13] These evils were hardly confined to Ireland but were widely present in the rest of the British Empire. "People, equally with the Irish, the Hindus, the Africans, and every other tribe and nation that dwell in the shadow of your pirate flag, are the victims of an infernal system," Ford proclaimed.[14] But he was not pessimistic about Ireland's future. A momentous change had taken place that would help Ireland to resist English control. "Never before," he argued, "were the bonds of sympathy that unite the Irish to their brothers on this side of the Atlantic stronger than they are today. England has now to deal with two Irelands. A blow dealt at Ireland is felt and resented by the Ireland across the Atlantic."[15] Patrick Ford, more than any other Irish-American leader, understood the possibilities inherent in the "Greater Ireland" emerging from the movement.

His belief in the need for radical social change in America and Ireland gradually led him toward the Land League movement. The success of the League in Ireland and Parnell's fundraising efforts in America presented him with an ideal opportunity to present his social agenda to a wider audience. For Ford the Irish land question was the "question of all questions." "National independence is all very fine," Ford remarked. "It sounds well in the courts of the world. But what will this thing mean in the cabins of Connemara?"[16] Overthrowing British rule without radical social reform would simply replace British tyranny with Irish tyranny, and "Ireland would have Pittsburg [*sic*] riots and armed insurrections long before she celebrates the first centennial of her independence."[17] In the pages of the *Irish World* Ford placed the Land League in the vanguard of a worldwide struggle for workers' rights and against the forces of monopoly.

If the Land League movement in Ireland was to be a success, Ford believed that it had to move beyond simply gaining relatively minor reforms in ownership and the terms of tenancy for farmers. What was needed was a movement that would alleviate the suffering of all Ireland's poor, including landless laborers. "The laborer who works for the farmer," Ford declared, "has just as much right to the land as the farmer."[18] A certain portion of the population might welcome reductions in the rents paid by tenant farmers, but if the Land League wanted to be a mass movement, it would have to expand its appeal. To solve the land problem in Ireland, the Irish needed not just to expel both British absentee and resident landlords but to topple the very institution of landlordism itself. Gradually transferring land titles from British or Irish landlords to Irish owner-occupiers (the former tenants), as Parnell and other moderates in the movement wanted, would merely be a stopgap measure. "It isn't on the Anglo-Irish we should expend all the fierceness of our energies," Ford argued, but "it is landlordism itself, whether English or Irish, we must lay siege to. . . . What matters it to the evicted whether the hand that directs the conquering crowbar belongs to a Celt or a Saxon?"[19] Instead of peasant proprietorship, Ford pushed for a system of land nationalization whereby the state would act as a trustee for its citizens and the size of farms would be restricted to what individuals could produce by their own efforts. Throughout the Land League agitation Ford continually pushed Irish leaders to broaden the goals of the movement beyond limited land reform.

Like Michael Davitt and John Murdoch, the crusading Scottish nationalist and crofters' champion who edited *The Highlander* at Inverness, Ford thought that the struggle of the poor in Ireland against landlordism extended beyond the shores of Ireland to the rest of the British Isles. Ford pleaded with Irish leaders to expand the Land League to include the English and Scottish working class. "The English people, whose interests in the question are identical with those of the Irish, the Scotch, and every other people," Ford argued, "are as ready now to accept the truth as the Irish themselves." Thus, Irish land reformers should "extend their labor into England and Scotland."[20] Though an Irish National Land League of Great Britain was established in 1881, these efforts did not amount to much in the face of Parnell's indifference.[21]

For Ford the relevance of the land movement was not confined to the British Isles. At stake was the future of the United States as well as that of Ireland. Part of Ford's interest in bringing the Land League to Britain stemmed from his fear that the "British system"—England's monarchial government and its practice of land monopoly—was spreading to the United States like a "dark shadow . . . creeping over the Republic" and threatening America's democratic promise.[22] "England driven out in the body," Ford warned his readers, "has returned upon us in the spirit and rots into the very soul of our circumventing classes, lives in our monopolies, breathes through our marts, growls through our press, putrefies our politics, and corrupts our courts."[23] The negative effects across American society were noticeable to anyone willing to look at how the "terrible monopolization of enormous tracts of land by railroad and other corporations, and even by individuals, and the wholesale murdering of the soil by machine farming are ruining the millions of small farmers throughout our country."[24] Both Ireland and the United States were fighting facets of the same system, and Americans needed to recognize this fact and support the Land League. "Rent, usury, disinheritance, and eviction are all right under the folds of the star-spangled banner," Ford warned.[25]

During the years of Land League activity Ford advocated changing the status quo not through organized and sustained political organization but through winning hearts and minds to "true" principles. Any attempts to achieve reform through the British Parliament would end in disappointment and the compromising of the Land League cause. Ford believed that the Irish people should ignore the "Home Rule humbug" and keep their focus on the question of radical land reform.[26] The *Irish World* argued that the goal of the Land League should be to institute a social movement that would triumph by the righteousness of its "moral force" and not through political negotiation and compromise with the British government.

Ford's distaste for the Land League's involvement in British politics extended to any involvement with American politics as well. Though a supporter of the Greenback Party (an American third-party political group), he believed politics to be inherently flawed and corrupting and urged supporters to avoid entangling the Land League in American political intrigues. "At all hazards," Ford insisted to his readers, "the politicians must be kept from all leadership in the Land League."[27] As with his aversion to mixing American politics with the work of the Land League, Ford also argued that it was dangerous to try to expand the League's reform agenda too broadly beyond land and economic reform. A strong supporter of various other reform movements during the 1870s, Ford nevertheless believed that the land question trumped all other concerns. He placed such issues as temperance, women's suffrage, and others outside the appropriate goals of the movement, claiming that they "would uselessly lumber it up and distract it."[28] Only after solving the land problem could other questions be tackled and effectively settled.

Ford directed his appeals primarily to the Irish-American working class, as he believed that the land and labor questions were indissolubly linked. "Every wage slave in America—every workingman—has a direct and vital interest in this movement," Ford asserted. "Liberate the soil and you liberate the loom and the forge."[29] He called on workers to organize Land League branches in every factory, village, and town. Ford pushed the poor in both countries to look beyond their narrow communities and to see themselves as part of a larger brotherhood of workers that extended across the Atlantic. It was this inclusive view of social reform that Ford advocated in the pages of the *Irish World*.

Keeping the Land League a social movement would also help workers in America to overcome the ethnic tensions and divisions that weakened working-class resistance to oppression. "The average mechanic and laborer who is not endeared to Ireland by tie of nationality," Ford wrote, "is as yet not level-headed enough to understand that despotism of property is not a national evil but a radical human evil."[30] By educating readers of the commonalities in labor's struggle across national boundaries, Ford believed that the Land League would be the start of a new era of industrial emancipation. Ford's idealistic view that the logical force of his arguments would ultimately win out against any opposition led him to dismiss the fact that many critics within the Land League rejected his arguments. His inability to compromise with opponents would later prove to be a serious handicap and hamper his effectiveness in guiding the movement.

In addition to the conservative members of the official American Land League who distrusted him, many members of the Catholic hierarchy in America denounced Ford's principles. The authorities of the American Catholic Church frequently criticized Ford's views as "un-Catholic" and radical. In 1879 Bishop Gilmour of Cleveland banned the circulation of the *Irish World* in his diocese, claiming that the paper was "doing the work of the devil" and that no good Catholic should subscribe to its tenets.[31] Ford expressed genuine surprise at the attacks by Catholic leaders on the *Irish World*. The biggest area of friction centered on Ford's belief that the Catholic Church in America should take a leading role in helping the poor and needy; he openly criticized church leaders unwilling to accept this responsibility. "Without *justice*," Ford argued, "religion is impossible. And this justice must be made manifest in our social and political life—in all our relations toward our neighbor."[32] What Ford was pushing church leaders to embrace was a version of the Catholic "social gospel," the belief that the church should attempt to alleviate social problems and address the needs of the poor. He issued his call years before the papal encyclical *Rerum Novarum* (1891), and the position of the Catholic Church at that point toward trade unions and its efforts at social reform remained cautious.[33] In Ford's mind the Land League and the labor movement were essentially "moral movements," and if churchmen did not render support, they risked losing their influence over their flocks.[34]

Ford's pleas to Catholic leaders did yield some ecclesiastical converts. Father Edward McGlynn, the Catholic pastor of New York City's St. Stephen's Church, became an early supporter of the Land League and of Ford and Henry George. The son of Irish-born parents, McGlynn was educated in Rome, where he received his doctorate in theology. He belonged to a debating society of liberal clergymen called the "Accademia," whose members argued for a distinctly American Catholic Church that would adapt itself to American conditions instead of primarily following Rome's direction.[35] This group was part of a larger ideological division among the American Catholic bishops. The liberal "Americanists" in one camp believed that the laity should be empowered to address social issues and become more actively involved in the church and in American life more broadly, whereas ultramontane conservatives in the other camp resisted experimental attempts to adjust Catholicism to fit American conditions.[36]

As the pastor of St. Stephen's Church, one of the poorest parishes in the city, McGlynn had a reputation as a brilliant orator, a friend of the poor and the working class, and an outspoken critic of Catholic conservatism. Almost from its inception he associated himself with the Land League.[37] Like Ford, McGlynn believed that fundamental changes needed to be made to both Irish and American society. Talking about evictions in Ireland, he bemoaned the conditions of the poor in New York. "I am told that there are some twenty thousand evictions in New York City every year for non-payment of rent, a greater number than in all Ireland," McGlynn asserted. "These sentences of eviction are to the street, with the poor little pots and pans and sticks of furniture, and from the streets to the hospital, to fill a premature grave in the Potter's field, unmarked, unknown."[38] McGlynn would later become a convert to the theories of the economic thinker Henry George, and the two men shared a close personal and working relationship for the rest of their lives.

In the pages of the *Irish World* Ford articulated a vision of the Land League that extended beyond the limited goal of reforming the system of land tenure in Ireland. Instead, he argued for the linkage of far-reaching agrarian reform in Ireland to the necessity for broad economic and social change in the United States. Believing that supporters of the Land League in America could be won over to his views, Ford set out to secure adherents to his cause.

The *Irish World* and the Radical Faction of the American Land League

Viewing the official American Land League as overrun by place seekers and politicians, Ford sought to swing Irish Americans behind his radical interpretation of the Land League. In February 1881 he established a rival branch of the American Land League with its own constitution based on the principles advocated by the *Irish World*. He then printed and mailed five thousand copies to readers. "God made the world for man's use and benefit," the "Declaration of Principles" proclaimed, and since God had created mankind with the same necessities, "He likewise created them with equal rights to His free gifts." Since land, air, light, and water were essential for the lives of all, the declaration continued, "they were made for no *special* class but are the natural inheritance of *all* and can be alienated by *none* without contravening the law of God." Thus the struggle in Ireland was "the dawn of humanity's emancipation the world over," and the *Irish World* called on all men and women, regardless of nationality, to band together "until landlordism, *root and branch*, shall have been abolished, and the equal right of *every* man to share in the bounties of God, free of rent or other immoral exaction, shall have been acknowledged and established, never more to be denied or abridged."[39] These sentiments stood in stark contrast to the conservative principles embraced at the Buffalo convention.

Irish World–affiliated Land League branches grew at an even faster rate than those of the official Land League. On 4 January 1881, 246 branches had notified the *Irish World* of their existence; by 26 March 1881 the total had soared to 1,046, with branches present in all thirty-eight states.[40] The Land League organized by Ford was really a loose confederation of local branches. Unlike the official Land League established at Buffalo, *Irish World* branches lacked any central executive or bureaucratic machinery. Ford did not believe that a centralized governing body was necessary in the United States.[41] Members were asked to pay only an initiation fee of one dollar, along with monthly dues of ten cents, and to forward their monies to the *Irish World* for acknowledgment in its columns and direct transmission to the Land League in Ireland.

To further spread his ideals, Ford attempted to extend the *Irish World*'s influence across the Atlantic to Ireland. Ford called on his readers to "institute a propaganda" and "spread the light" to working men and women in both countries.[42] Key to Ford's ideology was his belief in the need for spreading knowledge and educating workers about the true conditions facing them. "The mission of the *Irish World* is to *teach*," Ford told his readers.[43] Such efforts were necessary preconditions to initiating a successful social revolution in the United States and Ireland. The *Irish World*'s "Spread the Light Fund," in which subscribers paid for copies of the newspaper to be sent to friends and relatives in Ireland, was a huge success. Ford claimed a weekly Irish circulation of over sixty thousand copies, effectively making the *Irish World* the major newspaper of the movement on both sides of the Atlantic. The Irish journalist and land reformer William O'Brien said of the paper's presence in Ireland, "There was scarcely a cabin in the West to which some relative in America did not dispatch a weekly copy of the *Irish World*, flaming all over from the first line to the last . . . , as if some vast Irish-American invasion was sweeping the country with new and irresistible principles of liberty and democracy."[44] The British government was concerned enough by the impact of the *Irish World* that the British consulate general in New York sent a copy of the paper weekly to the British undersecretary at Dublin Castle.[45] The distribution of the *Irish World* in Ireland was also banned, and the British authorities seized any smuggled copies that they discovered. But such efforts, rather than reducing Ford's influence or the paper's circulation, simply enhanced the *Irish World*'s reputation.

Ford was a highly effective fundraiser and throughout his career as editor was able to collect significant sums for various movements. The Land League was no exception. A comparison of the receipts of the *Irish World* "Land League

Fund" with the first-quarter reports of Father Walsh shows that Ford's newspaper enjoyed a substantial lead amounting to about $47,500.[46] Ford's exceptional ability as a fundraiser made it difficult for Land League leaders who did not share his social radicalism to openly criticize him. The *ICBU Journal* lamented that "Patrick Ford has only to call for money for any or no purpose and get it—and plenty too."[47] After placing an ad on 10 January 1880 stating that the *World* would accept donations and forward them to the Irish Land League, Ford became its primary fundraiser. By the end of 1882, when he closed subscriptions, Ford had forwarded as much as $343,000 to Patrick Egan, the Land League treasurer in Paris, as compared with approximately $180,000 from the official American Land League.[48] Without the *Irish World* the Land League in Ireland would have been able to accomplish far less. Even Parnell, who distrusted Ford's radicalism, had to admit this truth.[49] Much to the chagrin of Irish and Irish-American nationalists uneasy with Ford's social radicalism, he became an indispensable asset to the Land League cause. His ability to raise money greatly increased the profile of the Land League in the United States and abroad, and conservatives were forced to tolerate his presence in the movement.

There were several reasons for the *Irish World*'s popularity among so many Land League supporters. Ford was a trustworthy bookkeeper and devoted considerable space in his columns to acknowledge the receipt of funds and to print letters from local branches describing their activities. Ford's critics argued that Irish Americans affiliated themselves with the *Irish World* not because of genuine sympathy with its radical views on the land question but because of his prompt recognition of donations (Father Walsh published receipts in a much slower and less detailed manner) and the thrill of seeing their names in print.[50] Scholars also disagree over why so much money was sent to the *Irish World*. Some argue that the contributions represented conscious political decisions in support of Ford's social radicalism, while others believe that they resulted from a combination of convenience and the novelty of seeing one's name and home location in print.[51] Certainly not everyone who sent money through the *Irish World* agreed with its views on the land question or social reform. But to dismiss its popularity simply as a reflection of the vanity of local groups greatly underestimates the very strong radical and working-class elements of the Land League.

Radical and working-class support was demonstrated in the letters sent by many branches to the *Irish World* along with their donations. The Transatlantic branch of South Boston repudiated the Buffalo convention and declared its motto to be "the land for the people and no surrender."[52] Jeremiah Kelly, president of the Jersey City branch of the Land League, proclaimed that "the social war is not an Irish question only—it appeals to a common humanity." The Jersey City branch also protested against the action of the Buffalo convention in dropping the word "industrial" from the American Land League's title.[53] In Cleveland, Ohio, the Parnell and Davitt branches pledged to send all their money through the *Irish World*, and in Philadelphia a new branch was formed after disagreements emerged over whether to send the local league's money to Ireland through Ford.[54] Thus, for many branches, sending money through the *Irish World* was a deliberate endorsement of Ford's beliefs in the need for far-reaching social reform in both Ireland and the United States.

The vast majority of donors to Ford's Land League Fund were found among the Irish-American working class. The writer of a *New York Times* editorial believed that "the money that has kept the Land League together has come mostly from the day laborers and servant maids of America."[55] While all classes of Irish Americans donated to Land League coffers, the contributors to the *Irish World* were overwhelmingly working class. Ford himself claimed that of the members of the Land League in America, "fully nineteen-twentieths were poor and unpretentious workingmen."[56] The vast amounts of money flowing to Ireland through the *Irish World* were the product of hundreds of thousands of small donations. One historian has determined that nearly 82 percent of contributions to the *Irish World* Land League Fund were of one dollar or less.[57] Ford's supporters did not fail to notice the absence of wealthy Irish Americans among the lists of contributors. The Land League of Reading, Pennsylvania, wondered if rich Irish Americans had "forgotten all about the dear old land in the hoarding of their ill-gotten wealth, which was brought them by the hard labor and sweat of others."[58] By a huge margin working-class donors fueled the *Irish World*'s fundraising success.

The working-class background of the *Irish World*'s supporters is further illustrated by the geographical distribution of contributors. Eric Foner has found that the greatest strength of the *Irish World*'s donors was found not in the large cities of the East Coast or the Midwest but in the mining regions of Pennsylvania and the West as well as in small industrial centers across the United States.[59] Despite their relatively small size, mining communities gave generously to the Land League cause. For example, up to February 1881, the branch in Leadville, Colorado, with $3,400 in total donations, had outpaced Chicago, New York, New Orleans, Philadelphia, Boston, and San Francisco; the anthracite region of Pennsylvania was also a hot spot for Land League fundraising activity.[60] Textile towns like Fall River in Massachusetts were also drawn to the *Irish World*'s message. The Fall River men and ladies' Leagues voted to send all their contributions through the *Irish World* and advocated the need for radical reform in both Ireland and the United States; one observer was prompted to remark, "You cannot say anything that is too radical for a Fall River audience."[61] In industrial towns across the United States workers flocked to support the Land League and the *Irish World*'s principles.

Why were members of the Irish-American working class so heavily attracted to Ford and the *Irish World*? One British journalist, touring the slums of New York, wondered why the poor of these "vast nurseries of poverty" were willing to "pay out their hard-earned dollars to keep up a political agitation thousands of miles away, in which they can never have actual hand or part or derive any benefit whatever."[62] There were several reasons. One of the simplest is that industrial workers in the United States increasingly saw their economic prospects steadily declining. Robert Blissert, an activist in the Knights of Labor and the New York Tailors' Union, when asked by an interviewer why he supported the Land League, replied simply that if things did not change, his children (of whom there were eight) would have to work harder than he did to live at the same level as they were now—a predicament that in his view was a poignant reminder of the failure of the American economy to meet the needs of its citizens. Blissert's example helps to demonstrate why so many American workers, looking at their own personal situation, were drawn to accept Ford's arguments that the problems facing the Irish poor had relevance to the problems confronting workers in the United States. Radicals and members of the working class came to appreciate the need for fundamental change in American society as a result of the Land League agitation and the nature of the Irish-American response.

It is necessary to emphasize, however, that not all members of the Irish-American working class supported a radical understanding of the Land League's purposes. As we have seen in chapter 4, many skilled and white-collar workers sided with the conservative faction of the American Land League. It is important not to be deterministic in attributing working-class support for the Land League to economic considerations alone. While workers generally belonged to occupational communities shaped by working-class culture, they were also individuals who often based their political and social views on their own personal experiences and concerns. Nevertheless, the evidence does suggest that huge numbers of Irish-American and other workers found Ford's ideas attractive and relevant to their own situation.

Ordinary men and women workers in the Land League linked their daily struggles in industrializing America with the problems faced by the toiling agrarian masses in Ireland. Louis F. Post, editor of the New York-based daily labor newspaper *Truth*, believed that the Land League cause should appeal to the "self-interest as well as the sympathy of every man who worked, whether with muscle or brain, with capital or without, regardless of his race or nationality and in whatever corner of the world he might be found."[63] For workers in America the problems facing the Irish in Ireland often rang true in their own lives. As the *Irish World* declared rather too optimistically, "Destroy the occupation of the landlord in Ireland and you sound the doom of the factory lord of America."[64]

Workers in the Land League also took up the producer-focused ideology espoused by Ford and others and denounced such nonproducers in American society as bankers and landlords. "Rent and usury," the coal miners of Thomastown, Ohio, exclaimed in their letter to the *Irish World*, are the "twin monsters that are breaking the backs of laboring men in every country on the globe today."[65] It was necessary to try to halt the advance of this system. In a speech before the Fall River Land League, Michael Connolly expressed confidence that "the benefits to accrue to the Irish people in driving the landlords out of Ireland will be felt by the workers the world over. . . . We have the same gigantic evil in this country." He finished by warning that "the public domain is rapidly passing away into the hands of the large corporations, and in time the people here will be in no better condition than those of Ireland."[66] As the Land League continued to grow through the middle months of 1881, many branches, influenced by Ford's rhetoric, adopted a more radical tone. The British consul in New York, E. M. Archibald, confirmed this change; he worriedly reported to London that the speeches at many Land League gatherings were becoming increasingly more radical and revolutionary.[67]

The Land League and the American Radical Tradition

The appeal of the Land League to workers in the United States extended beyond Irish Americans to the larger American working-class community. Attacks on monopolies and calls for land reform in Ireland held a special appeal for workers in the late nineteenth-century United States, many of whom believed they were under assault from the same hostile forces. As David Montgomery has astutely observed, "The closer one looks, the more strands appear connecting the labor movement, land reform, and Irish nationalism."[68] Several labor leaders and reformers joined Patrick Ford in linking the land movement in Ireland with labor reform in America. Terence V. Powderly, vice president of the American Land League and Grand Master Workman of the Knights of Labor, expressed the belief that the American labor movement and Irish land movement were "almost identical."[69] Workers' mass participation in the Land League challenged conservative control of the movement while advancing an extensive critique of American society in the Gilded Age.

American working-class support for the Land League also helped bring together Irish nationalism and broader currents of American radicalism. Radicalism in the Gilded Age spawned the rise of the Knights of Labor and the enormous popularity of the economic principles of Henry George. The "big tent" nature of the American Land League helped to draw these movements within its fold, as radicals tied together the problems facing the poor in Ireland and the United States with great regularity. Radicals in the movement also embraced elements of an earlier American reformist tradition. The Land League, one historian has plausibly argued, "reveals a conjunction of Irish-America with the Protestant reform tradition."[70] The radical element within the Land League combined with an earlier American reform tradition to create a wide-ranging constituency for the League that stretched far beyond the Irish-American community.

To understand why working-class and radical Irish Americans were attracted to the Land League, it is necessary to place it within the larger historical context of American land reform. Within the United States there was a long history of agitation for land reform prior to the Civil War. In the 1840s and 1850s antebellum land reformers had pushed for the opening of public lands to homesteaders.[71] George Henry Evans, a New York–based newspaperman, was the leading thinker of this movement, which consisted of a loose coalition of agrarian reformers known as the National Reform Association. Evans and other National Reformers were concerned with the negative effect of land monopoly on the democratic potential of the United States. Land monopoly, they argued, undermined the independence of working people while giving a small elite increasing control over the nation's political, economic, and social life.[72] Though successful in securing passage of the 1862 Homestead Act, many workers and radicals felt by the 1880s that much of the public land set aside for homesteaders had been snatched up unfairly by railroads and corporations, preventing workingmen from achieving the independence that would have come from owning their own land. A speaker before the St. Louis Central Land League insisted that "the continued growth of monopolies in America threatened the republican institutions" under which Americans lived.[73] Some reformers also feared that the shrinking availability of public lands kept workers from escaping the overcrowded conditions of cities, thus leaving urban centers ripe for eruptions of class, ethnic, and industrial conflict.[74] "Land-robbers 'must go,'" proclaimed the Jersey City Land League. "First in Ireland, then in America—both the old wolf and the sucking cub."[75] The Land League harkened back to these earlier movements and revived many of their tenets against land monopoly.

Further links between the Land League and earlier movements can be found in a few long-lived reformers who continued their antebellum activism during the Land League era. The most notable antebellum agrarian reformer associated with the League was the writer and newspaperman Thomas Ainge Devyr. Born in County Donegal in 1805, Devyr was a member of Daniel O'Connell's Catholic Association before leaving for England in 1834 and joining the Chartist movement. In 1840, fleeing British coercion, he immigrated to the United States, where he quickly became associated with the National Reform movement, gaining a reputation as an important, though often argumentative, thinker. Devyr's life illustrates the transatlantic character of early nineteenth-century land reform.[76] His activism did not end with the demise of the National Reform Association in the 1840s, for in 1876 he joined the *Irish World* staff. When the Land League agitation began, Devyr embraced it as a reawakening of the agrarian activism of the prior generation. "The great issue is indeed upon us," he wrote. "Let us accept it at once. And whilst with one hand we throw help and encouragement over to our friends in Ireland, with the other hand let us take our own domestic traitors by the throat."[77] Yet Devyr did not unconditionally accept everything about the Land League. Feisty even in his old age, Devyr, while attending a speech by Parnell in New York, was thrown out of the hall for hissing Henry Ward Beecher.[78] Besides Devyr, another National Reformer, J. K. Ingalls, contributed to the *Irish World* during the Land League era. The ideological similarities between the Land League and earlier American agrarian movements, and the embrace of the League by such old-time reformers as Ingalls and Devyr, suggests at the very least that Irish Americans might have been attracted to the movement not only because of the nature of the current crisis in Ireland but also because of their acceptance of an earlier American reform tradition.

It is necessary to mention as well the other movements for American agrarian social reform emerging outside the Land League in the early 1880s. These were the years of the Farmers' Alliance in the South and of the first stirrings of the Populist movement in the West. Providing the closest link between Irish-American nationalism and these other movements was Mary Elizabeth Lease, the Kansas Populist orator who famously called on farmers to "raise less corn and more hell." She began her public speaking career as a lecturer on behalf of the Irish National League, the successor to the Land League.[79] Though there is no direct connection between the American Land League and these movements, it is significant that they emerged in the United States at about the same time. That these movements coexisted, albeit separately, suggests that an anxiety over land reform was part of the intellectual and social milieu of late nineteenth-century America. John Swinton, the American labor leader, recognized this moment, telling a crowd at the Chicago Social Democratic Festival, "Thick is the driftwood and many are the floaters. Here is anti-monopoly, there anti-land grabbing; here is Grangerism, there trade unionism, here is anti-rack rent, there anti-tax shirking."[80] This proliferation of reform movements marks the 1880s as a period of great unrest within American society and shows that the Land League was part of this larger experience. The Land League served as a bridge between earlier American agrarian movements of the 1830s and 1840s and the Populist movement of the 1890s. The lasting legacy of the League was highlighted by the decision of the Texas-based Renters' Union, an alliance of poor Mexican and white American sharecroppers, to rename their organization the Land League in 1914.[81] Though it endured for only a few momentous years, the Land League achieved a striking popularity in the United States that helps to demonstrate and explain the continued significance of landed property as a social and political question in American history through the end of the nineteenth century.

The most significant American radical to associate himself with the Land League was the political economist Henry George, author of *Progress and Poverty*. George, as mentioned in chapter 2, had befriended Ford and Davitt in late 1880. Born in Philadelphia, George spent his late teens engaged in a variety of occupations, including seaman, apprentice typesetter, and clerk, often tasting failure, before settling in California in 1858 and finding work as a newspaperman.[82] In California George witnessed and was perturbed by the economic and social conflict of the 1870s. His experiences led him to question the tenets of the post–Civil War United States and to ask why, despite the widespread growth in economic production and the efficiency of the American economy, there were numerous signs of increased poverty alongside rapid progress. In his book *Progress and Poverty*, published in 1879, he argued that the monopolization of land by large landholders and speculators artificially inflated its price, leading to hardship across the economy and eventually to a depression in wages, business profits, and overall economic well-being. The answer to this problem, George believed, was to limit the amount of land that individuals could own. Existing taxation would then be replaced by a single tax—a tax on land values (specifically on unearned increases in value) that would fund all public necessities. George's hope, as one of his biographers has described it, was in effect to "achieve the goals of socialism without the growing pains."[83]

The principles enunciated in the pages of *Progress and Poverty* appealed greatly to Patrick Ford's beliefs in land reform. Though he disagreed with George's acceptance of interest payments and his unwillingness to seize landlords' holdings outright, Ford believed that he had found an ideological soul mate in George. Long before *Progress and Poverty* became the best-selling work of the nineteenth century on political economy, Ford and the *Irish World* had praised George's ideas. "The most important contribution to political economy which has appeared since Adam Smith's 'Wealth of Nations'" was J. K. Ingalls's accolade in his review of the book in the *Irish World*.[84] Ford thought the work important enough to arrange for the printing of a cheap seventy-five-cent edition and encouraged local Land League branches to circulate the book among their members. "Between the covers of 'Progress and Poverty,'" Ford declared, "there is enough of seed thought, if scattered widely enough, to revolutionize the world."[85]

George himself quickly realized the benefits of associating himself with the Land League movement. He joined the League early in 1881 and spent the spring of that year touring New England, New York, and Canada on its behalf. In his speeches he argued that the struggle in Ireland possessed the radical potential to inspire economic and social change worldwide. "The question is not an Irish land question, or an English land question; it is *the* land question — the fight of the times for the regeneration of mankind," George asserted to the Brooklyn Spread the Light Club. There was only one logical principle upon which the land movement could proceed — that "either the land is rightfully the possession of some people, or it is rightfully the possession of all people."[86] This belief he applied to both Ireland and the United States. George denounced "time-serving politicians" in the movement who were "willing enough to denounce Irish landlordism . . . but . . . tried to prevent all reference to American landlordism."[87] Such ideas pushed George into the vanguard of the radical faction of the American Land League.

His profile among Irish Americans was further enhanced by the publication of *The Irish Land Question* in 1881. This pamphlet, an expansion of a previous article written by George for the *Sacramento Bee* in 1879, distilled the concepts found in *Progress and Poverty* in a clear and forceful style. Despite its title, the pamphlet advocated a cosmopolitan view of the land question that extended well beyond the thirty-two counties of Ireland. "What is involved in this Irish land question is not a mere local matter between Irish landlords and Irish tenants," George wrote, "but the great social problem of modern civilization."[88] The pamphlet began with the argument that many of the preconditions of the crisis in Ireland were already present in the United States. "That Irish land titles rest on force and fraud is true," George agreed, but how many land titles in the United States, particularly in the West, had "been got by fraud and perjury and bribery — by the arts of the lobbyist or the cunning tricks of hired lawyers, by double-barreled shotguns and repeating rifles!"[89] In fact, he argued, "Standard Oil Company probably owns more acres of Western land than all the London companies put together own of Irish land."[90] George's analysis placed supposedly Irish problems firmly in an American context. Even Irish emigration, George was convinced, had its mirror image in America: "Is there not a constant emigration from the Eastern states of the Union to the Western — an emigration impelled by the same motives as that which sets across the Atlantic?"[91] If Ireland and the United States both shared the problems of land scarcity, absentee landlordism, and emigration, what was the root cause of these troubles?

George maintained that the chief cause of poverty was the centralized ownership of land in the hands of the few instead of the many. "It is this," George declared, "that produces the hideous squalor of London and Glasgow . . . , that makes want jostle luxury in the streets of rich New York, that forces little children to monotonous and stunting toil in Massachusetts mills, and that fills the highways of our newest states with tramps."[92] He criticized the Land League's motto of "the land for the people" as too vacuous and as ultimately wrongheaded. What was needed was the total abolition of private property, not the transference of the ownership of land from one class of landlords to another. Referring to the Irish Land League's demands for fair rents, fixity of tenure, and free sale, George insisted that the "'three F's'" were "three frauds," and that "the proposition to create peasant proprietorship is no better." Instead, he claimed, "The only true and just solution to the problem, the only end worth aiming at, is to make *all* the land the common property of *all* the people."[93] Under George's plan the state would appropriate the rent that normally went to the landlord. Once again, the solution was the taxation of land rent. Such an approach could be applied to landless tenants and smallholders in Ireland as well as urban workers in the United States, who saw their rents continue to rise while their wages slipped. George's theories represented an antidote to the fears among radicals of an America that was being overrun by corporate monopoly, the scarcity of homestead land, and increasing industrialization.

Not everyone welcomed George's intervention in Irish affairs. For physical-force nationalists who saw the Land League as the first step toward Irish freedom from British rule, George's most contentious suggestion was not the abolition of private property but his dismissal of the importance of Irish national independence. "Talk of Irish independence is as harmful as it is wild and vain," George asserted. "The English people could no more consent to separation than we could consent to secession, and if they did, it would be a step backward."[94] The key to the success of the Land League, George believed, was an alliance between the Irish poor and the English working class. Irish leaders could facilitate such a union by reaching out to English radicals and making common cause around the need for social reform throughout the United Kingdom. If the land agitation remained confined to Ireland alone, it would surely fail. "Ireland is only a lever with which to stir up England," George trumpeted. "Then from England the movement is to spread to America, and the American branches of the Land League are to be centres of the new social revolution."[95] This was a severe repudiation of claims for Irish political independence. John Devoy, the Clan na Gael leader, found such sentiments to be heresy. "It is for Ireland we fight," he declared, "not for the human race. Let us put that issue squarely and put our foot down on cant."[96] The influence of George and Ford on the movement increasingly troubled Devoy, and he worked tirelessly to prevent radical attempts to shift the mission of the Land League toward universal social reform.

Radical members of the Land League, however, responded favorably to George's writings. Patrick Ford told his readers that the *Irish Land Question* pamphlet "is one that we should like to see in the hands of every Land Leaguer in the country."[97] According to Eric Foner, American radicals did not necessarily understand or believe George's prescriptions, but they were impressed by the fact that George identified the three central problems of the Gilded Age: the unequal distribution of wealth, the growing squalor in the cities, and the declining status of labor, with a solution all laid out.[98] Land League branches across the country wrote to the *Irish World* praising George's ideas. The California Land League (San Francisco) showed its appreciation by extending the "thanks of the civilized world" to George for "his bold, uncompromising, and able exposition of the land question in his works."[99] Mrs. Still of the Jersey City, New Jersey, Ladies' Land League informed her fellow members that "the only book that I know of at present of any value is Henry George's 'Progress and Poverty.' I would advise every workingman and every workingwoman to read it. If it does not give you any new ideas, there is one thing it will do—cause you to get rid of your old ones."[100] The members of at least several branches of the Land League did read George's work, alongside other political tracts, as many branches established reading rooms and sponsored group discussions to circulate radical views on the Land League and political economy. In his writings and speeches on behalf of the Land League, George found an audience among working-class Irish Americans that was highly receptive to his economic and political ideals.

Radical nationalists in the Land League were also closely linked with another key element of Gilded Age radicalism, the Knights of Labor. The Knights attempted to organize workers nationally, regardless of skill (though they excluded Chinese immigrants), occupation, or gender, in an attempt to form one great "union for all." It was meant to be an alliance of the "producing classes" (workers, farmers, and small manufacturers) against nonproducers (lawyers, bankers, land speculators, and liquor dealers, all of whom were excluded from membership).[101] The connection between the Land League and the Knights began at the top, with its leader, Terence Powderly, who, as previously noted, was also elected the Land League's second vice president in 1881. Powderly was born in 1849 in Carbondale, Pennsylvania, to parents of Irish birth. Employed as a machinist in the 1870s, Powderly was dismissed from his job because of his union activities before eventually joining the nascent Knights of Labor in 1874.[102] In 1878 he was elected mayor of Scranton and became Grand Master Workman of the Knights in 1880. Under Powderly's capable leadership the

Knights of Labor became one of the dominant workers' organizations of the Gilded Age.

Alongside his labor activities Powderly was a fervent Irish nationalist. A member of Clan na Gael, he served as the organization's finance chairman before becoming involved in the Land League. Powderly recognized the potential of the Land League to provide a radical critique of late nineteenth-century American society. "The key note which will reach the American heart," he argued in 1883, was the attack on "the alien landlord who first drives his victim from Irish soil and [then] heads them off in this land by buying (stealing) up the land and compels his slave to go up in an eight story tenement in a large city and live on a crust or pay an exorbitant price for land which God made for all honest men instead of for thieves."[103] Powderly, like Ford and George, saw the problem of landlordism extending beyond the shores of distant Ireland and into the urban rookeries of the United States.

The links between the Land League and the Knights of Labor also existed on the local level. Branches of the Knights in many areas of the country served as de facto branches of the Land League. Powderly confided to a friend that he found it "to be the rule nearly all over that the men engaged in one are engaged in all reform movements," and he himself often combined his Land League and Knights' activities, giving a public speech on behalf of the Land League during the day in various cities and then, in the evenings, quietly organizing a branch of the Knights of Labor, which at the time was still a secret and oath-bound society.[104] Historians who have studied the Knights of Labor have also highlighted the connections between the League and the Knights. Paul Buhle has found that such industrial cities as Providence, Pawtucket, and Central Falls in Rhode Island, which were strongholds of the Knights, also possessed active Land League branches.[105] In Chicago, as another historian has noted, "Land League clubs became a magnet for socialists, trade unionists, Knights, and Greenbackers."[106] Similar connections were also found in the anthracite region of Pennsylvania and in mining communities in Colorado.[107]

The relationship between the Knights and the Land League went beyond an overlap in members and exhibited important ideological connections. "The Land League bequeathed an impressive ideological legacy to the Knights of Labor," David Brundage has argued. "The Land League also prepared the way for the emergence of a broad working-class movement, a movement which could finally overcome the limitations of both the trade unions and the immigrant organizations."[108] Many workers, especially members of labor organizations like the Knights of Labor, agreed with Patrick Ford's belief that "the struggle in Ireland is radically and essentially the same as the struggle in America—a contest against legalized forms of oppression."[109] The ideological importance of the Land League did not end with its disbandment in 1883. The League's critique of land monopoly and overweening corporate power, the need for workers' cooperation across ethnic lines, and its incorporation of women (discussed in the next chapter) were taken up and pursued later by the Knights of Labor.

The American working-class community and its spokespersons provided further support for the radical social vision advocated by Ford and others. The New York labor newspaper *Truth* prophesied that the "signs of the times all over the world are that the tremendous conflict which has been impending between capital and labor for many years past, the weapons for which have been steadily sharpened and improved on both sides for centuries, will be precipitated upon us with something like universal unanimity before many months are past." Its editors maintained that the movement for land reform in Ireland would soon reach America: "We regard the Irish Land League agitation . . . as the entering wedge of a vast popular movement that cannot fail to spread to the United States."[110] Such sentiments were not confined to the East Coast. In St. Louis, P. J. McGuire, a member of the Socialist Labor Party of America and secretary of the United Brotherhood of Carpenters and Joiners of America, speaking before a meeting of the Central Branch of the Land League, praised the Irish people for being "the first to register their protest against the evil of monopoly of the soil, the chief cause of the poverty of the inhabitants of that fruitful country"; he also warned that the "continued growth of monopolies in America threatened the republican institutions under which we live."[111] A *Sacramento Bee* editorial writer during Davitt's visit to the United States told Californians to welcome him because "he is laboring now not alone for Ireland but for all mankind through all the ages that are to come . . . [to] abolish land monopoly, and no people will ever again allow its wrongs to be repeated among them."[112] To workers struggling to resist their own deteriorating living conditions in late nineteenth-century America, the situation in Ireland served as a beacon for both a better Ireland and a better United States.

The incorporation of the boycott in American labor struggles further underscores the ideological connection between the Irish agitation and American labor activism. Boycotting in Ireland, as noted in chapter 2, was a system of economic and social ostracism used against landlords and land agents who attempted to charge unjust rents or evict tenants, and against tenant farmers who defied Land League orders by taking evicted holdings or paying rent behind the backs of fellow tenants. Increasingly in the United States, mass strikers moved away from physical force toward "moral force," a shift that, in the words of one historian, "owed much to the popularity of the boycott, which grew out of the agitation of the Irish Land League."[113] But as Michael A. Gordon has argued, the boycott "was an *adaptation*—not an *adoption*—of the Irish prac-tice."[114] Crucial to understanding the rise in popularity of labor boycotts in the United States was workers' increasing association of Old World oppression in land tenure with the growth of industrialization in America. In other words, many workers adopted the transatlantic vision of social reform championed by radicals in the Land League. Streetcar workers in Chicago, inspired by the example of Irish boycotting, launched the first successful public boycott in the city's history in April 1881. A Just Rent League was organized in New York City in April 1881 to resist the increase of rents through boycotting landlords who practiced "injustice" toward their tenants.[115] These examples and others that could be cited provide evidence of workers' attempts to translate the tenets found in the *Irish World* and elsewhere in the Land League movement into their daily lives in the United States.

While Irish Americans comprised the vast majority of Land League mem-bers, another function of the League in many working-class communities was to help to dampen ethnic division, albeit briefly, among workers. In the Home-stead Steelworks in Pennsylvania, League membership served as an important first entry into working-class organization for Swedes and Eastern Europeans who were excluded from the local union, the Amalgamated Association of Iron and Steelworkers (AAISW). John J. O'Donnell, president of the Homestead Michael Davitt Land League branch, boasted that during the 1882 workers' strike the League enlisted "Germans, Dutchmen, Swedes, Scotchmen, English-men, [and] Welshmen as well as Irishmen . . . to battle with capital for our rights here."[116] "Honorius" (the nom de plume of Henry Appleton), an *Irish World* correspondent, reporting on a meeting at Cooper Union in New York City in support of the Irish agitation, was pleased to note that with one-third of the audience consisting of Germans and three speeches given in German, the gathering showed that "all the workingmen are beginning to realize that the bottom causes of oppression are everywhere the same."[117] At the same meeting S. E. Shevitch of the New York German-American newspaper *Volkszeitung* pro-claimed "in the name of all workingmen, in the name of the socialist workingmen of New York [and] those now struggling in Russia . . . , in the name of the ni-hilists . . . , in the name of the heroes of the world, a welcome to the Irish revo-lution."[118] Though the cooperation engendered by the League proved to be transitory, these instances of ethnic collaboration within the Land League repre-sented attempts to overcome the stratification along national lines that so often plagued American working-class organizations.

The efforts of Patrick Ford and the *Irish World* were crucial in shaping a radical alternative to the beliefs of conservatives within the American Land League. Ford continuously pushed Irish leaders to expand the goals of the movement beyond its calls for rent reductions and peasant proprietorship and into a drastic reconfiguration of the existing land system that linked radical agrarian reform in Ireland inextricably to the urgent need for land reform in the United States. Such ideas attracted working-class and radical Irish Americans into the Land League, who in their meetings and in their speeches openly declared their support for the *Irish World.* Radical nationalists struggled against the social evils of land monopoly and big business, favoring instead a producer ideology that sought to restore the lost dignity of labor. The American Land League also influenced the general reform culture of the Gilded Age. Together, the various supporters of the *Irish World* faction of the League challenged both conservative dominance of the land movement and the economic and social status quo of late nineteenth-century America.

6

"Let Us Rise to Action"

Gender, Ethnic Nationalism, and the Ladies' Land League in the United States

Now, I ask my Irish countrywomen in America what are *they* going to do to help us to get this liberty and these just laws? What are *they* going to do to help these three million[s] of people, more than two million of whom are women and little children? Have they read what happened at Carraroe, when the women threw themselves in front of the bayonets of the soldiery, and tore the processes from the process-servers, and saved their husbands and their children from eviction and starvation? These women were as noble as the old heroines of Rome and Sparta. Are the women in America going to do anything to help them and those like them in Ireland? I fear that this winter heroic women as well as heroic men will be wanted in Ireland. Irish *men* in America are giving splendid help; now let Irish *women* put their shoulders to the wheel also, for the war that will have to be waged this winter will be for the cause of women and children.

Fanny Parnell, "The Coming Struggle"

Thousands of Irish-American women created and participated in an energetic Ladies' Land League in the United States in the early 1880s. These women embraced Irish nationalism and, through their activism, asserted a public role in their communities. Most historians have neglected the involvement of Irish-American women in Irish nationalism in the United States during the late nineteenth century. The few who have mentioned their participation in nationalist movements have largely dismissed their contributions. Instead, historians have focused primarily on their impact as economic actors, particularly their roles as domestic servants and teachers.[1] A reexamination of the historical record, however, indicates that thousands of Irish-American women were active in Irish nationalism and that their participation provided them with an opportunity to declare their desire for a public voice and inclusion within the male-dominated realm of Irish-American nationalist activity and public life.

The history of the Ladies' Land League in the United States reveals the contested nature of the Victorian ideology of domesticity. Whether they were housewives, domestic servants, factory workers, or teachers, Irish-American women experienced a fluid blurring of public and private activity in their everyday lives. During the widespread mobilization of Irish-American females in the Ladies' Land League, women sought to claim their right to participate publicly in the movement. This involvement had an important effect on a generation of Irish-American women.

Irish-American women benefited significantly from the "Greater Ireland" created through the Land League. Though intended at first simply as a way to strengthen Irish-American support for Ireland, the Ladies' Land League in the United States quickly became a vehicle for Irish-American women to assert their own American-based concerns and ideological convictions. Women's ideological divisions mirrored those that existed among males in the movement: on the one hand, a conservative belief that the movement should focus exclusively on social and political reform in Ireland, and on the other hand, a more radical view that far-reaching agrarian reform in Ireland should be linked to social reform in the United States. These differences of opinion demonstrate women's conflicting ideological conceptions of Irish nationalism and belie claims made by some historians of women's aversion to public activity and Irish nationalist politics. They also reveal the willingness of many Irish-American women to challenge male authority, including that of male leaders of the Catholic Church. When the church took positions against their interests, women often ignored its leaders and sometimes directly challenged them. Women's participation in the Ladies' Land League demonstrates how events in Ireland profoundly influenced the Irish-American experience in the United States in the 1880s and beyond.

Traditional Opposition to Public Activity
by Irish-American Women

Historians have challenged the use of the metaphor of separate spheres to describe women's public and private activity in American society. Separate-spheres ideology leaves us with only a partial picture of the full range of women's experiences. Instead, Linda Kerber has urged historians to treat the "language of separate spheres itself as a rhetorical construction that responded to changing social and economic reality."[2] An examination of the prescriptive literature directed toward women, when compared with the actual experiences of Irish-American women, helps to demonstrate the challenges and opportunities surrounding women's public participation within the Irish-American organizations of the late nineteenth century.

Many Irish-American Catholic leaders gave strong support to confining women's activity to the home. These leaders, eager to gain equal status and respectability within native-born American society, advocated an idealized view that women's proper role was in the home, and that it was there that women could best exercise their superior moral and spiritual rule over their families. Women who participated in the public arena were challenging the Victorian ideal of "true womanhood" advocated in American religious literature, advice manuals, and women's magazines and represented by "four cardinal virtues— piety, purity, submissiveness, and domesticity."[3] In his popular advice manual, *Mirror of True Womanhood* (1876), Father Bernard O'Reilly of New York City wrote that "no woman animated by the spirit of her baptism . . . ever fancied that she had or could have any other sphere of duty or activity than that home which is her domain, her garden, her paradise, her world."[4] The public world of men was tainted and corrupt, O'Reilly argued, and women had to remain outside of politics to maintain their purity. Ensconced in the home, women were expected to provide a sanctuary for their husbands from the rough and tumble of the outside world, while also raising the next generation and teaching them sound Catholic morals. For a woman to move outside the home not only endangered her and her family but also challenged the orderly running of society. This ideal of true womanhood was often reinforced and encouraged by clerical and lay leaders, in many newspapers and magazines (religious and secular), and sometimes by women themselves.

Of course, for many Irish-American women "true womanhood" was an idealized state that was both unrealistic and unwelcome in practice. Instead, Hasia Diner argues that "Irish women viewed themselves as self-sufficient beings, with economic roles to play in their families and communities."[5] Irish women were engaged in a variety of occupations in the late nineteenth-century American economy. They were some of the first labor activists and organizers in America's mills and factories. After the Great Famine large numbers of Irish immigrant women settled in New England's burgeoning textile towns and came to constitute a large percentage of the workforce.[6] Irish women were also prominent in the Knights of Labor, and they participated in a variety of boycotts, strikes, and other forms of economic protest.[7] American-born Irish women embraced such occupations as teaching as careers and women generally experienced significantly higher occupational mobility than Irish males in the United States in the second half of the nineteenth century.[8] Women's wages were a crucial element in the economic health of Irish-American households and helped to support their families in the United States and Ireland. For such women, a life removed from the public world of wage labor and capitalist production was utterly beyond their normal experience.

Irish-American women were most prominent in domestic service. Predominantly unmarried, these servants enjoyed an autonomy unheard of in Ireland.[9] Irish-American female servants also received relatively good wages, with their room and board provided by their employers, and as Diane Hotten-Somers has demonstrated, they "increasingly entered the public sphere as consumers," purchasing the latest fashions and attending theaters and other forms of popular entertainment.[10] Despite their relative autonomy and economic power, Irish-American women—outside of their participation in church activities—were excluded from male-dominated Irish Catholic reform movements.

The reasons for this exclusion can be found within the ideology and practice of late nineteenth-century Catholic reform. Catholic reformers (in movements such as temperance), often drawn from the newly established Irish-American middle class, were eager to assert their respectability and fitness for American society and to disprove Protestant claims of Irish laziness and drunkenness. These concerns resulted in certain important differences between Protestant and Catholic temperance efforts. Catholic men excluded women from temperance reform in order to avoid charges from other Catholics of "unmanliness," for some men saw temperance reform as an attack on the male-dominated world of social drinking and camaraderie. In contrast, women dominated the Protestant temperance movement and tended to view alcohol abuse, in large part, as an inherent problem of immigrant culture.[11] Protestant reformers attempted to enact temperance by pressing legislators to adopt prohibition statues. Catholic reformers were skeptical of the wisdom of pursuing legislative solutions and preferred to base their appeals on moral suasion and abstinence. To overcome criticisms of being overly gloomy and dull, Catholic temperance reformers also attempted to add an element of fraternal sociability to their gatherings and organizations in order to bring men together under the banner of moral reform.[12] Women were not welcome at such gatherings, even though women and children were often the ones who bore the brunt of the terrible costs of men's alcohol abuse.[13]

Just as in the temperance movement, so too in Irish-American nationalist and benevolent organizations: Irish-American women had been precluded from participation. Irish and Irish-American nationalists committed to the violent overthrow of British rule in Ireland saw their activity as a manly pursuit beyond the realm of women's participation. There were two main exceptions to this exclusion. One exception was the presence of women in the American Repeal movement in the early 1840s. As Angela Murphy notes, Irish-American women in Philadelphia and other cities provided financial and moral support to the cause of repeal.[14] The other exception to female exclusion was the Fenian Sisterhood of the 1860s, but it was short lived and lacked much widespread appeal.[15] The traditional social segregation of Irish-American men and women reinforced separation by gender. The world of the saloon and fraternal sociability belonged to men and was a sanctuary walled off from the influence of women.[16] Within the AOH, the great Irish-American benevolent and social organization (founded in 1836), the ladies' auxiliaries were given official recognition only in 1894.[17] Thus women's public participation in the Land League struggle in the 1880s represented a new form of political activism for a multitude of Irish-American women.

The Founding of the Ladies' Land League in the United States and Ireland

The impetus for involving women in the American Land League movement came from Charles Stewart Parnell's sister, Frances (Fanny) Isabel Parnell. Her American-born mother, Delia Tudor Stewart Parnell, raised Fanny and her sister Anna alone, after the early death of her husband. Delia was the daughter of an American naval hero, Captain Charles Stewart, commander of the frigate U.S.S. *Constitution*.[18] Under Delia's care the sisters gained a much more independent upbringing than most women of their class. They always valued their autonomy, and neither of them married.[19] Although their father's estate provided for their education, little else remained of their inheritance, and the sisters were left in a financially precarious position throughout their lives. Despite this financial uncertainty, Anna and Fanny Parnell were able to make their living through writing, and they both acquired a modest amount of literary success. Fanny, a talented poet, was active from an early age in Irish nationalist literary endeavors. Her first published foray into poetry had come in 1864 at the age of fifteen in the *Irish People*, a Fenian newspaper edited by John O'Leary. Fanny Parnell acquired minor fame for her poems in Ireland and America, while Anna published the article "How They Do in the House of Commons: Notes From the Ladies' Cage," an account of the British parliamentary session of 1877, memorable for the carefully staged obstructionist tactics employed by her brother and a small band of his followers that captured national attention in Ireland.

The Parnell sisters were active in the Land League from its inception. Fanny, residing at the time in Bordentown, New Jersey, with her mother and Anna, sent a letter to the Boston *Pilot* on 6 September 1879 calling on Irish Americans to alleviate the misery in Ireland. "Could not a subscription be raised," she asked, "to help the most distressing cases in some of the Western counties? Will not the Irish here, who can afford it, give something from their conveniences here to help our countrymen in their terrible need?"[20] The *Pilot* responded to this letter by opening a collection and encouraging subscribers to send money to be forwarded promptly to Ireland. In early 1880 the sisters helped organize their brother Charles Stewart Parnell's tour across the United States and were fixtures at the New York Land League branch office, where they worked ten-hour days for the relief committee. Anna Parnell returned to Ireland soon afterward, leaving Fanny (who would remain in the United States until her death) alone in New Jersey with their mother.[21]

Fanny Parnell's poetry provided important inspiration in the early days of the Land League movement. Though she remained an advocate of nonviolent agitation, her nationalist poetry, with its martial rhetoric and violent imagery, was a call for action and enthusiasm among Irishmen in the United States and Ireland in the 1880s. Several of her verses were published in the Boston *Pilot* and were widely reprinted elsewhere. Her best-known poem, "Hold the Harvest," was addressed to Irish farmers in 1880:

> Oh, by the God who made us all—
> The seignior and the serf—
> Rise up! and swear this day to hold
> Your own green Irish turf;
> Rise up! and plant your feet as men
> Where now you crawl as slaves,
> And make the harvest fields your camps,
> Or make them your graves.[22]

Dubbed by Michael Davitt the *Marseillaise* of the Land League movement, this poem, as well as others, pleaded with Irish men and women to pursue the struggle in Ireland until victory was achieved.[23] Fanny Parnell hoped that the Land League would lead to Ireland's eventual political independence.

Surveying the progress of the American Land League in the summer of 1880, however, Fanny Parnell concluded that the movement was not growing rapidly enough. After consulting with Michael Davitt, she decided to form a Ladies' Land League of America in the hope that competition from women would spur the male fundraising efforts already underway. On 12 August 1880, she sent a letter titled "The Coming Struggle" to the *Irish World* and several other newspapers, inviting Irish-American women to organize. "Compassion and enthusiasm," she argued, "are woman's attributes, and these are two things that are essentially needed in this Land League work."[24] Fanny Parnell appealed to female patriotism, beseeching Irish-American women to lend their aid to Ireland in this time of crisis.

Irish-American women rallied behind Fanny Parnell's call to organize. On 15 October 1881 a meeting was held in New York City to establish the New York branch of the Ladies' Irish National Land League. The participants elected Delia Parnell as president, Ellen Ford (sister of Patrick Ford) and Fanny Parnell as vice presidents, and Jane Byrne as secretary. Over a hundred women promptly joined the organization, which adopted the constitution and bylaws of the men's Land League of America. Irish-American newspapers across the United States reported on the new league, and Fanny Parnell was "overwhelmed with applications for copies of our constitution, for letters to be read out at meetings, for advice how to organize, etc."; for two months she "wrote letters incessantly, day and night."[25] Shortly after the establishment of the New York branch, local women organized Ladies' Land League branches in St. Louis and San Francisco.[26]

Branches of the Ladies' Land League quickly spread across the country, from Boston to Kansas City, Savannah to New Orleans, and as far west as California. Local Irish-American women organized these leagues and shaped their agendas, and the national leadership had little direct control. Women chaired the meetings, though men were often in attendance, and members elected their own officers, gave speeches, and passed resolutions. Thus participation in local branches allowed Irish-American women to carve out their own spaces within their communities and to define their own priorities for themselves.

It is impossible to know exactly how many women joined the Ladies' Land League, as no membership data have survived, but it is possible to make an educated estimate. In January 1881, Ellen Ford reported that twenty-five Ladies' Land Leagues had already been organized, with a total membership of 5,000 and an average of 200 women in each branch.[27] A tally of the announcements from October 1880 to December 1882 about Ladies' Land League branches in the *Irish World* newspaper, which provided the best coverage of the Land League, yields a total of 203 branches.[28] This total includes only branches that corresponded with the *Irish World*, and thus the actual number was undoubtedly higher. If we add these numbers to Ellen Ford's earlier report and conservatively estimate that each branch possessed sixty members, then it appears that the Ladies' Land League had over 225 branches, with a total membership over at least 17,000.[29] The real number may actually have been

Table 2. Number of new Ladies' Land League branches per quarter

Source: *Irish World*, October 1880–December 1882.

substantially greater. The city of Hartford in Connecticut alone had three branches, with 2,000 members altogether, while Philadelphia had 600 members and Woonsocket, Rhode Island, over 300.[30] Regardless of the precise total, the large number of women involved underscores the necessity of examining women's participation in the Ladies' Land League more closely in order to expand our understanding of Irish-American women's activities in the late nineteenth century.

The growth of the Ladies' Land League was connected tightly with developments in Ireland. The announcements found in the *Irish World* of the founding of Ladies' Land League branches in the United States allows us to illustrate this development (see table 2). After Davitt's arrest and the passage of a coercion bill in Ireland in February 1881, the number of Ladies' Land League branches founded skyrocketed. Another jump in membership occurred in early 1882 when Irish Americans organized a convention in Chicago to endorse the No-Rent Manifesto. Similar to their male counterparts, the Ladies' Land League in the United States grew fastest during periods of crisis in Ireland.

By examining this data from the *Irish World* further, we can also gain a picture of the regional breakdown of Ladies' League activity. Before we discuss these results, one major caveat must be recognized. These numbers represent

Table 3. Number of Ladies' Land League branches by region

Region	Number of branches
Mid Atlantic	86
New England	72
Midwest	24
West	15
South	6

Source: Irish World, October 1880–December 1882.

only branches that were announced through the *Irish World*, and some Ladies' Land League branches may have chosen not to self-report to the newspaper either for practical or for ideological reasons. But with that qualification recognized, the data shows that the Ladies' Land League seems to have been at its strongest in the New England and Mid-Atlantic regions, with the Midwest, West, and South trailing significantly (see table 3). It is difficult to fully identify the exact reasons for this geographical distribution, but the evidence suggests a few possibilities. Perhaps the simplest and most logical explanation for the eastern tilt of the Ladies' Land League is that the vast bulk of Irish Americans in 1880 were still primarily concentrated along the Eastern Seaboard.[31] It was also in New England and the Mid-Atlantic regions that Ellen Ford and Delia Stewart Parnell had been most active in organizing branches. It is possible that some branches in the West and the South did not support the *Irish World* and chose not to report their activities through the newspaper or reported their activities elsewhere, but unfortunately, evidence from regional newspapers is too scarce to know for sure. From the evidence that we do have, the Ladies' Land League in the United States appears to have been a mostly eastern phenomenon.

The activity of Irish-American women initiated through the formation of the Ladies' Land League brought to the cause of Irish nationalism talents previously lacking in earlier movements. The journalistic background of many leading women in the Ladies' Land League was a boon to the cause in the United States. Ellen Ford, Alice May Quinn, and Margaret F. Sullivan, to name just a few such members, were employed as newspaper correspondents and editors. Quinn began her journalistic career as a traveling correspondent for the *AOH Journal* of Richmond, Virginia, before settling in Chicago and assuming editorship of the Chicago *Sunday Telefone*. She lectured frequently across the United States, often on behalf of the Land League, and was very popular among working-class audiences. "Whenever I go in the coal regions," she declared on the eve of one of her lecture tours, "I anticipate a rousing accession of the League, as miners are still aware of the meaning of the word coercion and tyranny when applied to legalized robbers and plunderers."[32] Margaret Sullivan, also of Chicago, had served as a schoolteacher before accepting a position on the editorial staff of the *Chicago Times*. Sullivan traveled as a correspondent in Ireland and authored a history of the Land League in 1881 titled *Ireland of To-Day: The Causes and Aims of Irish Agitation*.[33] She also undertook another tour across Ireland in 1883, incognito, collecting notes for a comparative study of Irish, French, and Belgian daily life.[34] Both women were acknowledged across the United States as leading figures of the Ladies' Land League. Their journalistic responsibilities, of course, allowed them to travel much more frequently and widely than the average Irish-American woman. Working long hours, traveling extensively, and working alongside men, these two women greatly helped to expand the Ladies' Land League while undermining the neat separation of public and private in women's lives advocated by Victorian moralists.

The large amount of money Irish-American women sent back home to Ireland was one of the most important contributions that Irish-American women made to Ireland during the Land League era. This usually took the form of remittances to family members and friends, and these funds were used for a variety of purposes, including the payment of rent. Somewhere between 50 and 80 percent of all remittances from the United States to Ireland were sent by women.[35] Most of the remittances sent were in small amounts of a few dollars or pounds, but taken together, these remittances had a substantial impact on Irish families and the Irish economy.[36]

Members of the Ladies' Land League were also active in raising money for Ireland. Irish-American Catholic women were able to draw on extensive prior fundraising experience from their participation in parish church fairs, in which women were the chief organizers, workers, and collectors of money.[37] This expertise aided female Land Leaguers' financial activities. It is not possible to quantify all the funds sent by women to Ireland, as branches sent money through several sources, including the *Irish World* and the official Land League treasurer, Father Lawrence Walsh, or often directly to Ireland. But a tally of the donations made to the "Land League Fund" of the *Irish World* by local branches of the Ladies' League from 31 January to 31 October 1882 amounted to almost $22,500.[38] The overall total, however, must have been substantially higher, as the New York Central Branch of the Ladies' League alone, of which Fanny Parnell was secretary, transmitted some $1,400 directly to Ireland.[39]

Initiation fees could be as low as twenty-five cents, as they were in Woonsocket, Rhode Island.[40] These low membership expenses allowed Irish-American women across the whole economic spectrum to participate. This strategy echoed the example of Daniel O'Connell's "Catholic Rent" in the 1820s in Ireland, whereby a penny a month was collected from Catholics of all classes in a mass movement that raised substantial sums because of the huge numbers reached by local organizers.

The efforts made by Irish-American women in support of the Land League did not go unnoticed in Ireland. Inspired by the success of the Ladies' Land League in America, Michael Davitt founded a Ladies' Land League in Ireland on 31 January 1881. Davitt argued that since the male leaders of the movement were increasingly being arrested and jailed, and Land League meetings suppressed under the coercion act, Irish women should be recruited to carry on the cause. Davitt believed that women would provide critical leadership and support to the movement. Furthermore, if the British government used the coercion act to imprison Irish women, it would place the British authorities in the uncomfortable position of attacking Irish womanhood and garner additional support for Ireland's cause abroad.[41] Anna Parnell accepted the presidency, and the Ladies' Land League in Ireland proved to be a vigorous organization.

Anna Parnell was a driven and inspiring leader of the Ladies' Land League in Ireland. Katherine Tynan recalled of Anna Parnell that she "had the heart of a revolutionary" and was "of the stuff of which heroines are made."[42] She gave speeches across Ireland exhorting Irish women to take a firm stand against evictions. One famous (or infamous) example of her courage came in 1882 when she grabbed the reins of Lord Lieutenant Earl Spencer's carriage horses and demanded to know what he meant "by interfering with the houses I am building for evicted tenants?"[43] Under Anna Parnell's stewardship the Ladies' Land League in Ireland propelled the agrarian movement forward. Indeed, after the arrest of almost all the male leaders by mid-1881, the Ladies' Land League in Ireland became the driving force in the land agitation.[44]

The Ladies' Land League of Ireland had a much more contentious existence than its American counterpart. From the beginning, most male Irish leaders, with the exception of Davitt and a few others, were uneasy about incorporating women into the Land League struggle. Davitt recalled that Charles Stewart Parnell and John Dillon were especially opposed to the idea.[45] This uneasiness among the male leadership of the League toward women's participation slowly poisoned relationships between men and women in the movement and eventually led to a bitter split between Irish Ladies' Land Leaguers and Parnell.

The Ladies' Land League of America:
Irish-American Women and Ethnic Nationalism

In the United States a new enthusiasm for the Irish nationalist cause and for the Land League prompted women of Irish birth or descent to assert themselves in Irish-American nationalist politics and to demonstrate their leadership capacities publicly in their local communities. Women in the Ladies' Land League worked independently of men and determined their own priorities. Their embrace of Irish nationalism presented a new and exciting opportunity for women to contribute to Irish-American nationalist politics and to promote their own interpretation of the movement in Ireland and the United States.

Local Irish-American women organized branches and shaped their agendas, as the national leadership exercised little direct control. In the early stages of the movement many women were tentative in asserting their independence at meetings. At one of the first meetings of the New York branches, for example, Delia Parnell requested that a gentleman come forward and make a few remarks, as "we women are not yet quite accustomed to going alone."[46] Such uncertainties, however, were quickly overcome, and Ladies' Land League meetings became lively and self-assured.

The assertiveness of Ladies' Land Leaguers did not extend to women's suffrage. No evidence has been found that any female League branch advocated or supported voting rights for women. In several instances individual members or specific branches of the Ladies' Land League repudiated suffrage. As Fanny Parnell put it, "I am not a woman's rights woman, but I believe that every woman has the right to do good."[47] The Buffalo Branch No. 1 of the Land League, which was composed of both women and men, unanimously adopted a resolution denouncing women's suffrage after it was reported that the branch had attempted to form a women's suffrage association under the auspices of the Land League.[48] John Boyle O'Reilly, an ardent supporter of the Ladies' Land League and a friend of Fanny Parnell, declared: "Woman's suffrage is an unjust, unreasonable, unspiritual abnormality. . . . It is the antithesis of that highest and sweetest mystery—conviction by submission, conquest by sacrifice."[49] Though Irish-American women argued forcefully and articulately for the rights of Irish men and women vis-à-vis Britain, they did not challenge the disenfranchisement of women in American society.

Irish-American women joined the Ladies' Land League for a variety of reasons. Many welcomed the opportunity to demonstrate their intelligence and competence. Women "were possessed of as much intelligence as men," Delia Parnell declared to a Ladies' Land League audience in Jersey City, and they "had formerly proved themselves to be as strong, both mentally and physically, as the sterner sex."[50] Unfortunately, however, the greater occupational mobility enjoyed by Irish-American women in the late nineteenth century had not translated into leadership roles in American society. Participation in the Ladies' Land League allowed women to experience a sense of pride and to exhibit their fitness for public leadership in their local communities.

Membership in the Ladies' Land League was also seen as part of a larger, humanitarian mission to save Ireland from British misrule. Mrs. M. J. O'Connor of the San Francisco Ladies' Land League argued: "We have struggled for families, for selves, for freedom, but never once for humanity. Awake women! Let us rise to action and help our brothers in the battle for humanity and natural rights."[51] The Pawtucket, Rhode Island, Ladies' Land League declared, "Our object shall be to aid and encourage the persecuted people of Ireland to beat down that inhuman monster called landlordism and to do all in our power to raise funds to aid Charles Stewart Parnell and his noble co-workers baffle the British lion."[52] This was to be a community effort, and for those women unwilling to help Ireland, the Pawtucket members expressed the view that "every young lady in Pawtucket who did not rally and join the just cause deserved to be boycotted by all who had a drop of Irish blood in their veins."[53]

Some women in the movement argued that they were not challenging gender boundaries but merely practicing their traditional womanly domestic roles. Concern for the home, they insisted, must extend to the homeland. Fanny Parnell was convinced that "this Land League business is essentially a woman's business because it is essentially a work of philanthropy and humanity."[54] Her mother echoed this conviction in declaring that "the characteristic of a virtuous woman is to raise her voice for those who are condemned to destruction."[55] Belief in the necessity of providing for despondent and suffering Irish kinsfolk placed the responsibility for action on Irish-American women and justified their inclusion in male-dominated nationalist politics. Rallying public opinion against British injustice and oppression was another important responsibility falling on Irish-American women. As Ellen Ford asserted, "I believe in women's rights—that is, woman's right to protest against injustice. It is charitable to feed the hungry but uncharitable not to protest against laws that make paupers."[56] Thus, despite the fact that the lives of most Irish-American women were not confined to the home, women in the Ladies' Land League were still comfortable in using the rhetoric of domesticity to assert their fitness for public participation in Irish nationalism.

Membership in the League was also a way for Irish-American women to assert their respectability in American society. This concern can be seen in their decision to style their organization "Ladies' League" instead of women's or females' league. In a newspaper interview Delia Parnell claimed that while many members of the Ladies' Land League were "servant girls," the "word 'lady' has been enlarged to include almost all women in this country. As long as the 'German ladies' hold their festivals and the 'colored ladies' go on a picnic, the Irish ladies propose to manifest also their own dignity and *amour propre*."[57] Using the term "ladies" was a conscious decision by numerous Irish-American women to assert their gentility, which was often challenged in American public culture by such stereotypes as "Bridget" (the young, lazy, and gullible newly arrived immigrant domestic) and "Biddy" (the older, oafish, and rebellious servant). Irish-American women active in the Irish cause insisted that they were as worthy of respect as their Anglo-American counterparts. Female League members were also eager to emphasize to men and to Catholic bishops and priests that despite their participation in the hitherto male-dominated national-ist movement, they retained their respectability and femininity.[58]

The adoption of the term "ladies" was also an expression of the attempts of middle-class Irish-American women to create and impose their own definition of the nature of Irish-American womanhood on their poorer countrywomen. Kerby Miller has argued that "middle-class [Irish-American] immigrants could not gain status in American society until they had both mobilized the Irish American masses, to demonstrate their political leverage, and imposed bourgeois norms on them, to reassure the host society's governing classes that the group was sufficiently 'civilized.'"[59] While Miller focuses primarily on Irish-American men, such a conceptual framework could help explain part of the motivation of middle-class women in joining the movement. If such a motive was preva-lent, however, these well-heeled women faced a difficult task in imposing their bourgeois norms on the movement in general. Severe ideological disagreement existed within the Ladies' Land League, as will be discussed shortly, over the purpose and goals of the agitation and led to acrimony and strife among its members.

The Ladies' Land League also provided a forum for sociability. "The meetings of the Ladies' Land League of the Seventh Ward [in New York City]," declared the *Irish-American*, "partake more of the character of social reunions than of the stereotyped, stiff-necked business meeting."[60] Many branches sponsored picnics and hosted weekend excursions, combining their concern for Ireland with recreational outings. Colleen McDannell has found that Amer-ican Catholic reformers in the late nineteenth century, uneasy with the rowdi-ness and often alcohol-driven sociability of Irish-American men, argued that "honor, character, orderliness, future-orientation, and piety ripened in the company of women" and pressed Irish-American men to "integrate their al-ready too tight male bonds with domestic sentiments."[61] Irish-American men and women were brought together in social settings under the banner of the

Land League. Thus, alongside their political goal of securing Irish freedom, the men's and women's Land Leagues provided an outlet for Irish-American male and female sociability.

The Ladies' Land League urged women to act not in a subordinate role but to assert themselves morally and intellectually. Delia Parnell and Ellen Ford undertook several barnstorming tours across the eastern United States and in their public addresses called on Irish-American women to join the Land League cause. At a meeting in Brooklyn, Delia Parnell praised the knowledge of Irish-American women: "They understand the land question; they don't want anyone to preach to them about the value of land." She also exhorted women to "go to lectures on religion, education, and industrial matters."[62] By educating themselves, women could make their own decisions on the pressing political and economic issues of the times in Ireland and America. Participation by Irish-American women in the Land League cause would spur not only the Irish in America but also their kinsfolk in Ireland. "The women are firing the first shot," Ellen Ford declared, "and are going to keep this thing going until it goes round the world."[63]

Despite the earlier exclusion of women from nationalist activities, many male Land Leaguers in America seemed to welcome women's participation in the Land League movement. John Boyle O'Reilly, editor of the Boston *Pilot*, remarked of the Ladies' Land League that it "is one of the most interesting and may grow to be one of the most potent phases of this great movement."[64] Support for the Ladies' Land League was not confined to the Irish Catholic laity. Many priests vigorously supported the Ladies' Land League in their communities and welcomed women as fellow workers in the cause of Irish freedom and agrarian reform. At a reception in Boston for Fanny Parnell, commentators noted that no fewer than a dozen Catholic priests were present.[65] The pastor of the parish of the Ladies' Land League in Central Falls, Rhode Island, dedicated all parish collections to the branch for a month.[66]

Some members of the American Catholic hierarchy, however, did not share this favorable opinion of women's participation in the movement. On 17 March 1881, Bishop Thomas Grace of St. Paul, Minnesota, denounced the formation of Ladies' Land Leagues in his Saint Patrick's Day address. "There is something about the calling out of mothers and daughters from their homes at night to form leagues and hold meetings that does not seem right," he declared. "The movement, I know, did not originate with the women themselves. It is in opposition to all their womanly instincts." This claim, that the women were the dupes of conniving males, was actually a gross distortion, but that was of little consequence to Grace. He finished his exhortation to his flock by pleading that Irish-American womanhood be left alone and not constrained "to adopt the rough, unfamiliar ways of men by holding public meetings for discussion."[67]

Grace's remarks spurred a vigorous defense of the Ladies' Land League. William Markoe, a prominent Land Leaguer in St. Paul, disagreed with Grace's assessment and wondered "whether it is outside of the sphere of a woman's modesty or woman's love to tender to the poor, crushed, joyless, heartbroken mothers and children of Ireland."[68] Other commentators questioned the hypocrisy of engaging women in the solicitation of funds for church purposes while denouncing their benevolent concern for their distressed kinsfolk in Ireland. As Ellen Ford pointed out with some heat, "No one thinks it wrong for women to beg for church fairs, sell tickets for lotteries, picnics, lectures, etc.; and why should they not form clubs or societies to-day for the relief of the wives, mothers, and sisters in Ireland?"[69] The response to Grace's address starkly illustrates the hazy line between the public and private aspects of many Irish-American women's lives. In the end Grace's warnings were largely ignored.

Why did Irish-American men so willingly accept women's participation in the Land League movement? One reason may have been that members of the Ladies' Land League made no mention of taking up of arms against the hated enemy England. Physical warfare and military action was reserved exclusively for males. With such clear gender norms in place, the fear of women adopting manly and aggressive behavior was tempered by the knowledge that if the movement turned violent, Irish-American women would once again be relegated to the sidelines. Another possible explanation is that some men may have been convinced that women's participation in the Ladies' Land League served as a practical lesson in patriotism and commitment to the homeland that women could pass on to the next generation of Irish-American patriots.[70]

The most likely reason for male acceptance of women's involvement in the movement, however, may be the simplest: many men did not see women's activism in the Ladies' Land League as a serious threat to existing gender and social relationships. In fact, the paucity of protests against women's participation could indicate that, far from embarking on a completely new path by joining the League, women were already increasingly active outside the home. Many Irish-American women, in their employment as domestic servants, factory workers, and schoolteachers, were engaged in work that passed beyond the direct oversight and control of their male family members. As Timothy Meagher has observed, once unmarried women were permitted "the freedom to work outside the household, it proved difficult to rein them in and restrict them to the natural place for all women: the home."[71] Seen in this way, opposition to the Ladies' Land League by men like Bishop Grace could have been an attempt to reassert rather than maintain traditional boundaries. But for the many men who saw the Land League as a movement based on moral suasion, such a move would not have been appealing. For them, what could have been more natural than to engage women, with their widely ascribed moral and spiritual influence, in pursuit of the noble work of the Irish cause? Many women also shared this view of their activities. As the Ironsides Branch of the Philadelphia Ladies' Land League declared, "We deny in advocating the cause of Irish liberty [that] we are doing what is immodest or unwomanly, but on the contrary we are engaged in holy work."[72] Through their active and passionate support of the Land League, women demonstrated to men their value as partners in serving the holy cause of supporting the homeland.

Ideological Disagreement within the American Ladies' Land League

Ladies' Land League organizers obscured for a time the ideological differences among their members by crafting a broad appeal for the participation of Irish-American women in the movement. Once women became engaged publicly in support of the movement, however, differences of opinion about the purpose and goals of the organization emerged. A conservative faction within the Ladies' Land League wanted to limit its mission to generating funds and other forms of support for the Irish agitation, while a radical element advocated the necessity of fundamental economic and social reform in both Ireland and the United States. While this difference of opinion ultimately hurt the effectiveness of the Ladies' Land League in America, the fact that women were willing to openly air their differences demonstrates their comfort with their new public roles. Rather than simply defending their participation and closing ranks in response to opposition, as might have been expected if women were overly defensive about their position, they instead insisted upon their prerogatives in helping to shape the direction of the movement.

For conservative members the primary purpose of the Ladies' Land League was to provide much-needed financial and moral support to the Land League agitation in Ireland. Female leaders of the Buffalo branch called on their fellow women "to give of your moral influence, of your worldly substance. Is it charity we ask? Not so; suffering humanity claims aid as its right; justice claims adherence as its right."[73] Members would spur the growth of the movement in Ireland through their generous donations and activism in the United States. At a meeting in New York, Delia Parnell pointed the way forward: "A change has come over the spirit of the Irish; they have felt as yet but the first ripple of the immense return tidal-wave of their emigration to this land."[74] Conservatives argued that if Irish-American women kept the funds coming, it would be only a matter of time before Irish nationalists and agrarian reformers emerged triumphant.

Fanny Parnell was the most influential member of the conservative faction of the Ladies' Land League. While she hoped that the Land League would lead to Ireland's eventual political independence, her vision of Ireland's future did not include social revolution. She favored peasant proprietorship (the gradual purchase of landed estates by tenants), denounced schemes favoring land redistribution or nationalization, and resisted attempts to connect the Irish nationalist struggle against Britain with economic reform in the United States.[75] Parnell eschewed class conflict in the belief that "between every producing class in a nation there is solidarity of interests."[76] This stance led her to distrust the *Irish World* and its contention that the Irish agitation was the first step in a worldwide struggle against the forces of monopoly and economic tyranny. For Fanny Parnell and other female conservatives the Land League in the United States was an auxiliary movement meant to support and follow the direction of Land League leaders in Ireland.

While many conservative Irish-American women focused their efforts on sending relief to Irish victims of eviction and the coercion act and on promoting Irish freedom, many radical Irish-American women linked land reform in Ireland to the need for sweeping social reform in the United States. Like their male counterparts, radical women were generally convinced that the economic problems in Ireland and the United States were two sides of the same coin.

From the beginning of the Land League many radical labor reformers advocated that women involve themselves with the movement. The members of the Workingwomen's Union of Chicago, a socialist organization that included the African-American anarchist Lucy Parsons and Elizabeth Rodgers, a member of the Knights of Labor, encouraged female participation in the Irish cause. The Workingwomen's Union, while not officially affiliated with the Land League, pronounced itself in favor of its tenets.[77] The Workingwomen's Union had nearly one thousand members, mostly housewives, but it also comprised women from a variety of trades. The stated aims of the Workingwomen's Union were the reduction of working hours, higher wages, workplace inspections, the abolition of contract convict labor and the truck system, employer responsibility for industrial accidents, and the prohibition of child labor.[78] Elizabeth Rodgers, who would become the first female Master Workman of the Knights of Labor, was elected president of a mixed-sex Land League in Chicago. Many men advocated the recruitment of women to the cause. Terence Powderly, Grand Master Workman of the Knights of Labor and vice president of the Land League, declared to a female Knights of Labor member that "if the women take an interest in a movement, the men *must* follow."[79]

Ellen Ford, an editor for her brother Patrick's newspaper, was a strong advocate of coupling the issue of land reform in Ireland with that of social reform in the United States. Though she was not working class herself, Ford articulated a brand of economic and social radicalism that appealed to many working-class and radical women and brought these women into Irish nationalist politics for the first time. Like her brother, Ellen Ford believed that the battle against landlordism in Ireland was the cause of the victimized classes the world over. She anticipated that "the day is not too far distant when the Land League war must be fought in the land of the so-called free."[80] Speaking to large audiences across the country, Ford forcefully maintained the radical potential of the land movement in Ireland. "A government that can make a pauper of a man and then abuse him for being a pauper," she exclaimed, "deserves to be destroyed."[81]

Evidence of support for these radical ideals is to be found in letters to the *Irish World* from Ladies' Land Leagues across the country. In Boston the secretary of a branch of the Ladies' League informed the *Irish World* that she and her female colleagues "have taken to the study of Henry George's *The Irish Land Question*."[82] The women's branch in Paterson, New Jersey, voted unanimously, over the objection of male Land Leaguers, to send all their money through the *Irish World*.[83] The female branch in St. Louis, Missouri, passed a motion to dispatch money that would allow the *Irish World* to be distributed in Ireland, as its members believed that "it would also be well to send knowledge along with bread."[84] And in Fall River, Massachusetts, the Sarah Curran Branch declared that its members firmly believed in the principles advocated by the *Irish World*.[85]

The tenets of the *Irish World* were particularly appealing in the mill towns of New England and the anthracite region of Pennsylvania. Eric Foner has shown that some of the Land League's strongest support for the *Irish World* was found "in the belt of southern New England textile towns stretching from Fall River, Massachusetts, down to Providence and Pawtucket in Rhode Island."[86] While Foner has convincingly demonstrated the active support in these areas of Irish-American men, he overlooked that of Irish-American women workers.

A close examination of the Ladies' League of Woonsocket, Rhode Island, serves as an illuminating example of the level of support among Irish-American female industrial workers for the women's Land League. Woonsocket had a long history of supporting Irish causes. In 1847, at the height of the Great Famine, the Irish-American community in Woonsocket was able in just one week to raise $3,400 for famine relief.[87] On 19 February 1881 a branch of the Ladies' Land League was formed in Woonsocket, with 300 members. Of these 300 women, 119 can be conclusively identified in the 1880 census record. This data, while not complete, provides a glimpse of the occupational breakdown found in this branch of the League (see table 4).

Table 4. Woonsocket, Rhode Island, Ladies' Land League members by occupation

Occupation	Number of women	Percentage of total
Cotton mill	53	44.54%
Keeping house	26	21.85%
Woolen mill	24	20.17%
Rubber works	6	5.04%
Clothing trade	5	4.20%
Domestic servant	3	2.52%
Boarding house manager	1	0.84%
Braid factory	1	0.84%
Total	**119**	**100.00%**

Source: Membership list with members' street addresses found in the *Irish World*, 19 March 1881, 8. Demographic information found via United States Census (1880) using www.ancestry.com.

The strong industrial makeup of this branch is evident in the census results.[88] What attracted these women to the Ladies' Land League? The majority of its members were relatively young, with an average age of almost twenty-five, and most were unmarried. Women could have been attracted to the movement by their concern for relatives at home in Ireland or because of their own emigration experience from Ireland. But we learn from the census data that close to 60 percent of members employed in the mills were second-generation American-born Irish Americans. Thus it is impossible to attribute these women's activism only to feelings of "exile" or longing for a faraway homeland. For members of the Ladies' Land League working in the northeastern textile and rubber mills of late nineteenth-century America, Patrick Ford's dictum that the cause of the impoverished tenant in Ireland was the cause of the factory worker in the United States may have exerted an especially powerful appeal.

As demonstrated above in the example of Ellen Ford, the economic radicalism found among many Ladies' Land League members cannot be traced solely to class background. The Worcester, Massachusetts, branch of the Ladies' Land League was arguably the most radical and successful such branch in the United States. Led by Maria Dougherty, an unmarried milliner who ran her own shop, the Worcester branch was hailed by the *Irish World* as the "banner branch of the Land League" and had over four hundred members. In his work on the Irish in Worcester, Timothy Meagher has found that "teachers and professional women played critical roles in the branch."[89] Further census research supports Meagher's conclusion, as an executive committee list for the Worcester branch appearing in the *Irish World* of 4 December 1880 lists three unmarried schoolteachers, two middle-class housewives, one unmarried store clerk, and one unmarried domestic servant.[90] But if their radicalism did not derive from their class background, what explains the Worcester women's radicalism? According to Dougherty, "the articles about the movement in Patrick Ford's Irish World," which they had "read diligently," shaped their views of the Land League. Perhaps, alongside their reading of the *Irish World*, membership in the Ladies' League, Meagher asserts, provided a "sense of gender solidarity" and allowed women "to prove their competence as well as challenge the male leaders of their community."[91]

Whether female members were economic radicals with respect to both countries or concerned solely with the issues of agrarian reform and self-government in Ireland, the Ladies' Land League provided Irish-American women with an unprecedented opportunity to assert themselves publicly, and they reveled in the chance to express their opinions.

PART III

THE END
OF THE LAND LEAGUE

7

"Ireland Is Fighting Humanity's Battle"

The No-Rent Manifesto,
Land Nationalization, and the Radical
Challenge in the United States

We believe . . . the No-Rent manifesto is . . . the initiation of a mighty revolution
that is destined not to end till the disinherited, not only of Ireland, but of all
lands, are restored to the inheritance of which they have been robbed.

Patrick Ford, October 1881

In late 1881 the British government responded to the Land League agitation in
Ireland with a dual strategy—the creation of limited land reform with the
passage in August of the Irish Land Act (embodying the famous "Three Fs")
and the outlawing of the Land League in October.[1] Charles Stewart Parnell
and other Irish leaders were imprisoned a week before the League was declared
"an unlawful and criminal association." The Land League's response was the
No-Rent Manifesto, which called for a general rent strike across Ireland until
the jailed leaders were released and the rule of law was reinstated in Ireland.
In the United States, Land Leaguers responded to the banning of the Irish
Land League and to the No-Rent Manifesto with increased agitation and
fundraising.

In New York City on 30 January 1882, some 12,000 men and women assembled to express their support for the imprisoned Irish Land League leaders and for the manifesto. The impetus for this gathering came from the combined efforts of New York's various labor unions. "Ten thousand workingmen of New York, representing American trades unions of all nationalities," declared a resolution passed at this meeting, "ask Ireland to hold on with a death grip to the 'no-rent' manifesto. The workingmen of America stand by her. God Save Ireland that Ireland may save humanity."[2] As this resolution helps demonstrate, many American workers supported the Land League. They drew from the Land League movement in Ireland inspiration for tackling and resolving the problems facing an industrializing United States in the Gilded Age.

The No-Rent Manifesto issued by the Irish Land League had a huge effect on the movement in the United States. In America, Land Leaguers responded to the No-Rent Manifesto with a new round of agitation. But the effect of the startling developments in Ireland in October 1881 laid bare the ideological divisions that existed among the different elements of the American Land League. Some conservatives and physical-force nationalists were suspicious of the No-Rent Manifesto, while others denounced it. Radical Land Leaguers, however, saw the manifesto as a positive development, and they reiterated their view that the Land League was a force for dramatic social reform in Ireland and the United States. While the No-Rent Manifesto presented an opportunity for radicals to reassert their agenda, it would also ultimately begin the final breakdown of the "Greater Ireland" formed during the heyday of the Land League movement.

The Road to the No-Rent Manifesto

At the same time that the Land League movement was spreading in the United States, the Land League in Ireland reached a crossroads. After Michael Davitt's arrest in February 1881, the League executive in Dublin was left with the difficult decision of determining what the future course of the Land League should be. Members of the League considered two options: increasing the scope and intensity of the land agitation or resisting the passage of the coercion bill at Westminster. Davitt and other radicals favored an immediate withdrawal of Irish MPs from Parliament and a general rent strike to broaden and escalate resistance in Ireland. They also wanted Parnell to return to the United States to spur Irish-American financial and moral support.[3] Moderate constitutionalist members were fearful that these measures might lead to open revolution; they much preferred to wage a militant struggle against the coercion bill in Parliament.

Faced with these two competing factions, Parnell steered a middle course. At a meeting of the Land League executive on 14 February 1881 in Paris, Parnell sketched out an alternative plan. Leaving for America at this juncture, he argued, would be an abandonment of his duty. He advocated instead that Land League treasurer Patrick Egan relocate to Paris to prevent the British government from seizing the League's funds. Parnell strongly favored continued participation by Irish MPs in Parliament while also advocating an attempt to "effect . . . a junction between the English masses and Irish nationalism."[4] This last suggestion followed a policy long promoted by Davitt. The Land League executive accepted Parnell's strategy in full.

Parnell's desire was to craft a way forward that could mollify constitutionalists and radicals in the League. Not a revolutionary at heart, Parnell believed that to desert Parliament was a step toward revolution that should be avoided.[5] He was concerned to secure the continued cooperation of Irish constitutionalists and radicals in the Land League while at the same time maintaining Irish-American support, particularly that of Patrick Ford and his followers, who advocated a more militant posture. The set of policies outlined above allowed Parnell to accomplish both goals. As one biographer has written, Parnell's strategy presented "the Irish public with an alternative that would look 'strong' instead of 'weak,' without being revolutionary in any real sense. His action . . . was that of a master of constitutional politics, adept at the cape-work of the pseudo-revolutionary gesture."[6] Despite his rhetoric about linking Ireland's struggle with that of the English working class, no concrete steps were taken to forge such a union. Yet Parnell's gesture did gain him praise from Irish-American radicals. His ability to craft a way forward acceptable to all elements of the Land League prevented the movement from splintering along ideological lines for a time.

Parnell's efforts notwithstanding, events in Ireland were not completely under Land League control. In the countryside mass agitation contributed to an alarming increase in agrarian violence, and by the beginning of 1881 there was furious agitation in many areas of Ireland. Evidence of this worsening situation was all too apparent in the growing percentage of agrarian "outrages" in the overall crime statistics; in 1879 agrarian "outrages" constituted 25 percent of crimes in general, whereas by 1881 the corresponding figure had risen to 58 percent.[7] Much of this violence drew on Irish traditions of organized and clandestine agrarian violence. Bands of "Moonlighters" or militant individuals in the countryside attacked dwellings, mutilated cattle, sent threatening letters, intimidated others from paying rent, and fired shots at landlords and their agents, often to frighten, sometimes to wound, and more rarely to murder.[8] "In the disturbed parts of Ireland," the Irish viceroy Lord Cowper believed, "the vast majority are, in the cases of agrarian nature, invariably on the side of the criminal."[9] The growing rural unrest alarmed British officials as well as many Land League supporters favorable under quite different circumstances to the violent overthrow of British rule in Ireland. William Mackey Lomasney, a prominent Irish-American member of Clan na Gael, warned John Devoy in a private letter that revolution in Ireland at this time would be an unmitigated disaster.[10] As conditions in Ireland continued to escalate, both the Land League and the British government strained to regain control.

The Gladstone administration first responded to the Land League and rural discontent with coercive legislation. In the winter of 1881, despite fierce opposition by Irish MPs, Parliament passed the Protection of Person and Property Bill on 28 February and an Arms Bill on 11 March. These bills suspended habeas corpus, conferred the power to seize newspapers and outlaw public gatherings, and granted authority to officials to imprison any "reasonably suspected" person without trial.[11] The authorities in Ireland quickly put their new powers into effect, arresting nearly a thousand individuals over the course of the next eighteen months.[12] Those arrested were mostly local activists accused of intimidation against the payment of rent and a variety of other agrarian offenses, but prominent national leaders like John Dillon were also incarcerated under the coercion act.[13] The draconian manner in which the special powers were enforced led Land League supporters to nickname the chief secretary of Ireland, William Edward Forster, "Buckshot Forster." Coercion, however, did not have the desired effect. Agrarian disturbances in Ireland increased dramatically from 2,500 in 1880 to 4,400 in 1881.[14] British officials increasingly came to believe that coercion was not enough, and that a political solution to the turmoil in Ireland was badly needed.

The British government followed coercive legislation with the introduction of the Irish Land Bill in April 1881. (It became law on 22 August of that year.) The purpose of the Land Act was primarily political rather than economic. As one historian has written, "The Land Act of 1881 reflected no principle, no hypothesis," and "there was no policy framed, only demands granted—and hastily."[15] The Land Act conceded to yearly tenants (but not leaseholders or those in arrears) the "Three Fs": fair rent, fixity of tenure, and free sale. In effect, these concessions provided many tenants with dual ownership of the land. The act also established land courts in which tenants who considered their rents to be too high could appeal to an impartial judge who would assess a "fair rent." During the first three years after the passage of the act, the land courts reduced the rents of appealing tenants by an average of almost 20 percent.[16] This law began to break down the class alliance within the Land League, since many farmers accepted the terms of the legislation rather than adhering to the policy proclaimed in the No-Rent Manifesto.

The Land Act left Land League leaders uncertain of how to respond. For Davitt and other radicals, the efforts of the Gladstone administration were seen as too little, too late. They also feared that the Land Act would drain away conservative support for the Land League. Davitt confided to John Devoy that even though he believed the Land Act did not go far enough, he thought that it would "satisfy a great number inside the League and be accepted by the bishops and priests almost to a man."[17] Parnell, on the other hand, wanting the movement not to become too radicalized or to pass out of his control, worked to craft a response to the land bill that would placate both radical and conservative elements of the League. In April 1881 a Land League convention was held in Dublin at which a resolution was passed proclaiming that nothing short of the abolition of landlordism would fulfill the demands of the Irish people.[18] The phrase "abolition of landlordism" was never defined exactly and left Parnell with some flexibility in deciding his next step. But matters came to a head a few weeks later when John Dillon was arrested and taken into custody for attacking the proposed land legislation in a speech.

Parnell struggled to keep the Land League united once the Land Act had been signed into law. He again found the basis for a compromise at the Land League convention held in September 1881. The convention accepted his recommendation that the League should neither accept nor reject the Land Act; instead the League decided to present selected test cases to the land courts to determine the true usefulness of the new law.[19] This policy was adopted mainly as a means of preventing Land League supporters from abandoning the League for the land courts, but the plan caused deep uneasiness among some League leaders. The Land Act, according to John Dillon, would "in the course of a few months take all the power out of the arm of the Land League," and it would "be difficult, if not impossible, for the League to carry on a 'fighting' policy."[20] The decision to test the Land Act also created uneasiness and even anger among radical elements in Irish America. Patrick Ford demanded that there "be no compromise with the blasphemous thing called landlordism."[21] It was a clear measure of Parnell's personal prestige within the movement at this time that he was able to push through his plan for testing the Land Act despite such vocal opposition from radicals in Ireland and the United States.

Parnell sought to mask the conservative nature of his policy by ratcheting up his rhetoric denouncing British rule in Ireland. Within the British government there was a growing impatience with conciliatory policies, especially since their reception in Ireland was lukewarm or worse. In a speech at Leeds, Gladstone warned that he would react forcefully to Parnell's continued attacks on the government.[22] Parnell responded by publicly mocking Gladstone as "a masquerading knight-errant" and in effect dared Gladstone to arrest him.[23] With the government's patience finally exhausted, the decision was made to arrest Parnell and outlaw the Land League. On 13 October 1881, Parnell was arrested and sent to Kilmainham prison. Parnell welcomed his arrest. "Politically, it is a fortunate thing for me that I have been arrested," he secretly confided to his lover, Katharine O'Shea, "as the movement is breaking fast, and all will be quiet in a few months, when I shall be released." Four days later, the remaining male Land League leaders were arrested as well.

Rather than ending the agitation, Parnell's arrest initiated the last great phase of the Land League movement. On 18 October the imprisoned leaders issued the No-Rent Manifesto, which called on Irish tenants to "pay no rents under any circumstances to their landlords until the government relinquishes the existing system of terrorism and restores the constitutional rights of the people."[24] The No-Rent Manifesto was the last official act of the Land League, as the British declared it an illegal organization two days later.

It is unclear what exactly the leaders hoped to accomplish other than keeping the movement afloat. The No-Rent Manifesto had been issued from a position of weakness rather than strength, as most of the leadership of the Land League was imprisoned. Michael Davitt, whose name had been signed to the declaration *in absentia*, believed that the manifesto "was an act of desperation" that "suggested . . . a spirit of retaliation more in keeping with the temper of a man unfairly fought by his assailants, who strikes back blindly and passionately as best he can, than a blow of cool and calculating purpose."[25] He was also convinced that the passage of the Land Act had further undermined any prospects of success. Fanny Parnell shared Davitt's assessment, confiding to Patrick Collins that "the failure of the No Rent Manifesto . . . resulted from its being issued six months too late."[26] Parnell himself seemed to believe that the future lay not in conflict but in accommodation with the British government.[27] Whatever their actual motivations, after the No-Rent Manifesto, Parnell and the other jailed leaders lost control over the movement. In Ireland, Anna Parnell and the Ladies' Land League stepped to the fore, directing and sustaining the movement for a time themselves.

The American Land League and "No Rent"

Like Davitt's arrest seven months earlier, the incarceration of Parnell and the issuing of the No-Rent Manifesto helped to spark a resurgence of activity among American Land Leaguers. But the manifesto also had negative effects on the movement. Earlier, the American Land League, despite disagreements between social radicals and conservatives, had been able to overcome or set aside ideological differences, and indeed for an extended period both factions operated in healthy competition with each other. But the No-Rent Manifesto pushed Irish Americans into making a choice: Was the Land League going to be a radical movement dedicated to achieving transformative social reform in Ireland and the United States, or had the land agitation largely fulfilled its purpose, making the next step a final push for Irish legislative independence? In the United States the No-Rent Manifesto pushed different groups of Irish Americans into open warfare with each other.

Radical nationalists in the American Land League, led by Patrick Ford, warmly embraced the No-Rent Manifesto. Ford had been urging a general rent strike since the beginning of the Land League, and he welcomed the dramatic new development in Ireland. "A thousand cheers for that glorious manifesto," Ford declared to his readers. "It is the bravest act of the Land War."[28] According to Ford, the Land League was now on the path of ensuring redemption for Ireland's landless poor and in the vanguard of an international current of social reform. As he put it, "We believe . . . the No-Rent Manifesto is . . . the initiation of a mighty revolution that is destined not to end till the disinherited, not only of Ireland, but of all lands, are restored to the inheritance of which they have been robbed."[29] He also arranged for Henry George to travel to Ireland and report on the situation there as a correspondent for the *Irish World*.[30] "You have landlordism by the throat," Ford congratulated the Irish leaders. "Do not let go of your grip until you have strangled it."[31]

Conservative nationalists were less enthusiastic about the imprisoned Irish leaders' change of course. Among conservatives, two main reactions emerged in response to the No-Rent Manifesto. Some conservatives argued that the manifesto was a temporary measure forced upon the Land League leaders by the repressive tactics of the British government. Martin Griffin, editor of the *ICBU Journal*, denied that the policy of no rent had been adopted as a "universal principle"; instead he insisted that it was a war measure.[32] John Boyle O'Reilly, editor of the Boston *Pilot*, echoed Griffin's interpretation of the manifesto. "The man or party or paper," O'Reilly declared, "that would advise Irish tenants to pay no rent under any circumstances is either a fool or a rogue."[33] But for other conservatives the No-Rent Manifesto, regardless of the circumstances surrounding its adoption, was seen as a dangerous slide toward radicalism. The *Western Home Journal* of Detroit denounced the manifesto as the "rash act of imprisoned leaders" and warned its readers that "the principle that wrong may be done because wrong has been done—the policy of retaliation" was immoral.[34] The publishers of this conservative newspaper also believed that the *Irish World* had pushed the Irish leaders into this policy, and that "anything which can be traced to the office door of that vile sheet should be condemned at once."[35] Disagreement over the acceptability and advisability of the policies of the Irish Land League threatened to tear the Land League in America apart.

Irish-American Land League leaders quickly sought to craft a compromise that would prevent the League from splintering. At the center of these efforts was John F. Finerty, the editor of the Irish-American newspaper the *Chicago Citizen*. T. P. O'Connor, a visiting Irish Land Leaguer, also supported his efforts. In a series of telegrams, Finerty and O'Connor attempted to persuade Patrick Collins, president of the Land League, and Patrick Ford to agree to an emergency convention of Land League supporters in Chicago to frame a united response to the crisis in Ireland. Collins at first rejected Finerty's request for a convention, as the League had already held its annual convention. He also resented Ford's demand to be given a prominent role in the meeting.[36] Collins was eventually persuaded to call a convention but insisted on a number of conditions. First, the organizers must "use their best efforts to confine the resolutions and deliberations of the convention to the *Irish Question*, excluding . . . all reference to subjects upon which American citizens friendly to the Irish cause entertain diverse opinions." He also demanded "strict adherence to the policy and programme of the Irish National Land League" and the "exclusion of Ford's policy and programme."[37] Whether all of these conditions were accepted is unclear, but an agreement was reached to issue a call for an Irish Race Convention to be held in Chicago on 30 November 1881, to which all branches of the Land League and all organizations in America "friendly to the Irish cause" were invited.[38]

The leaders of the competing elements within the American Land League urged their supporters to attend the convention and to fight for their agendas. In a circular sent out to *Irish World* Land Leagues, Ford pointedly asked members to voice their support for the Irish leaders' new policy. "We must sustain this manifesto with all the resources at our command," Ford insisted. "We must make a demonstration in force . . . that will convince both the British government and the Irish landlords of the intensity of our feeling and the fixedness of our resolution." He also declared his wish that no central treasurer be reappointed for America, a policy meant to protect the *Irish World*'s status as the preeminent source for the transmission of funds to Ireland.[39] "Ireland is fighting humanity's battle," Ford argued, and he expressed the hope that the Chicago convention would make the *Irish World*'s radical principles the official policy of the American Land League.[40]

Conservative supporters of the Land League rallied to resist Ford's influence on the movement. Fanny Parnell insisted in a letter to Patrick Collins that Ford and his followers must be stopped. "The time has come now," she wrote, "when it will be no longer possible for the party of common sense and honesty to avoid an open rupture with the *Irish World*."[41] Parnell wanted the delegates to repudiate the *Irish World* once and for all, regardless of the consequences for Irish-American unity. "When one is attacked," she counseled Collins, "I think one should either crush one's enemy by one's defence, or else not attempt to defend oneself at all."[42] Conservative delegates left for Chicago determined to assert their control.

Physical-force nationalists saw the Chicago convention as a chance to re-establish themselves in the movement. Clan na Gael leaders had been disappointed by the conservative domination of the Buffalo convention, but they also rejected Ford's social radicalism. In August 1881, Clan na Gael elected a new executive, with Alexander Sullivan serving as chairman. Sullivan, a Chicago-based lawyer and politician, believed that the Clan needed to reassert itself and use the Chicago convention to replace the Land League with a centralized Irish-American organization that would fuse the various nationalist factions together, but which would be secretly controlled by Clan na Gael members.[43] To accomplish this goal, Clansmen who were members of the Ancient Order of Hibernians and other benevolent and fraternal societies were directed to make sure that they were elected delegates to the convention.[44] Rather than being a demonstration of Irish-American unity and support for the imprisoned Irish leaders, the Chicago convention became a battleground in which conservatives, radicals, and physical-force nationalists battled for domination of the movement.

On 30 November, the Irish-American delegates convened in Chicago's McCormack Hall for the three-day meeting. Ford and Collins both attended the meeting, as did the three representatives of the Irish Land League currently touring on behalf of the movement in the United States: T. P. O'Connor, Tim Healy, and Father Eugene Sheehy, an Irish priest heavily involved in the movement. The turnout for the convention was impressive, with 845 delegates attending. Clan na Gael's efforts to stack the convention were fairly successful, since as many as 400 delegates were members of the Clan.[45] The large turnout of Clansmen was partly the result of their mobilization efforts, but the location of the convention was also important, for the Midwest was a hotbed of physical-force nationalism, and New England and New York were underrepresented in Chicago.[46] Despite their numbers, however, the Clan na Gael members failed to completely dominate the convention because the remaining delegates, including fifty Catholic priests, refused to fully cede control of the Land League to Clan na Gael.

John Finerty called the convention to order and pressed the delegates to unite in their support for the Irish cause. "The convention," he said, "had met to give a definite expression and proclaim a definite policy for the

Irish-American people . . . , to align themselves with the people of Ireland—to go with them as far as they went, and as much further as they were prepared to go."[47] The delegates did not, however, "wish to dictate" or "force . . . any ideas" on the Irish leaders."[48] Finerty also addressed American critics who believed that Irish Americans were being disloyal in their opposition to a government friendly to the United States. From the American Revolution onward, he argued, "the Irish-American heart had beaten true to the United States, the Irish-American sword had flashed in the van of its battles, and Irish-American blood had reddened with a deeper crimson every strife that glorified the banner of the free."[49] Despite their American citizenship, Irish Americans possessed the right to "sustain Ireland" and "to do everything that Ireland demanded of them . . . for her sustenance."[50]

Conservative and physical-force delegates united in their efforts to repudiate Patrick Ford and the *Irish World*. The delegates voted to support the No-Rent Manifesto, but only as a temporary "wartime" strategy—a clear dismissal of Ford's social radicalism. Ford's supporters were also harassed and marginalized at the convention. Delegates from a socialist Chicago Spread the Light Club were denied credentials because of their support of socialism.[51] A resolution thanking Patrick Ford for his efforts on behalf of the Land League was also voted down.[52] The delegates did pass a resolution promising Irish-American support for the struggle of "the Irish people" against British policy in Ireland and pledged to raise $250,000 for the Irish Land League by 17 March 1882.[53] Clan na Gael delegates attempted to have donations flow through Dennis O'Connor, the treasurer of the Illinois State Land League and a loyal Clan member, but were defeated by opposition from Collins and Ford. It was decided instead that donors could forward money through any channel of their choosing—a confirmation of long-standing practice.[54] Delegates also voted against the Clan's desire to replace the Land League with a new, centralized Irish-American organization. As a compromise, a permanent "Irish National Executive Committee," including Ford, Collins, and five others, was established in a halfhearted attempt to overcome disagreements between the various Land League factions, but personal antagonisms and distrust doomed the enterprise from the start.[55] The delegates ended the convention with a public pledge of unity and continued support for the Irish cause.

When delegates returned home on 2 December, it seemed that Ford's principles had been soundly defeated by the conservative and militant coalition, but for some conservatives the partial acceptance of the no-rent policy was still too much to endure. "The idea of 'no rent' is a fallacious and mischievous one," declared the *Western Home Journal* of Detroit in lamenting the results of the Chicago convention.[56] The *Catholic Universe* warned its readers that the policy advocated at Chicago would "drag an unarmed people ruthlessly under martial law . . . into all the horrors of the present Irish situation [and would] never release a solitary Irish prisoner."[57] Father Abram J. Ryan, an Irish-American Catholic priest, proclaimed his belief that "No Rent" was "not a Christian, nor a Catholic, nor, therefore, an Irish cry." On the contrary, he insisted, "No Rent" was "a phrase full of danger and destruction."[58]

Some important members of the American Catholic hierarchy were angered by the League's stance at Chicago. Bishop Bernard McQuaid of Rochester, New York, for example, withdrew his prior support of the Land League. McQuaid explained his reasoning directly from the pulpit in a Sunday sermon. He addressed his sermon "only [to] those who do not deny the authority of the church in teaching questions of faith and morals," and chided the priests who had been present at Chicago, claiming that "wild revolutionists" had infiltrated and directed the convention.[59] "It is dangerous," he argued, "to arouse hopes and expectations [those of the Irish people] by wild talk . . . , [since] when the fighting begins, the victims of this talk will be found on the other side of the Atlantic, not on this."[60] McQuaid later forbade a parish priest in Rochester from taking up a collection in church for the imprisoned Irish leaders.[61]

In a public lecture in Cleveland, Ohio, Bishop Richard Gilmour echoed McQuaid's concerns over the new direction of the Land League. Unlike McQuaid, Gilmour acknowledged the conditional right of the Irish people to rebel against British misrule, but he believed that since an Irish rebellion had no real chance of success, any such move was "folly" and a "crime."[62] Instead, Gilmour argued that the Irish Land League should continue on its old course and look to peaceful and parliamentary means of achieving Home Rule. The No-Rent Manifesto, Gilmour declared, was "clear, unqualified theft . . . , based on the communistic doctrine, 'property is robbery.'"[63] Unhappy with the Chicago convention, Gilmour declared himself unwilling "to fight under the battle-cry of 'no rent.'"[64] Across the United States, similar ecclesiastical denunciations were voiced against the Land League, and the earlier support for the movement among church authorities waned.

John Boyle O'Reilly was also unhappy with the partial acceptance of the No-Rent Manifesto. Instead he wanted the Irish leaders to move away from land agitation and to direct their energies toward Home Rule. In an article titled "Ireland's Opportunity—Will It Be Lost?" published in the *American Catholic Quarterly Review*, he laid out his argument. According to O'Reilly, the Land League was adrift, having already achieved success by pressuring the British government into passing a "law that will lower rents, more or less," and now the movement needed a new plan to take it forward.[65] O'Reilly rejected the social revolution advocated by Patrick Ford and his supporters, and he

dismissed their claims that the No-Rent Manifesto called for the complete abolition of all rents in the future. That was "a social theory which no country has
yet accepted," O'Reilly angrily declared, and "no sensible person expects poor
Ireland, struggling for her very life, to voluntarily burden herself with a socialistic
millstone that would probably sink the United States."[66] He also rejected the
plans of any group for fomenting violent revolution in Ireland, arguing that the
Irish populace was completely unready for such a step and that any such attempt
would end up a terrible failure. What was urgently needed, O'Reilly believed,
was for the Irish people "to agitate for and demand her own government."[67]
O'Reilly's article signified further the uneasiness many conservatives felt about
the future of the Land League movement.

Physical-force nationalists also expressed disquiet over the course of events
in Ireland and over Ford's influence among a large segment of Irish Americans.
John Devoy, one of the original framers of the New Departure, was especially
infuriated at the direction of the movement in the United States. After the Chicago convention Devoy resigned from the Clan na Gael executive and founded
his own New York–based newspaper, the *Irish Nation*.[68] The first issue of the *Irish
Nation* was full of invective against Patrick Ford and his supporters. "The most
mischievous form of the cant which afflicts the land movement is the humanitarian," Devoy mockingly wrote. "The Irish people, it seems, are not battling
for their own rights and interests but for those of the whole human race."[69] Dismissing Ford's call to action, Devoy believed that a total refusal to pay any rent
would plunge Ireland into violent revolution—a conflict for which the Irish
people were grievously unprepared. "No rent," Devoy insisted, "means social
revolution, defeat, disaster, ruin."[70]

While for numerous conservative and physical-force members of the Land
League the No-Rent Manifesto was an unwelcome new direction, many other
Irish-American men and women embraced the principles contained in the
manifesto. Among radical nationalists there was a new burst of energy and
activity in favor of the Land League that was clearly prompted by the change of
policy in Ireland. Radicals saw in the No-Rent Manifesto ideas that appealed
to them and seemed to be based on their own lives and experiences in the
United States. It is this radical Irish-American embrace of the No-Rent Manifesto that the rest of the chapter will explore.

Irish-American Radicalism and the No-Rent Manifesto

After the Chicago convention Ellen and Patrick Ford pushed supporters to
continue to back the No-Rent Manifesto. Patrick Ford urged readers of the

Irish World to ignore the claims of conservatives that the No-Rent Manifesto was only a temporary measure. "It was said [the manifesto] was conditional," Ford observed. "Yes, and so was Lincoln's Emancipation Proclamation conditional. Both were war measures. But who is the man in this republic today that regrets that Lincoln's manifesto turned out to be absolute?"[71] The real danger to the Land League, according to Ford, was the threat of conservatives abandoning the land agitation on the eve of success for a strategy of achieving a Home Rule parliament. "In Ireland as well as in America," he warned, "there is a Whig element in the ranks of the Land League that is far more dangerous and needs more watching than the open enemy."[72] Rather than attacking the No-Rent Manifesto openly, conservatives were trying "to kill it by explanations."[73] Ellen Ford also implored Land Leaguers not to view the manifesto as only a temporary expedient. "We are not going to have any patching with landlordism but to abolish it," she told a meeting of the Manhattan Land League. "We are not going to put down one set of landlords to build up another."[74]

The Fords also maintained that the principles enshrined in the No-Rent Manifesto were important in the United States as well as Ireland. Patrick Ford warned that the problems facing the Irish people were slowly creeping into the United States. "The rent banditti are here," Ford thundered. "They are already hard at work among us, and like flights of vultures, every breeze across the Atlantic comes loaded with them; and bonanza robbers and railroad robbers open wide their arms to receive them."[75] But the problems facing Americans were not limited to the monopolization of land by individuals and corporations. He believed that "the Land League movement is distinctively a labor movement."[76] "Is there an intelligent workingman," Ford asked rhetorically, "be he American, English, French, German, Spanish, or Italian—be his race or color what it may . . . , who cannot see that if the Irish people succeed . . . , they will inaugurate a revolution that is bound to affect directly the interests of every workingman in every land under the sun?"[77] With this appeal, Ford called on Irish Americans to respond to his call for action and rally to the *Irish World*.

Readers of the *Irish World* responded to the No-Rent Manifesto with a dramatic outpouring of donations on behalf of the Land League. From 10 January 1880 to 8 October 1881 the *Irish World* Land League Fund had received almost $152,400.[78] But from the issuance of the No-Rent Manifesto on 18 October 1881 to 29 April 1882 alone, a span of just over six months, donations to the *Irish World* amounted to over $151,600.[79] In February and March 1882 the monthly totals were as much as $43,560 and $30,390, respectively.[80] Alongside this flood of money for Ireland, the *Irish World* reported in May 1882 that 341 new American branches of the Land League had been founded since the previous

October.[81] Ford was ecstatic over this huge monetary response. "This is an American endorsement of the manifesto," he boasted, "which cannot be misinterpreted," and he changed the name of his collection from the "Land League Fund" to the "No Rent Fund."[82]

Radical Irish-American support for the no-rent policy is evidenced not only by the massive donations to the *Irish World* but also in many of the letters accompanying these contributions. "The home rule we believe in is free homes for the farm laborer as well as the tenant, and the free homes will make us freemen," declared members of the Robert Emmet branch of the Land League in North Cambridge, Massachusetts. "We believe that while political freedom may not bring about a social revolution, a great social revolution like the one inaugurated by the Land League will surely bring political freedom."[83] In the West, railroad workers from Umatilla, Oregon, beseeched the Irish at home "not to falter nor rest content until landlordism is forever banished from Ireland."[84] Praise for the manifesto was not confined only to male Land Leagues. The women of the Michael Davitt Ladies' Land League of South Coventry, Connecticut, pledged their full support for the no-rent policy and considered it their "duty as Irishwomen to help old Ireland in her struggle with the land thieves, and every dollar we send . . . , we will regard as so many nails in the coffin of landlordism."[85]

While the bulk of the American Catholic hierarchy was suspicious of the No-Rent Manifesto or hostile toward it, there were pockets of support for the manifesto from American clergymen who encouraged their flocks to continue their engagement with the Land League. Father Edward McGlynn of New York City was increasingly interested at this time in the teachings of Henry George and favored a radical Land League policy in both the United States and Ireland.[86] Father J. P. Ryan, speaking at a farewell meeting for Tim Healy in New York, told the crowd, "A people have a right to live on the land that God gave them." He also dismissed Bishop Gilmour's attacks on the morality of the Land League. "We were told recently that a certain American bishop has said that the No Rent doctrine was opposed to the eternal laws of God. When I heard that statement, I declared it was eternal nonsense. . . . When civil law conflicts with justice, it deserves neither respect nor obedience."[87] In Virginia City, Nevada, Father Patrick Minogue, coadjutor to Bishop Eugene O'Connell of Grass Valley, California, declared his unreserved endorsement of the No-Rent Manifesto.[88] Those priests who did reject the Land League sometimes faced reprisals from parishioners. Land Leaguers in Natick, Massachusetts, outraged that their local Catholic priest, Father Walsh, had refused to meet with the visiting Irish envoy Tim Healy, voted not to donate any money to the church and promised to boycott religious services until Father Walsh was recalled.[89] Several branches elsewhere in the country boycotted priests critical of the Chicago convention and the manifesto.[90] Like their dismissals of earlier ecclesiastical censures of the Ladies' Land League, Irish Americans were willing to ignore or reject clerical demands when they deemed them unwise.

Perhaps the most important reason why many Land Leaguers in the United States supported the No-Rent Manifesto was that they believed its principles to be crucial both for ending landlordism in Ireland and for achieving social reform in America. The members of the Land League branch in Pigeon Falls, Wisconsin, mostly composed of Norwegian immigrants, declared that "anti-usury, anti-rent, and anti-monopoly are the fundamental principles that must be adopted by the laboring masses in order to successfully check the wild schemes of the aristocratic class in the Old and New Worlds."[91] The same viewpoint could also be found in urban areas. The New York labor newspaper *Truth* told its readers to support the Irish cause in order to protect their own interests. "Let Americans remember while thus aiding the oppressed of another country," one editorial urged, "that the time may not be far distant when a similar land question will arise in America."[92] Labor radicals welcomed the manifesto as the beginning of an international struggle for workers' rights. "The war is not against the English people," said Robert Blissert, the New York–based labor activist. "I'm at war with the English government; I'm at war with the American government; I'm at war with every government which crushes labor under foot."[93] In supporting Irish nationalism, workers and their leaders made the case that there existed a brotherhood of labor that stretched across the Atlantic, and that workers across the world were facing many of the same struggles.

The best demonstration of the linkage between Irish and American labor radicalism was the founding of the Central Labor Union in New York City in early 1882. The impetus for the Central Labor Union arose from a call by Robert Blissert for American trade and labor unions to organize publicly in favor of the No-Rent Manifesto. Blissert declared, "Brothers, the cause of labor is everywhere the same, [whether] in Ireland, in the refusal of the tillers of the soil to give the fruits of their labor as rent to the so-called owners of the soil, [or] American and European workmen who demand just remuneration of their labors, fewer hours of toil, and a full recognition of the dignity and usefulness of their callings."[94] Whether in Ireland or the United States, Blissert argued, workers confronted the same forces of oppression. "We have but one common enemy—the non-producing class—people who reap where they did not sow, and who are a constant menace to the happiness, if not to the very existence, of the producers."[95] A committee of trade bodies and labor unions seeking to organize a mass meeting was established soon afterward. Altogether, over fifty organizations joined the committee, including several German-American unions, and this joint body represented more than seventy thousand workers.[96] The date of the mass meeting was set for 30 January 1882.

On that night more than twelve thousand workingmen gathered at Cooper Union and declared their sympathy for the No-Rent Manifesto.[97] Draped above the stage was a banner proclaiming, "The No Rent battle of Ireland is the battle of workingmen the world over."[98] Several labor leaders addressed the meeting and hammered this theme home in their speeches. Louis F. Post of *Truth* called on those present "to let the whole Irish people know that we look upon them as leaders in a new revolution which could not be confined between the coasts of Ireland . . . but which would grow broader and broader . . . until it sweeps the civilized world, terminating in another victory of right over might and the banishment of involuntary poverty from the face of the earth."[99] John Swinton, another American labor activist, seconded Post's sentiments and asserted that "from Ireland light will arise and the sunburst shall be for mankind."[100] German-American representatives also made speeches pledging solidarity with Ireland and linking the struggle of the Irish people with national movements elsewhere.[101] The great Cooper Union demonstration and the intensive organizing drive that preceded it show the wide appeal of the No-Rent Manifesto for Irish-American and other workers in this teeming urban metropolis. In this case common support for the Land League also helped New York workingmen overcome ethnic differences in favor of broader labor and class concerns.[102]

Two weeks later, representatives from the various unions that had sponsored the no-rent meeting formed the Central Labor Union of New York. In drafting the declaration of principles, which one historian has called "one of the clearest expressions of producer ideology and worker radicalism in the Gilded Age," these representatives reemphasized their cosmopolitan view of labor reform.[103] "The land of every country," the Central Labor Union platform began, "is the common property of the people of that country."[104] By June 1882, between fifty and sixty thousand New York workingmen were affiliated with the new organization.[105]

The No-Rent Manifesto clearly ignited a firestorm of support for the Land League among non-Irish workers and radicals, who embraced a cosmopolitan view of labor radicalism that sought to link Ireland's struggles with workers' movements across the globe. But rather than being a moment of triumph for League radicals, the No-Rent Manifesto exposed the deep ideological divisions present in the American Land League and led to a conservative backlash that ultimately destroyed the "Greater Ireland" created by the movement.

8

The Road from Kilmainham Jail

The Death of the Land League and the Triumph of Conservative Irish Nationalism in the United States and Ireland

> It seems to me a most regrettable thing that a great movement promising so much for Ireland and the world, as did the Land League movement and with success within its grasp, should have so easily been switched off; and I could not address any Irish meeting without saying so. The main lesson of the Irish agitation to me is that radical men should not allow themselves any consideration of a temporary expediency to put themselves under the leadership of politicians or to abate one jot or battle of their principles.
>
> Letter from Henry George to Terence Powderly, 1883

Through the early months of 1882 the Irish Land League leaders remained in jail. In the Irish countryside, despite the efforts of the Ladies' Land League, the land agitation was escalating into widespread violence, and its direction became very uncertain. Wanting to end the violence and reassert control of the movement, Parnell secretly crafted an agreement with the British prime minister William Gladstone to secure his release and end the land agitation. The "Kilmainham Treaty" pushed Parnell and the Irish Parliamentary Party closer toward an alliance with the Liberals to secure Home Rule for Ireland.[1]

Two events in Ireland quickly threatened Parnell's new accommodation with Gladstone: the assassination of two British officials in Dublin and Michael Davitt's conversion to a scheme of land nationalization in Ireland. Parnell survived both threats and by the end of 1882 emerged as the dominant Irish nationalist leader of his era. Parnell's achievement of dominance marked the triumph of a conservative Irish nationalism in Ireland that eschewed mass agrarian agitation in favor of a strategy of gradual parliamentary progress toward Irish Home Rule.

This shift in Ireland led to the end of the Land League in the United States. As discussed in earlier chapters, the Land League movement had presented Irish-American women and radical nationalists with opportunities to assert their aspirations and priorities within Irish America and the broader American society—opportunities that they had eagerly seized. But by linking their public participation so closely to the political and social movement for land reform in Ireland, Irish-American women nationalists came to depend on the continued success of mass agitation in Ireland. Radical nationalists had come to the fore because of the agrarian struggle in Ireland, but they found Parnell's shift toward Home Rule less germane to their American agenda. Ultimately, the influence of women and radicals on the Irish nationalist movement was limited by a combination of Irish-American conservative resistance in the United States and the emergence of a conservative Irish nationalism in Ireland. These forces increasingly alienated radical nationalists from Irish nationalist endeavors and reduced women's participation, as conservatives and physical-force nationalists mostly dominated Irish-American nationalism through the remainder of the 1880s and 1890s.

The Kilmainham Treaty and the Phoenix Park Murders

While the No-Rent Manifesto sparked a resurgence of Land League activity in the United States, its effects in Ireland were an increase in violence and demoral- ization within the movement. As evictions increased, so too did violent responses by Irish tenants against landlords and officials.[2] But instead of rallying around the manifesto, many Irish tenants sought to take advantage of the "fair rent" provisions of the 1881 Land Act and proved unwilling to follow a radical Land League policy. Still enjoying general support almost everywhere in the Irish countryside was peasant proprietorship, the gradual conversion of tenants into owner-occupiers, but this goal was likely to take decades to achieve.[3] Meanwhile, in County Mayo, where the Land League had originated, the movement had largely collapsed. Small farmers in that county, feeling that the agitation had become too focused on the interests of large farmers and graziers, and having lost faith in the Irish rural economy, often chose to emigrate instead.[4] The Land League agitation continued in Ireland, but in a disorganized and weakened fashion.

With the male leaders in prison, control of the movement fell to the Ladies' Land League under the leadership of Anna Parnell. For a while, the Ladies' Land League did quite well, providing funds and shelter for evicted tenants and managing to keep the official newspaper of the Land League, *United Ireland*, in circulation. Anna Parnell, faced with a difficult situation, decided that "the programme of a permanent resistance until the aim of the League should be attained" was the "only logical" option.[5] This militant stance became a problem, however, since for Parnell the No-Rent Manifesto was meant only as a ploy to place pressure on the British government. Instead, as Paul Bew has argued, "'No Rent' was never designed to succeed, it was designed to create a context in which Land League failures could be blamed on government repression; not bad leadership or flawed tactics, still less the nature of the Irish agrarian movement itself."[6] The women ignored this strategy and persisted in attempting to turn the rhetoric of the manifesto into reality.

The level of activity from the Ladies' Land League during this period was impressive. Anna Parnell and others took to the countryside and urged Irish men and women to maintain their allegiance to the Land League. But events soon turned against them. The British government began arresting women Land Leaguers under a statute formerly used to curb prostitution.[7] Once imprisoned, women were not given the political-prisoner status or the rather lenient treatment afforded to the arrested male leaders. There was also a marked increase in agrarian unrest in Ireland. From October 1881 to April 1882 there were seventy-five agrarian "outrages"—fourteen murders and sixty-one instances of shots being fired at landlords or their agents or bailiffs.[8] Until relatively recently, Irish historians have often linked this rise in violence to the "reckless" and "radical" leadership of the Ladies' Land League.[9] This characterization misses the mark since members of the Ladies' Land League did valuable work in keeping the movement going, and since Anna Parnell loudly denounced violent retribution against landlords, local magistrates, and land agents.[10] The surge in agrarian violence was more attributable to increasing evictions, anger at British coercive policies, and economic turmoil in the Irish countryside.

Charles Stewart Parnell, still imprisoned in Kilmainham jail, and troubled by the unsettled conditions in Ireland, increasingly believed in the necessity of reaching an accommodation with the British government. Contemporaries and historians have disagreed over Parnell's mindset while in Kilmainham.

Michael Davitt thought that imprisonment was psychologically repugnant to Parnell, despite the very lenient treatment given to him by his jailors.[11] Davitt also alleged that Parnell, alarmed by his loss of control over the Irish country-side, feared that the "League movement would be used not for the purposes he approved of, but for a real revolutionary end and aim."[12] Parnell's biographer F. S. L. Lyons and other historians have argued that his shift was an example of Parnell's political opportunism.[13] Alongside Parnell's uneasiness over the di-rection of the movement, there was a personal element pushing him toward accommodation. His lover Katharine O'Shea had recently given birth to their child and Parnell was eager to see the infant. Parnell's unhappiness over the course of the movement and his desire to leave prison prompted him to reach out to Gladstone in search of a settlement.

Within the British cabinet Gladstone and other ministers had decided, despite the opposition of the Irish chief secretary W. E. Forster, that coercion in Ireland had failed.[14] Working through intermediaries, Gladstone and Parnell agreed on terms for a settlement. In a letter shown to Gladstone, Parnell, with-out consulting his colleagues, pledged that if the Land Act were amended to include leaseholders and those in arrears, and if its provisions for land purchase by tenants were extended, these concessions would amount to "a practical settlement of the land question." Parnell expressed his belief that this set of changes would enable the Irish Parliamentary Party to "cooperate cordially for the future with the Liberal party in forwarding Liberal principles." In exchange Gladstone would work to amend the Land Act to cover tenants in arrears, to free the imprisoned Irish leaders, and to revoke emergency rule in Ireland.[15] Gladstone was able to carry his cabinet with him on these points, though Forster resigned as chief secretary in protest. This agreement later came to be known as the "Kilmainham Treaty."

These negotiations had been carried out in secret, and Parnell's secrecy left him vulnerable to attack from radicals who were unhappy with the moderate terms of agreement. Henry George, staying in Dublin at the time, was already suspicious of Parnell and warned Patrick Ford that conservative members of the Land League were pushing for a settlement with the government.[16] Back in America, Patrick Ford cautioned his readers that Home Rule was "a will-o'-wisp of the very first quagmire," and that the Land League should persist in the no-rent agitation.[17] There was also a danger that Parnell's leadership would be challenged by physical-force nationalists who considered Home Rule a pale substitute for national independence. Despite these possible difficulties, Parnell concluded that he would be able to execute the shift in direction.

On 2 May 1882, Parnell was released from prison and Michael Davitt was freed four days later. Owing to the news embargo imposed by prison authorities, Davitt was in the dark about the situation in Ireland. Parnell, Dillon, and J. J. O'Kelly, an ardent Parnellite MP, accompanied Davitt on his train ride to London and informed him of events since his imprisonment. "We are on the eve of something like Home Rule," Parnell told Davitt. "The Tory party are going to advocate land purchase, almost on the lines of the Land League programme, and I see no reason why we should not obtain all we are looking for in the League movement."[18] Parnell did not confide to Davitt or the others his agreement with Gladstone, but he did reveal his unhappiness with the current direction of the Land League movement. He was convinced that the no-rent manifesto had failed and that a "frightful condition" had existed in Ireland over the past six months.[19] Davitt, though suspicious about Parnell's dealings with the British government, did not press the issue. Parnell also criticized the leadership of his sister Anna and the other chief members of the Ladies' Land League. Davitt defended their management of affairs and stressed how the women had kept the movement going in Ireland under difficult circumstances. "I am out now," Parnell responded, "and I don't want them to keep the ball rolling any more. The League must be suppressed, or I will leave public life."[20] While Davitt's uneasiness with the Kilmainham Treaty and Parnell's unhappiness with the Ladies' Land League soon boiled over, it seemed that with the release of the prisoners the Land League had weathered the worst from the British government and would be moving forward from a strengthened position. A terrible development in Ireland, however, dramatically changed the political context.

The event that sent shockwaves throughout Britain and Ireland was the brutal murder of the new chief secretary of Ireland, Lord Frederick Cavendish, and his undersecretary, Thomas Henry Burke, outside the Vice-Regal Lodge in Phoenix Park in Dublin on 6 May 1882. The two officials had been taking a late afternoon stroll when they were brutally stabbed to death by their assailants. Members of a secret splinter group of the Irish Republican Brotherhood called the Irish National Invincibles carried out the assassinations and escaped after killing the two officials with twelve-inch-long surgical knives. The bloody deed and the murderers' escape sent British officialdom into a panic and created fears of further political assassinations. That evening in London Davitt was told about the murders, but believing the report to be a hoax, he ignored it and went to bed. At 5:00 a.m. the next day Henry George woke him and confirmed the rumors. Davitt was horrified at the news and wrote in his diary that this was the "blackest day that has perhaps ever dawned for Ireland."[21] Parnell too was deeply disturbed by the murders. He was so distraught that he sent a message to Gladstone offering up his resignation from politics, but Gladstone dissuaded him from this course of action. Instead, Parnell, Dillon, and Davitt issued a declaration condemning the murders. "We feel that no act has ever been perpetrated in our country during the exciting struggles for social and political rights of the past fifty years," they declared, "that has so stained the name of hospitable Ireland as this cowardly and unprovoked assassination."[22] Ten thousand copies of this declaration were printed, and it was cabled to John Boyle O'Reilly for distribution in several Irish-American newspapers.[23]

The murders of Cavendish and Burke outraged public opinion in Britain and the United States. Cavendish had been very friendly toward Irish aspirations, and his appointment as chief secretary signaled for many people a genuine effort to improve the situation in Ireland. In the first few days after the murders many of London's churches, societies, and clubs issued condemnations of the crime.[24] In the United States, Americans had experienced their own bout of political assassination with the recent killing of President James Garfield in September 1881. But while denouncing the Phoenix Park murders, Irish Americans commonly placed some of the blame on the British government's coercive policies in Ireland. Expressing his outrage at the murder, John Boyle O'Reilly declared at a mass meeting at Faneuil Hall in Boston that the real perpetrators were "the office-holders in Dublin Castle, the paid magistrates who commanded the military power, the officers of the brutal constabulary, the virulent 'emergency men.'"[25] Still, the Irish Americans assembled at this Boston meeting offered a reward of $5,000 for the apprehension of the killers.[26] Patrick Ford also condemned the murders, but he put the onus for the crimes on Irish landlords. "It was their [landlords'] disregard in the past of every principle of justice," he insisted, "that bred the hatred that more than once has found expression in murder."[27] Alongside League leaders, hundreds of local Land League branches in America issued their own declarations of dismay or condemnation.

The British government reacted quickly to the murders. Conservatives in Parliament attempted to link the murders to the Land League and clamored for more coercion in Ireland. The Gladstone administration responded with new legislation. Despite opposition from Irish MPs, parliament passed the Prevention of Crimes (Ireland) Bill on 11 May 1882.[28] This measure again suspended trials by jury, expanded the authority of magistrates, placed certain districts under curfew, and greatly increased overall police powers in Ireland.[29] The Phoenix Park murders did not, however, completely destroy the understanding reached between Parnell and Gladstone. No attempt was made to re-arrest the Irish leaders, and a few weeks later, Gladstone partly fulfilled his pledges to Parnell by amending the 1881 Land Act so as to include some 150,000 tenants in arrears. The foundations of the Kilmainham Treaty were shaken by the murders, but they did not collapse.

While the Phoenix Park murders made an alliance with the British government more difficult for Parnell, the fallout from the killings actually improved
his political standing in Ireland. As mentioned earlier, Parnell's secret negotiations with Gladstone had left him in a vulnerable position with physical-force
nationalists and radicals in Ireland and the United States. The negative reaction
immediately discredited any advocacy by physical-force nationalists of violent
resistance in Ireland and strengthened the desire of conservative nationalists
for a shift away from mass agrarian agitation and toward a parliamentary pursuit
of Home Rule.[30] It also suggested to many observers the correctness of Parnell's
attempt to reach a moderate settlement of the land question, as Ireland seemed
on the brink of spinning out of control. Davitt believed that except for the
killings, the majority of Irish and Irish-American nationalists would have challenged Parnell's leadership and rejected the Kilmainham Treaty as too conciliatory toward the British.[31] As one historian has noted, the Phoenix Park murders
were an Irish version of the "Haymarket bombing" and led to a similar conservative backlash against radicalism.[32] Rather than being weakened by the dramatic
events in Ireland, Parnell's authority was strengthened, and he moved to consolidate it further.

Parnell still faced powerful opposition to his polices from Dillon and Davitt.
Dillon was unhappy with Parnell's plans to establish a successor organization
to the Land League that would be constitutional, dominated by the Irish Parliamentary Party, and under the direct control of Parnell.[33] But Dillon, who
suffered from ill health his entire life, decided to immigrate to the United States
and stayed there (in Colorado) for the next two years in an attempt to regain his
health. Only in 1885 did he return to Ireland.

Parnell faced a much more serious challenge from Davitt, who strongly disagreed with the Kilmainham Treaty and wanted to continue the land agitation
in Ireland. As Philip Bull has argued, "For Davitt the Land League represented
an empowerment of the people most oppressed by the existing social and political order, and no matter what part it played in the advance of the nationalist
cause, its existence was also to be defended in the long term as a social mobilization with the potential eventually to change and reform the social order."[34]
Parnell, in contrast, had used the land agitation to mobilize the Irish population
in support of self-government, and rather than obliterating the Irish landed
elite, he hoped to convince Irish landlords to accept a moderate solution of the
land question for their own good and to convert them in significant numbers to
his nationalist project.[35] Soon after his release from prison Davitt declared his
conversion to land nationalization in Ireland, a policy diametrically opposed to
Parnell's desire for moderate land reform. Having extracted large concessions
from the British government, the Land League now became embroiled in this

conflict between Parnell and Davitt. This split between the two leaders had lasting repercussions in Ireland and the United States and destroyed the remaining vestiges of unity within the Land League.

Michael Davitt, Land Nationalization, and the Last Gasp of Irish-American Radicalism

During his sixteen-month imprisonment in England, Davitt spent this time reexamining his views on the future of the land agitation. He believed that the Land League had become too oriented toward supporting large farmers to the detriment of smallholders, agricultural laborers, and the urban poor, and he struggled to articulate a new direction.[36] His thinking was greatly influenced by Henry George's *Progress and Poverty*, which he reread twice during his incarceration.[37] The solution to which he turned was that of nationalizing the Irish land system.

Davitt first publicly announced his new direction at a speech on 21 May 1882 at Manchester before a local land-nationalization society. He presided at this meeting despite Parnell's expressed wish that he refrain from participating.[38] With Henry George beside him, Davitt stated that the Land League's work was far from over. "The Land League movement was organized to effect the complete abolition of Irish landlordism," he asserted; "until that work is fully and completely accomplished, there can be no alliance between the people of Ireland and the Whig party in this country."[39] A few weeks later in Liverpool, Davitt openly declared his support for land nationalization. Under his plan the state would own all land (after compensating landlords for their estates), and farmers would be subject to a small land tax that would pay for the civil administration of Ireland and eventually become the main source of public revenue.[40] Davitt believed that this scheme would cause Ireland's land to become the national inheritance of the people, administered by the state "with a single eye to the welfare of entire people."[41]

Parnell and conservative Irish nationalists regarded Davitt's conversion to land nationalization as a dangerous attempt to revive the land agitation. Parnell never fully supported the No-Rent Manifesto and its radical implications. The last thing that Parnell wanted was a further radicalization of the Land League, and he openly denounced Davitt's plan.[42] Conservative elements in Ireland and the United States blamed Patrick Ford and Henry George for corrupting Davitt and for pushing him in this new direction. "Mr. Davitt is the dupe of his American friends," the *Dublin Review* editorialized, "and his scheme is a scheme not so much for the regeneration of Ireland as for making that unhappy country a *corpus vile* on which to try the experiment of American communism."[43] Others accused Davitt of trying to overthrow Parnell and usurp control of the movement. "I know what they din into his ears," George wrote to Ford. "'George has captured you for the *Irish World.*' But whatever happens now, Davitt will be to those moderates . . . a bull in a china shop."[44]

Realizing that the balance of forces was against him in Ireland, Davitt prepared to leave for a short tour of the United States. Though he claimed to be going there to raise money and to garner support for Parnell and the Ladies' Land League, in reality he was attempting to rally Irish Americans behind his policies.[45] Before leaving Ireland, Davitt denied that there was any split between the leaders of the Land League. Much to the chagrin of Parnell, he asserted that he was going to tell Irish Americans "what I told the English people in Liverpool—that what Ireland wants is the nationalization of land administrated in Dublin by an Irish parliament."[46] The internecine conflict between Parnell and Davitt now shifted across the Atlantic to the United States.

On the eve of Davitt's return to the United States, Irish America remained fractious and divided. When the annual convention of the American Land League was held in Washington, DC, in April 1882, Patrick Ford and supporters of the *Irish World*, still angry at their treatment in Chicago, boycotted the convention. Conservative and physical-force delegates once again united to pursue a course in opposition to Ford's social radicalism.[47] Patrick Collins resigned the presidency, and the delegates elected James Mooney, a Buffalo insurance agent and Clan na Gael member, to replace him. In a further sign of rapprochement between the Clan and conservative nationalists, John Devoy urged his readers to send their money for the Irish cause through Father Walsh, the official Land League treasurer.[48] Ford's response to the convention was an editorial plea to agree to disagree.[49] Even prior to Davitt's arrival, the movement in America was thus wracked by disagreement.

Davitt arrived in New York harbor on 18 June 1882. From the moment he stepped off the boat, the competing sides in the American Land League jostled to influence him. Patrick Ford maintained that if the Irish people followed Davitt's lead, landlordism would be destroyed, and "from its ruins will [a]rise an Ireland whose political independence will rest on that surest of all foundations—social independence."[50] Louis F. Post, a follower of Henry George, declared that American workers looked upon Davitt as the leader in a "new revolution which cannot be confined between the coasts of Ireland, . . . but which will grow . . . until it sweeps the civilized world, terminating in . . . the banishment of involuntary poverty from the face of the earth."[51] Conservatives attacked Davitt's scheme as strongly as reform-minded nationalists applauded it. "The scheme of the 'nationalization of the land,'" James Redpath argued, "is founded on the most sweeping theory of the confiscation of the property of the working classes ever conceived . . . [and] is a scheme worthy of the sophist of the sand lots of San Francisco."[52] Martin Griffith, the editor of the *ICBU Journal*, penned an editorial titled "Davitt the Destroyer," in which he accused Davitt of seeking to split the Land League.[53] Conservatives roundly rejected the belief of Davitt and the radicals that the Irish land struggle was part of a broader international movement for agrarian and labor reform. "We do not wish to see Irish national leaders," scoffed John Finerty, editor of the *Chicago Citizen*, "donning the rusty armor of Don Quixote to make the country the laughing stock of the civilized world. Ireland owes the latter very little, and she certainly is not obligated to the extent of having one of her foremost men become the champion of international principles and 'nationalization of the land.'"[54] John Boyle O'Reilly seconded Finerty's sentiments. "For God's-sake, Davitt, do not begin a split now," he implored. "Your position and power are unique, beautiful. Henry George cares as much for one country as another—he is only an abstract reasoner. We are Irishmen and we want to secure Irish national-ity."[55] The prior disagreements between radical and conservative nationalists caused by the No-Rent Manifesto were only amplified by the debate over land nationalization.

While many conservative supporters regarded the No-Rent Manifesto and Davitt's nationalization scheme as a dangerous slide toward "communism," many radical men and women in the United States saw these developments as the natural progression of the land agitation. Ellen Ford responded positively to land nationalization; she declared that "the nationalization of the soil is the surest means of making 'Ireland for the Irish and the land for the people' a substantial fact."[56] The male and female Leagues of Minneapolis, Minnesota, jointly declared: "We believe with Michael Davitt that rent for land under any circumstances, in prosperous times or bad times, is nothing more or less than an unjust and immoral tax upon the industry of a people . . . , without regard to their being Irish, English, Scotch, or any others under the broad canopy of heaven."[57] The Martha Washington Ladies' Land League of Philadelphia demanded that all of its donations continue to go toward supporting the No-Rent Manifesto, while the branch in Worcester, Massachusetts, "enthusiasti-cally approved of the nationalization of the land scheme."[58]

American labor circles also expressed strong encouragement for Davitt's ideas. The Knights of Labor of Chicago hailed Davitt as "the champion of popular rights, the advocate of correct principles, and the heroic defender of the poor against their oppressors."[59] The Jersey City freight handlers, then on strike, passed a resolution reminding Davitt that "it is the dimes and dollars of the workingmen in America that have been the backbone of the American

Land League movement," and "the nationalization of the land seems . . . to be the only means of forever destroying class monopolization of the natural source of opportunity to mankind—land."[60] In New York City some twelve thousand workers held a rally in support of Davitt in Union Square. A resolution adopted by the meeting praised Ireland for being "the first amongst the sisterhood of nations to inaugurate a war against monopolization" and pointed out that "her cry of the 'Land for the People' has found an echo on these shores, supplying American workingmen with a watchword for the future."[61] In other cities, mining camps, and industrial centers, working-class and radical men and women also gathered to voice their support for Davitt and land nationalization.

While most Catholic bishops and priests loudly criticized land nationalization, Father Edward McGlynn of New York City became one of Davitt's strongest supporters. McGlynn had been active in the Land League for quite some time, but he first came to national attention because of his support for Davitt at this juncture over land nationalization. "The doctrine of the land for the people is a gospel pregnant with a known truth and fraught with tidings of great joy to all mankind," McGlynn told a Jersey City audience, "and therefore [is] universal in its application." The acceptance of this doctrine would lead to "the improvement of society, the amelioration of the working classes, the diffusion of education, and the suppression of maladministration, the abolition of standing armies, and of those terrible crimes against God and men called wars."[62] McGlynn's backing provided important cover for Davitt and other radicals against charges of "communism." Henry George remarked to Ford with delight that "if Davitt's visit had no other results, it was well worth this. To start such a man [McGlynn] is worth a trip around the world three times over. He is 'an army with banners.'"[63]

Conservative branches responded by passing resolutions supporting Parnell's leadership as well as urging Davitt to turn away from his nationalization scheme. Fanny Parnell dismissed Davitt's land-nationalization plan as "nothing short of disastrous."[64] She also had Ellen Ford expelled from the executive of the Ladies' Land League for endorsing radical doctrines, and remarked of the *Irish World* that "while the paper is safe enough for educated people and contains some excellent ideas, it is a paper calculated to do much mischief in the hands of an only partially educated and simple-minded peasantry."[65] Such a perspective was not restricted to the national leadership. The Parnell Land League of New York City viewed "with alarm the efforts of the *Irish World* . . . to control the collection of Land League funds . . . in trying to create a new departure in Irish affairs . . . and [being] responsible for the unfortunate position occupied by Mr. Davitt."[66] In San Francisco, Branch No. 1 called on the Irish people to continue their adherence to peasant proprietorship.[67] And the Ladies'

Land League of Hartford, Connecticut, seized control of Davitt's visit to the city in June 1882 and barred from the stage any supporters of land nationalization.[68]

Davitt, dazed by the strong and frequently hostile feelings elicited by his plan, began a slow retreat from land nationalization shortly after his arrival in America. At his first speech in New York City, he gave a detailed denial to the various charges made against him. Davitt dismissed claims that he was seeking to replace Parnell's leadership or advancing a radical new departure from prior Land League principles. Instead, he argued that his advocacy of land nationalization was merely a proposal and not a rejection of peasant proprietorship.[69] He also refuted allegations that he had abandoned the struggle for Irish national independence by his support for the English working class. His speech did much to mollify conservatives in the audience. But while denying that he had fallen under the spell of Henry George or Patrick Ford, Davitt refused to denounce either man and praised their efforts on behalf of the Land League.[70] Davitt continued his tour of eastern and midwestern cities and at each successive stop he retreated further and further from his scheme. In Boston he declared: "I would sooner have my other arm severed than allow myself to be an obstruction to any plan laid down by Mr. Parnell. The nationalization scheme is my own, and I do not urge its adoption or even its consideration."[71] By the time he reached Chicago a few weeks later, he had abandoned all effort to push land nationalization forward.[72]

Within just a few short weeks Michael Davitt had suffered a terrible defeat and his nationalization scheme lay in ruins. Why did he capitulate so quickly? Davitt was temperamentally and politically unfit to lead any sustained drive to seize the leadership of the movement. He had been genuinely surprised and hurt by the rancor caused by his support of nationalization.[73] In a letter to John Dillon, Davitt complained, "It seems as if I can neither do or say anything that is not wrongly construed on both sides of the Atlantic."[74] He was unwilling to challenge Parnell directly. Unlike Parnell, Davitt lacked the ruthlessness and political ambition necessary for a prolonged and bitter leadership dispute. Tim Healy, one of Parnell's principal lieutenants, informed Patrick Collins that the worst was over: "So long as Parnell cares to make any effort, he has the whole country with him and he is today stronger than ever."[75] Davitt was also a patriot and was willing to subordinate his personal beliefs for what he thought was the benefit of the greater cause. "All danger of a split is over," he told John Dillon in June 1882. "I have to make many sacrifices in the matters of feeling and temper to effect this, but I of course do not regret it."[76] When Davitt returned to Ireland on 16 July, his attempt to reinvigorate the land agitation had failed.

Among radicals in the United States there was disappointment with Davitt's unwillingness to fight for the cause of land nationalization. "It is a pity he came here," Louis F. Post caustically remarked. "His mission is a failure, and he is a fallen idol. At Manchester, before his departure for this country, he lifted the colors of the labor army of the world; at Liverpool he began to furl them, and before his first public reception in America occurred, he had packed them away and swung out a little green flag with a harp on it."[77] Radicals within the Land League became increasingly disillusioned with the principles of the movement. In New York City the CLU signaled this feeling by its shift away from the more abstract principles of achieving social revolution in Ireland and toward a more practical focus on solving local problems facing working-men and women.[78] Even two of Davitt's biggest supporters, Edward McGlynn and Henry George, were dismayed by his withdrawal. In a speech before New York City workingmen McGlynn gently chided Davitt and told the audience that "if I had to fall into anyone's hands, I know of none that I would like to fall in better than those of Henry George."[79] George, for his part, wished that Davitt "would stand up and stop making apologies and offering compromises" and "frittering the strength of great principle."[80] After Davitt's defeat in America the Land League, in the eyes of many radicals like George, was slowly slipping into irrelevancy.

The Triumph of Conservative Irish Nationalism in Ireland and the United States and the End of a "Greater Ireland"

The shift toward a political movement for Home Rule in Ireland and the over-whelming disagreements among the various Irish-American factions destroyed the "Greater Ireland" that the Land League movement had helped spawn. In Ireland, Parnell moved to consolidate his control of the nationalist movement, pushing the nationalist agenda away from a focus on the land question and toward a political strategy. In the United States, infighting splintered the move-ment, leaving Irish-American radicals to seek other outlets for their passion and radicalism.

Davitt's unwillingness to press his challenge while in America strengthened Parnell and helped to remove any strong opposition to the conservative back-lash within the movement. By the summer of 1882 Parnell had effectively ter-minated central political support for the Irish land agitation and was ready to shift to a parliamentary campaign for Home Rule. Before doing so, he took care to rein in all elements in the Land League resistant to his control, especially the Ladies' Land League. Parnell had been unhappy with the stewardship of the movement by the Ladies' Land League during his imprisonment, and his anger only increased after his release. He was bitter about the large sums of money expended by the women leaders in maintaining the movement and about the criticism that he had received from the Ladies' Land League over the Kilmainham Treaty. "They [the women leaders] told me in Dublin after my release," Parnell confided to Davitt, "that I ought to have remained in Kilmainham."[81] Jessie Craigen's letter to her fellow Ladies' Land Leaguer Helen Taylor highlights this dissatisfaction with Parnell's decision making: "I made great sacrifices for the Irish cause . . . , but it was to fight for the liberty of the people and not to put political tricksters into power."[82] For the first few months after Parnell's release the Ladies' Land League and Parnell remained in an uneasy truce, with each side eyeing the other suspiciously.

The end of the Ladies' Land League in Ireland came on 10 August 1882, when the organization disbanded rather than accept Parnell's efforts to place it under the strict control of male leaders. Parnell had refused to pay the overdraft (then £5,000) of the Ladies' Land League unless the women leaders signed an agreement to disband the organization but still requiring them to continue considering applications from tenants in need of relief.[83] Anna Parnell later asserted that the male leaders "wanted us for a buffer between them and the country—a perpetual petticoat screen behind which they could shelter, not from the government, but from the people."[84] The women removed themselves from this predicament by changing the wording of the proposed agreement, making them responsible only for debts incurred by the Ladies' Land League itself, and this outstanding balance was quickly paid off. Davitt was convinced that "Parnell never made a greater mistake or a more mischievous blunder than in suppressing the Ladies in the manner he did."[85] Anna Parnell never forgave her brother for his treatment of the Ladies' Land League.

Having dealt to his satisfaction with the Ladies' Land League, Charles Stewart Parnell now worked to garner political support for his parliamentary quest for Home Rule. He had been reluctant to establish another nationwide organization as he feared a repeat of the Land League experience, but his colleagues eventually persuaded him of the utility of a centralized organization to promote the movement. In October 1882 a "land conference" was held and the Irish National League was organized in Dublin. The new organization was focused primarily on Home Rule, with agrarian concerns a distant second, and there was a noted emphasis on enlisting the support of the Catholic Church and its clergy. The National League was also structured very differently from the Land League. "Despite the appearance of democracy," one historian has noted, "the National League remained . . . an autocratically controlled body, ruled by a committee which it had not elected, and whose powers were undefined."[86] Davitt and other radicals were excluded from any real power within the organization during its founding and afterward. Tim Healy confided to

Patrick Collins that "Davitt did not suggest one line on the constitution of the League. Parnell drew up the land clause, [William] O'Brien the labour, and I did the others."[87] From this point forward Davitt would play the role of autonomous agent, speaking out in favor of the causes he supported and acting as an unofficial loyal opposition to Parnell. The new organization left no doubt as to its views on the relationship between women and politics; it described itself as "an open organization in which the ladies will not take part."[88] With the demise of the Ladies' Land League, Irish women were no longer a prominent part of the nationalist leadership.

This shift to a conservative, centralized parliamentary movement in Ireland profoundly affected Irish-American nationalism. The Land League had been unique in its ability to mobilize all elements of the Irish-American community into one organization. For Irish-American women and radicals especially, the Land League had provided them with opportunities to publicly assert their priorities within their communities. Ordinary men and women, as we have seen in earlier chapters, argued over and staked out their own claims to what it meant to be Irish and American in the Gilded Age. When the movement in Ireland changed to a gradualist constitutional strategy, a large part of the raison d'être for the perpetuation of women's presence in Irish nationalism was removed. Irish-American radical nationalists had been attracted to the movement because of the radical possibilities of the agrarian struggle in Ireland and its relevance to social problems present in the United States. The rise of a conservative Irish nationalism in both the United States and Ireland prompted radicals to reexamine their commitment to the movement, with the result that many soon abandoned it. When to this factor was added a conservative Irish-American nationalist backlash, women and radicals found themselves on the defensive and either quit the movement in disgust or were forced out.

But even before Davitt left the United States, there were signs that the American Land League was in decline. Donations sent to the treasurer Father Walsh slowly began to dry up. This decline in contributions was partly due to donor fatigue, which had been growing more pronounced since the Land League's founding two years earlier. The phases of League activity that elicited the most funds from Irish Americans were the responses to Parnell's 1880 tour, Davitt's arrest and the battle over coercion, Parnell's imprisonment, and the No-Rent Manifesto. All of these periods were marked by crisis in Ireland, and Irish Americans responded vigorously and generously to the Land League's calls for funds. But with the adoption of a parliamentary strategy for Home Rule, Irish Americans no longer had that earlier motivation to stave off dangerous crises. Dr. William Wallace of the New York Land League also believed that the same group of Irish Americans were being asked to shoulder too much of the financial burden. "When a person becomes a member of the League," he commented, "and has paid his dollar according to the pledge . . . , there is no reason why the few on this continent should be forced into paying such [an] amount of money as would compensate for the indifference of the greater portion of their race here."[89] Even contributors to the *Irish World*, normally so reliable, began to lessen their donations. The monthly totals of contributions plummeted from almost $45,000 in February 1882 to just under $4,000 in August, $5,000 in September, and only $1,500 in October.[90] A letter home from a newly arrived immigrant in Boston asked, "Is there anything going on? Some of the people whom I have met seem to be tired subscribing to the League."[91] After supporting the Land League for two years, Irish Americans became less generous with their contributions.

Alongside the dwindling donations a general apathy gripped the Land League. Numerous branches across the country dissolved or met infrequently. During the late winter and the spring of 1882 the number of active official American Land League branches fell from 900 to 500.[92] Many conservatives had left the organization when the No-Rent Manifesto was adopted. Without regular stimulation more Irish Americans simply began to lose interest in the movement. The Land League branch in Petersburg, Virginia, voted to dissolve after members had continually skipped meetings for months.[93] While visiting the United States, the noted Irish newspaper editor and Parnellite MP A. M. Sullivan described in a letter to Davitt the fluctuating interest of ordinary Irish Americans in the Land League. "If the people here see the public movement at home going on in a 'live' way, they are good for any amount of help," he remarked, "but any chilling idea or rumour of breakup, or division, or do-nothingism will dispel into thin air all further efforts on this side."[94] A combination of donor fatigue and membership apathy had thus set in among many Irish Americans before Davitt's ill-fated tour.

Within the American Land League members of the Ladies' Land League and social radicals had been among the most stalwart and energetic members. Both groups, however, increasingly came under attack from conservative critics. In Cleveland, Ohio, Bishop Richard Gilmour excommunicated members of the Cleveland Ladies' Land League for their radicalism and their refusal to disband. Gilmour had previously been a supporter of the Land League, but the issuance of the No-Rent Manifesto had soured his views on the League, and in a public lecture he claimed that the movement was edging dangerously close to communism.[95] On 15 May 1882 a branch of the Ladies' Land League was formed in Cleveland, with twenty members joining. Gilmour, already at odds with the local men's Land League and seeing the men as the driving force behind the formation of the new ladies' branch, cautioned them not to "turn our Catholic women into brawling politicians. . . . As you choose, you must abide, but you shall not further be permitted . . . to assail the modesty of our Catholic women by turning them, for your selfish ends, into noisy politicians or newspaper pests."[96] He called on the women's branch to disband immediately in order to maintain female propriety and to "save our common manhood the shame of seeing you shield yourselves [i.e., the male Land Leaguers] behind a petticoat."[97] For Gilmour the Ladies' Land League was both a challenge to Irish-American women's gender roles and a threat to Irish-American masculinity. Despite Gilmour's views, however, the women went ahead and held their regular meeting.

When his warnings were ignored, Gilmour issued a decree of excommunication against all members of the Cleveland Ladies' Land League and anyone who might join them. He insisted that "the Catholic woman must live within the modesty of the home; she must be the ornament of the family circle, and her womanly delicacy and gentle nature shall not be tainted with the noisy brawl of the virago. . . . Female modesty must be maintained, let the cost be what it may."[98] Gilmour's excommunication applied only to the members of the Ladies' Land League, and despite his belief that male Leaguers were the real culprits, no action was taken against them. It was the public activity of women outside the home that was the most serious threat in Gilmour's eyes.

Mary Rowland, president of the Cleveland Ladies' Land League, responded to Gilmour's excommunication order by declaring that "the stigma of immodesty, indelicacy, and political brawling you cast upon us, I fling it back."[99] Despite the excommunication, forty more members joined, the members posed for a group photograph, and 1,500 people attended their picnic in August 1882, all of which demonstrated the Cleveland women's hardened belief in the righteousness of their public activism.[100] Several male and female Land Leagues, including those in Denver, Toledo, Pittsburgh, Washington, DC, St. Louis, and Portland, sent resolutions of support to the Cleveland Ladies' Land League.[101] In Cleveland, however, the local Hibernian Rifles Club and Ancient Order of Hibernians denounced the female Leaguers, as did most of the Catholic press outside Cleveland. The editor of the *Catholic Columbian* of Columbus, Ohio, declared in an editorial, "See what a glorious spectacle that notoriety-craving woman who leads the Ladies' Land League of Cleveland would present if she could have her own way and dance about the stage of Parnell Hall with a mitre on her head and crosier in her hand."[102] In contrast to earlier attacks on women's participation in the Land League, the support shown for women in the movement was now less widespread and more muted, signaling the ascendency of conservative control.

But unlike its Irish counterpart, the American Ladies' Land League did not experience a dramatic ending. Irish-American women were never explicitly banned from participation in the Irish National League formed in the United

States, but the number of women in the organization steadily fell. The main reason for this decline was the shift from a dynamic movement for land reform in Ireland to an incremental and constitutional pursuit of Home Rule that removed much of the impetus for women's participation in nationalist politics. Delivering a further blow to the movement was the premature and sudden death of Fanny Parnell on 18 July 1882; this unexpected event removed a tireless advocate for the Ladies' Land League.[103] One editorial declared that the demise of Fanny Parnell and the reported death in Ireland of Anna Parnell from exhaustion (accounts of her death were false) were proof that "the constitution of woman is too weak to bear the excitement necessarily connected with political life. . . . How can women stand the noise, the strife, the contradiction, the disappointment of political life, toilsome days, and sleepless nights?"[104] Such sexist nonsense aside, her death was difficult to overcome because of Fanny Parnell's symbolic importance; without a clear national advocate to assert the need for women's participation, the Ladies' Land League in the United States limped on through 1883 with a marked drop-off in the number of women participating and in branch activity.[105] Women left the nationalist movement in droves, and though they soon gained admission to ethnic and benevolent societies like the AOH and CTAU, they were welcomed only as auxiliary members. Irish-American women also joined such labor organizations as the Knights of Labor, but even within this movement, despite its inclusive rhetoric, women were often not accorded equal status.[106] Unfortunately, women faced similar struggles even as they proceeded to form their own groups and organizations in the waning decades of the nineteenth century. Irish-American women were left behind by the new direction of Irish nationalism after 1882 and failed to reestablish a similarly important presence in Irish-American nationalism until the twentieth century.

In late 1882, Irish-American radical nationalists began to abandon the Land League. Edward O'Donnell has noted that in New York City labor organizers who had "drawn inspiration and strength from the radical elements within the early Land League struggle became disenchanted by its shifts away from those principles and decided to strike out on [their] own."[107] A similar process was found at work throughout the United States. In Denver the working-class men and women active in the Land League helped pave the way for the growth of the Knights of Labor in that area.[108] On 14 October 1882 even Patrick Ford withdrew his support from the League and closed his Land League fund. "The reason for this action," he told his readers, "is that *there is no longer a Land League in existence. What was the Land League is a thing of the past.*"[109] But Ford believed that the struggle for the emancipation of the world's workers would persist: "*The movement will go on!* There is no power on earth that can stop it. . . .

The light has been spread. The principle which the *Irish World* enunciated has struck its roots deep in the soil and will there abide. . . . England too is catching fire, and Scotland. And here in America what question is coming to the front like the land? A New World has been discovered, and all are crying out 'Land! Land!'"[110] Ford's abandonment of the Land League further undermined its effectiveness.

Ordinary Irish-American working-class and radical men and women retreated from Irish nationalism and refused to join the Irish National League, the conservative successor to the Land League. Their absence severely weakened the new organization since radical men and women had been the most numerous group of active workers among Irish-American nationalists. Henry George, despite his sympathy for the Irish people, refused to participate in the National League. "The Irish Land League could have commanded any services I could have rendered," he told Terence Powderly, "because it was clearly and ostensibly a great social movement making a struggle for a principle of worldwide importance, but shorn of this social element, the Irish National League seems to me a mere political movement, and . . . I have no faith in mere political movements of any kind."[111] The end of the Land League did not, however, mark an end to working-class participation in the struggle for American social reform. Rather, the demise of the Land League led to a divorce between Irish nationalism and economic radicalism, as radicals shifted their attention to non-Irish organizations and movements like the Knights of Labor and others.

Irish Americans and other workers built on their experience in the Land League to continue their efforts to enact economic and social reform. When Henry George ran for mayor of New York in 1886, male and female former Land Leaguers turned out in large numbers to assist and support the campaign. In Denver, Colorado, in the 1890s, former radical Land Leaguers went on to provide enthusiastic support for the Populist movement.[112] As David Montgomery has observed, "The Irish-American community and the American labor movement came of age together in the last quarter of the nineteenth century."[113]

Perhaps the clearest example of the continued influence of the Land League on American labor radicals was the adoption by American workers of the boycott. Michael Gordon has shown how American workers adapted the use of the boycott to try to wrest concessions from employers, and these tactics were quickly deployed across the United States.[114] In 1882 Jersey City freight handlers declared a strike and threatened to boycott any members who turned their back on the union and continued to work. The union president, Jeremiah Murphy of Cork, argued that anyone who crossed the picket line "should be shunned like a leper."[115] In Chicago, streetcar workers successfully deployed a boycott to force ownership to capitulate their demands for better pay and

ostracized workers who violated labor solidarity.[116] Boycotting would continue
to be employed by American workers well into the twentieth century.

What was left of the American Land League was officially dissolved at its
third convention, held in Philadelphia on 25–27 April 1883. Over 1,100 delegates
attended the convention, 468 of them representing the Land League and the
rest coming from the Ancient Order of Hibernians, the Catholic temperance
societies, and other, smaller fraternal organizations.[117] The delegates voted at
the end of the first day to disband the Land League and met the next day to
form the Irish National League of America. Clan na Gael, determined to take
control of the movement, stacked the convention with its members.[118] The
Chicago lawyer Alexander Sullivan, the leader of the Clan, was elected president
of the Irish National League. As a conciliatory gesture to conservatives, Father
Charles O'Reilly of Detroit was elected as treasurer, but the real power remained in the hands of Clan na Gael. The platform adopted by the convention
was designed to please everyone, and this task was made simpler by the absence
of most radicals. Ireland's right to self-government was recognized and divisive
issues were avoided. The delegates also pledged their allegiance to Parnell
and emphasized the new organization's auxiliary status to the movement in
Ireland.[119]

The Irish National League of America was a poor successor to the Land
League. Despite the strong showing at its first convention, its membership
never came close to matching that of its predecessor. Its major purpose was to
provide financial and moral support to the Irish National League in Ireland,
but it lacked the dynamic vigor of the Land League. Money flowed much more
slowly into the coffers of the new League. Treasurer O'Reilly declined to issue
regular public announcements of financial receipts because of the relative
scantiness of the donations received.[120] Poor leadership also plagued the National League. Conservatives played a much smaller role in the League, and
physical-force nationalists were firmly in control. Alexander Sullivan, while
serving as president of this open and constitutional movement, was secretly
ordering dynamite attacks in Britain. There were also rumors of the embezzle-
ment of League funds.[121] Sullivan stepped down in 1884, and Patrick Egan, the
former Irish Land League treasurer and recent immigrant to Lincoln, Nebraska,
was elected to replace him. Egan immediately created a furor when he publicly
endorsed the Republican candidate James G. Blaine, to the dismay of the
mostly Democratic membership of the League.[122] The Irish National League
continued for another seven years, but it was always a pale imitation of the
Land League. It would take, as Martin Griffith believed, a "long time to revive
the spirit of the old Land League times."[123] Griffith proved to be prophetic.
While Home Rule and other causes attracted the attention of Irish Americans,

it was not until the aftermath of the 1916 Easter Rising and the years of the Irish War of Independence that Irish Americans once again responded to Irish nationalism with the numbers, energy, and financial generosity found in the Land League era.

That the Land League did not endure should not lead us to underestimate its significance. In the United States the participation of so many ordinary men and women in the movement brought out into the open diverse and competing claims over what should be the future direction of Irish-American nationalism in the Gilded Age. The League also helped create and strengthen links between Irish Americans and American labor reform that endured well beyond the end of the movement. The Land League's influence was not confined to the United States but was felt in the homeland as well. Reflecting on the heady years of the Land League agitation in Ireland and the United States, Charles Stewart Parnell believed that had it not been "for the help of the Irish in America . . . , it would have been impossible for the people at home to have thought of such a movement as the Land League, much less to have sustained it to fruition."[124] Despite its relatively brief existence, the Land League had a lasting impact on American and Irish history in the late nineteenth century.

Epilogue

The preceding chapters have demonstrated the important impact of the Land League in the United States and Ireland. Before ending our discussion of the movement, it is worthwhile to briefly examine the Land League's continuing influence on Irish nationalism in the late nineteenth century. As previous chapters have shown, Irish-American men and women who mobilized in support of the Land League used the opportunity that such activity provided to voice their own individual, American-based concerns publicly in their local communities. Likewise, the Irish in Ireland found inspiration and felt the impact from the transference of money, ideas, and sentiments from the Irish in America.

After the Land League, however, the ascendancy of Charles Stewart Parnell and his domination of Irish politics curtailed Irish-American influence on Irish nationalism. Irish Americans remained a strong base of financial support for Irish nationalist leaders, but they no longer possessed the broader sway over the direction of Irish nationalism that they had enjoyed during the New Departure. From the Kilmainham Treaty onward, Parnell shifted the focus of Irish politics toward a parliamentary pursuit of Home Rule, and within a few years he successfully maneuvered the Irish question back into the forefront of British politics. The 1885 general election resulted in the Liberals winning 335 seats, the Conservatives 249, and the Irish Parliamentary Party 86, the exact difference between the two major parties, a set of results that seemed to put Parnell in a position to arbitrate the exercise of political power in Parliament. A year later, Prime Minister Gladstone declared his support for Irish Home Rule. In April 1886 he submitted a bill granting Ireland autonomy over its domestic affairs but maintaining the imperial link with Great Britain and keeping foreign policy under British control.

Irish Americans responded positively to this revival of Home Rule and supported Parnell's efforts with financial and moral assistance. But whereas the

Land League had drawn support from many reform-minded and working-class Irish Americans, Irish-American backing for Home Rule was dominated by the middle class and the wealthy. Well-to-do Irish Americans believed that the movement for Home Rule possessed a respectability and conservatism that had been lacking in the Land League.[1] The Irish Parliamentary Fund Association, a conservative offshoot of the Irish National League, provided important funding for the electoral campaigns of Irish politicians contesting seats in the British Parliament. The New York branch of the association, with the help of Tammany Hall politicians who collected money in their districts, raised $150,000 between November 1885 and August 1886.[2] Money from other Irish-American sources also continued to fill the Irish party's purse in anticipation of Ireland achieving Home Rule.

These hopes were dashed when Gladstone's Home Rule Bill went down to defeat in the British Parliament. The final vote in the House of Commons was 343 against to 313 in favor, a result caused primarily by the defection of a minority faction of the Liberal party. This group, which opposed granting Home Rule to Ireland, became known as the Liberal Unionists and soon afterward allied themselves with the Conservatives. Having failed to carry the bill, Gladstone's administration dissolved Parliament, and the Liberals were badly defeated in the next general election. Despite the failure of the Home Rule bill, Parnell remained optimistic that with continued Liberal support Home Rule for Ireland would eventually be achieved through a combination of political and public pressure that would overcome resistance in both houses of Parliament.

This optimism was shattered in 1890 when Captain William O'Shea named Parnell as a co-respondent in a divorce proceeding filed against his wife, and Parnell's lover, Katharine O'Shea. The public disclosure of Parnell's affair sent the Irish nationalist movement into chaos. Gladstone, under pressure from nonconformist Liberals, warned Irish leaders that he could not continue an alliance with Irish MPs if Parnell remained in power.[3] When Parnell refused to step down, the Irish Catholic hierarchy denounced him, and a bitter split occurred within the Irish nationalist movement as anti-Parnellite and Parnellite members viciously attacked each other. This infighting continued even after Parnell's death on 6 October 1891; the Irish nationalist movement would remain divided for almost another decade.

The fall of Parnell had a similarly disastrous impact among Irish-American nationalists. Parnell's personal leadership after the Land League had been a key motivator in keeping Irish Americans involved with their homeland, and his demise plunged Irish nationalist politics into a period of acrimony and inactivity. Irish Americans retreated from Irish nationalism, and the transatlantic transference of money, people, and ideas that had been so important in the

1880s fell into insignificance until interest in Ireland was revived in the early twentieth century.

While conservative Irish-American nationalism ebbed after Parnell, in the 1880s radical and working-class Irish Americans, alienated from Home Rule and Irish nationalism after the Land League, continued to participate in a variety of other American social and labor movements. "The labor consciousness that flowered in the 1880s," Eric Foner has argued, "owed a great deal to the Ford-George wing of the Land League."[4] A wave of labor militancy swept across the United States in 1885 and 1886. During this period of "great upheaval" the Knights of Labor grew from 110,000 to over 700,000 members, and on 1 May 1886, 950,000 workers, responding to calls from Samuel Gompers's Federation of Organized Trades and Labor Unions, took to the streets and struck for an eight-hour workday.[5] The boycott, adopted from the Irish example, became one of the important weapons used by labor activists to assert their rights. "I bless Ireland for St. Boycott," the labor leader Robert Blissert told a New York workers' meeting, "and we want those who try to crush it to know that it is but a baby as yet, but if they understood what a stalwart mother and father it has, they would respect it."[6] Irish Americans in the mid-1880s were in the forefront of labor's struggles. During the last days of the Land League Henry George had confided to Patrick Ford that though the League was nearing an end, a "seed has at least been planted. . . . We who have seen the light must win because much greater forces than ourselves are working with us."[7] The labor unrest that covered the United States in 1886 seemed to bear out George's prophecy.

The best expression of the continuing links between the social radicalism present in the Land League and the broader American society could be seen in New York City. The coalition of prominent reformers and working-class Irish Americans that had supported a radical interpretation of the Land League's purpose coalesced once again in late 1886 in support of Henry George's campaign for mayor. This campaign was launched when the Central Labor Union, which had first come together in support of the No-Rent Manifesto, decided that for labor to achieve its goals it was necessary to enter electoral politics. The decision of the popular Democratic mayor William Grace, New York's first Irish-American mayor, not to run for reelection left the race to succeed him wide open. A conference of labor delegates, held on 19 August 1886, voted to field a candidate for New York's open mayoral seat, and they chose Henry George to represent them.[8] George's opponents were the Democratic nominee Abram S. Hewitt, a former congressman, and a young Theodore Roosevelt, drafted by the Republicans.

George's candidacy posed a serious challenge to the political status quo. Despite the unlikelihood of a George victory, Democratic and Tammany officials feared that he would drain off enough Irish-American and working-class votes from Hewitt to give the election to Roosevelt. The George campaign, one historian has written, "cut across racial, ethnic, craft, political, and even class lines, bringing together revolutionary German socialists, genteel reformers, Irish land radicals, and 'pure and simple' unionists."[9] Their candidate claimed that the task facing New Yorkers was "removing industrial slavery. That is the meaning of our movement. This is at once a revolt against political corruption and social injustice."[10]

The rhetoric emanating from George's campaign echoed sentiments expressed a few years earlier in the Land League, and former Land Leaguers flocked to support him. "My great reason," George claimed, "for accepting this nomination was that it would bring into public discussion principles which it seemed to me were most necessary to be discussed."[11] James Redpath, Terence Powderly, Patrick Ford, and Edward McGlynn, brought together for the first time since the Land League, praised George and worked for his election. The *Irish World* declared itself "heart and soul for Henry George" and urged workers to "rally round Henry George and to stand by him with inflexible devotion until the last hour of the contest."[12] Father McGlynn, a close friend of George, claimed in an interview during the campaign that he knew "of no man I admire and love so much." "The movement [to elect Henry George]," he continued, "will go on until it shall have smashed irretrievably all the existing political machines, until it shall have emancipated labor throughout this country, until it shall have restored to the disinherited and landless class who have to pay rent for the use of land to landlords their long-lost inheritance, and until it shall have embraced in its beneficent action the whole world."[13] In many ways the arguments made for George in 1886 paralleled the language of the social-reform wing of the Land League. George's candidacy won strong support from the Irish Americans in New York City, who remembered his efforts on behalf of Ireland during the Land League. His supporters, however, did not include his close friend Michael Davitt, who spent late 1886 on tour in America. Davitt refused to back George's campaign for mayor owing to his belief that George did not have a chance of winning and because of Davitt's desire not to be seen as interfering in American elections.[14]

One further element of support for the radical candidate worthy of mention is the assistance given to George and McGlynn by Irish-American women. Though they lacked the franchise, Irish-American women expressed their backing by attending rallies and speeches. Historians and contemporaries have noted the large numbers of women involved in the Single Tax and Anti-Poverty movements.[15] There is also evidence that some of these women were active earlier in the Ladies' Land League. Marguerite Moore, a former organizer for the Ladies' Land League in Ireland, immigrated to the United States with her six children in 1884. She soon became active in American reform politics and gave two to three public speeches a night on behalf of George during his 1886 campaign.[16] In 1887 Father McGlynn, now excommunicated, founded the Anti-Poverty Society, a social-reform organization that was popular among both working-class Catholics and middle-class Protestant reformers.[17] Maria Dougherty, the former president of the Worcester, Massachusetts, Ladies' Land League, continued her support for radical causes. Her obituary mentions her long friendship with McGlynn and her willingness to stand by him after his excommunication.[18] Reform-minded Irish-American women did not end their public participation with the demise of the Ladies' Land League but instead continued to work in movements outside of Irish nationalism.

Many elements in New York did not approve of George, and his opponents included not just the other political parties but also most of the New York press and local Catholic Church authorities. The *Brooklyn Daily Eagle* denounced George's ideas as "absolute communism" and expressed the belief that "so long as schemes of this sort are confined to the pages of smoothly written volumes, they are comparatively harmless speculations. But when they are made into a political platform upon which a man asks to be elected to office, . . . and [propagated] . . . as means for establishing the millennium, they become rank demagogy, and the man who represents them is a pure demagogue."[19] Archbishop Michael Corrigan, despite his insistence that McGlynn stay out of politics, let it be known that he thought George and his ideas to be dangerous and harmful. Monsignor Thomas S. Preston, vicar general of the New York archdiocese, sent a letter to Tammany Hall that was published just prior to the election. "I can state with confidence that the majority of the Catholic clergy in this city are opposed to the candidacy of Mr. George. . . . His principles, logically carried out, would prove the ruin of the working-men he professes to befriend."[20] As in the last few months of the Land League, the Catholic Church came down heavily on what it perceived to be the growth of a destructive radicalism.

The election results in November 1886 did not yield a victory for George, but his supporters were still pleased with the outcome. The Democratic candidate Hewitt won the election with 90,500 votes, with George tallying 68,000 and Roosevelt coming in third with 60,000.[21] These were significant numbers for a third-party candidate. George's campaign had made important inroads among the second-generation German-American and Irish-American working class. Some supporters believed that the Catholic Church's opposition had been critical in George's defeat. "Noisy Land League supporters howled themselves red in the face until the Sunday before election day," one of George's supporters complained, "and then from every pulpit came a soft whisper more potent on the Thursday after than Moses on Mount Sinai."[22] But historians have found that George in fact did quite well among Catholics, with one investigator claiming that Catholics provided him with perhaps five-sixths of his support.[23] Much of the reason for George's defeat can be found in the choices of newly arrived immigrants (desiring Tammany Hall patronage and unwilling to flout the wishes of church authorities) to vote Democratic, along with the decision by some wealthier Republicans to desert Roosevelt in favor of Hewitt in order to ensure George's defeat.[24] But George and his supporters believed that there was a bright future ahead for labor and working-class politics. "This is the Bunker Hill," George exclaimed. "We have lit a fire that will never go out."[25]

This optimistic outlook soon proved to be based on false hopes. The coalition that George had formed in 1886 quickly began to splinter, and various elements headed off in their own directions. George was not blameless in this development. Shortly after the election he purged German-American socialists from the movement, claiming that their principles were anathema to him.[26] Within a year the Knights of Labor reverted to its old principle of abstaining from politics. Terence Powderly, the Knights' Grandmaster Workman, already fearful that the Knights would be branded as anarchists after the Haymarket bombing, was careful not to put at risk the Catholic Church's recent approval of the Knights of Labor by continuing to support George and McGlynn.[27] Even Patrick Ford, beginning a slow retreat from his earlier radicalism, abandoned George after criticisms of the Catholic Church by George and McGlynn became increasingly vocal.[28] The final blow to the labor coalition was struck when George announced that he believed that the Haymarket defendants, having exhausted all their appeals, did not deserve to be granted executive clemency by the governor of Illinois. Labor activists and workers denounced George as a traitor and withdrew their electoral support.[29] By 1887 the grand mobilization of reformers and ordinary working-class men and women first started in 1880 by the Land League had been fatally undermined, and individuals either retreated from reform or migrated to the vast array of other reform organizations available in the late nineteenth century. The link between social reform and Irish nationalism, which had been so powerful in the Land League, remained severed, and it would be left to another generation of Irish Americans to resurrect the radical potential of the Land League era.

Appendix

Cities Visited during Charles Stewart Parnell's 1880 American Tour

1 January—Arrives in New York City aboard the steamer *Sycthia*
4 January—First speech in Madison Square Garden in New York, New York
6 January—Newark, New Jersey
8 January—Jersey City, New Jersey
9 January—Brooklyn, New York
10 January—Philadelphia, Pennsylvania
12 January—Boston, Massachusetts
13 January—Lowell, Massachusetts
14 January—Fall River, Massachusetts
15 January—Lawrence, Massachusetts
16 January—Lynn, Massachusetts
17 January—Providence, Rhode Island
21 January—Indianapolis, Indiana
22 January—Toledo, Ohio
23 January—Springfield, Ohio
24 January—Cleveland, Ohio
25 January—Buffalo, New York
26 January—Rochester, New York
27 January—Albany, New York
28 January—Troy, New York
29 January—New Haven, Connecticut
30 January—Springfield and Holyoke, Massachusetts
31 January—Cambridge, Massachusetts
2 February—Washington, DC, in the United States House of Representatives
4 February—Washington, DC
6 February—Richmond, Virginia
8 February—Hazelton, Pennsylvania

9 February—Wilkesbarre, Pennsylvania

10 February—Scranton, Pennsylvania

12 February—Altoona, Pennsylvania

13 February—Baltimore, Maryland

15 February—Pittsburgh, Pennsylvania

16 February—Wheeling, West Virginia

18 February—Frankfort, Kentucky

19 February—Louisville, Kentucky

20 February—Cincinnati, Ohio

22 February—Detroit, Michigan

23 February—Chicago, Illinois

24 February—Milwaukee, Wisconsin

25 February—Madison, Wisconsin

26 February—Winona, Lake City, Red Wing, Hastings, St. Paul, and Minneapolis, Minnesota

27 February—Dubuque, Iowa

28 February—Davenport, Iowa

1 March—Des Moines, Iowa

2 March—Peoria, Illinois

3 March—Springfield, Illinois

4 March—St. Louis, Missouri

6 March—Toronto, Canada

8 March—Montreal, Canada

11 March—Departs for Ireland aboard the steamer *Baltic*

Cities Visited during Michael Davitt's 1880 American Tour

2 August—Wilkesbarre, Pennsylvania

4 August—Scranton, Pennsylvania

5 August—Washington, DC

7 August—Pittsburgh, Pennsylvania

8 August—Columbus, Ohio

10-11 August—Springfield, Ohio

12 August—Cincinnati, Ohio

13 August—Indianapolis, Indiana

14 August—Chicago, Illinois

16 August—Joliet, Illinois

17 August—Braidwood, Illinois

18 August—Terre Haute, Indiana

19-24 August—St. Louis, Missouri

25-26 August—Kansas City, Missouri

27 August—St. Joseph, Missouri

28 August-12 September—Omaha, Nebraska (Davitt bedridden for more than a week)

13 September—Cheyenne, Wyoming

14 September—Ogden, Utah

15 September—Salt Lake City, Utah

17 September—Sacramento, California

18 September—Oakland, California

19–26 September—San Francisco, California

30 September—Virginia City, Nevada

7 October—Denver, Colorado

9 October—Leadville, Colorado

12 October—Cheyenne, Wyoming

14–15 October—Chicago, Illinois

16 October—Cleveland, Ohio

22 October–3 November—New York, New York

5 November—Boston, Massachusetts

8 November—New York, New York; last public meeting at Cooper Union hosted by
   the newly organized Ladies' Land League

10 November—Leaves the United States for Ireland

Cities Visited during Michael Davitt's 1882 American Tour

19 June—New York, New York

20 June—Boston, Massachusetts

21 June—Albany, New York

23 June—Jersey City, New Jersey

24 June—New Haven, Connecticut

25 June—Hartford, Connecticut

26 June—Philadelphia, Pennsylvania

28 June—Chicago, Illinois

29 June—Buffalo, New York

30 June—Rochester, New York

1 July—Providence, Rhode Island

2 July—Worcester, Massachusetts

4 July—Troy, New York

5 July—New York, New York, meeting before New York Trade Unions

6 July—New York, New York, Fifth Ward Meeting

7 July—New York, New York, Davitt Branch Meeting

8 July—Fifth Ward Branch Meeting, final meeting

15 July—Leaves United States and sails for Ireland

Notes

Introduction

1. Quoted in Thomas N. Brown, *Irish-American Nationalism, 1870–1879* (Philadelphia: J. B. Lippincott, 1966), 108.

2. Brown, *Irish-American Nationalism*, 23.

3. Ibid., 46.

4. Eric Foner, "Class, Ethnicity, and Radicalism in the Gilded Age: The Land League and Irish-America," in Foner, *Politics and Ideology in the Age of the Civil War* (Oxford: Oxford University Press, 1980), 195.

5. Ibid., 151.

6. Victor A. Walsh, "'A Fanatic Heart': The Cause of Irish-American Nationalism in Pittsburgh during the Gilded Age," *Journal of Social History* 15, no. 2 (Winter 1981): 188. In his work on the Irish in Pittsburgh, Pennsylvania, Walsh has demonstrated the importance of regional origins on levels of support for the Land League among Irish immigrants. While I recognize the importance of Walsh's insights (though I do believe he generalizes his findings on the Pittsburgh Irish too much to the rest of Irish America), in this project I have made the decision to examine the Land League as a national movement rather than focus on a small sample of individual locales.

7. David Emmons, *The Butte Irish: Class and Ethnicity in an American Mining Town, 1875–1925* (Urbana: University of Illinois Press, 1990), 294.

8. Kerby Miller has also argued that the Irish-American middle class was able to use Irish nationalism to assert hegemonic middle-class values. See Kerby Miller, "Class, Culture, and Immigrant Group Identity in the United States: The Case of Irish-American Ethnicity," in *Immigration Reconsidered: History, Sociology, and Politics*, ed. Virginia Yans-McLaughlin (New York: Oxford University Press, 1990), 96–129. Matthew Frye Jacobson has challenged the primacy of this hegemonic control in the 1890s. See Matthew Frye Jacobson, *Special Sorrows: The Diasporic Imagination of Irish, Polish, and Jewish Immigrants in the United States* (Cambridge: Cambridge University Press, 1995), 29. This book demonstrates that such hegemonic control was also not in the ascendant during the Land League era.

9. A note on methodology is necessary here. This study is not a local study of one Irish-American community but instead examines the Land League in the United States in a national and transatlantic context. The American Land League was a national movement with national officers and nationwide support. But this does not mean that local and regional differences were not important. Just as class, gender, and ideology shaped Land Leaguers' reaction to the movement, local circumstances and regional distinctiveness shaped the organization. By focusing on local Land League activity when appropriate, this project seeks to incorporate the most useful elements of local case studies to fashion a more complete picture of the movement.

10. Quoted in Adrian Mulligan, "A Forgotten 'Greater Ireland': The Transatlantic Development of Irish Nationalism," *Scottish Geographic Journal* 118, no. 3 (2002): 232. Mulligan has also highlighted Irish and Irish-Americans' use of the idea of a "Greater Ireland" being created. Whereas he focuses primarily on the transatlantic flow of revolutionary ideology and capital, alongside the transatlantic movements of key Irish-American and Irish leaders, bolstered by the increased capabilities of global communications, this study emphasizes the instability and unsustainability of this transatlantic moment while also incorporating a much wider perspective of the Irish-American community in this era.

11. *Irish-American*, 9 July 1881, 4.

12. Quoted in Conor Cruise O'Brien, *States of Ireland* (New York: Vintage Books, 1973), 45 (emphasis in original).

13. When referring to Irish-American men and women, this book is focusing primarily on Catholic Irish Americans. There does seem to have been some support for the Land League from American Protestants, but Catholics dominated the movement. It is important to note that hundreds of thousands of Irish Protestants immigrated to the United States in the nineteenth century. However, the evidence suggests that by the 1880s many Protestant Irish Americans had assimilated fairly deeply into American society and lacked the interest in their homeland of Catholics.

14. See, for example, Hasia Diner's *Erin's Daughters in America: Irish Immigrant Women in the Nineteenth Century* (Baltimore: Johns Hopkins University Press, 1983), 128, and Victor A. Walsh, "Irish Nationalism and Land Reform: The Role of the Irish in America," in *The Irish in America: Emigration, Assimilation, and Impact*, ed. P. J. Drudy (Cambridge: Cambridge University Press, 1985), 260.

15. The activity of the Irish Ladies' Land League in Ireland, led by Anna Parnell, Charles Stewart Parnell's sister, has received increasing amounts of attention in the last twenty years. For example, see Margaret Ward's *Unmanageable Revolutionaries: Women and Irish Nationalism* (London: Pluto Press, 1995); Jane Côté, *Fanny and Anna Parnell: Ireland's Patriot Sisters* (London: Macmillan, 1991); and Anna Parnell's recollection of her Ladies' Land League activities, *The Tale of a Great Sham*, ed. Dana Hearne (Dublin: Arlen House, 1986). Some American historians have mentioned the Ladies' Land League in the United States but often just in passing. For example, see David Brundage, *The Making of Western Labor Radicalism: Denver's Organized Workers, 1878–1905* (Urbana: University of Illinois Press, 1994), 43–44; and Richard Schneirov, *Labor and Urban Politics: Class Conflict and the*

Origins of Modern Liberalism in Chicago, 1864–97 (Urbana: University of Illinois Press, 1998), 131–32. Timothy Meagher deals more substantially with the Ladies' Land League in Worcester, Massachusetts, in *Inventing Irish America: Generation, Class, and Ethnic Identity in a New England City, 1880–1928* (Notre Dame, IN: Notre Dame University Press, 2001), 183–88, 190–95.

  16. For American agrarian movements in the 1830s and 1840s, see Reeve Huston, *Land and Freedom: Rural Society, Popular Protest, and Party Politics in Antebellum New York* (New York: Oxford University Press, 2000); and Jamie Bronstein, *Land Reform and Working-Class Experience in Britain and the United States, 1800–1862* (Stanford, CA: Stanford University Press, 1999). For populism, see Steven Hahn, *The Roots of Southern Populism: Yeoman Farmers and the Transformation of the Georgia Upcountry, 1850–1890* (New York: Oxford University Press, 1983); Lawrence Goodwyn, *The Populist Moment: A Short History of the Agrarian Revolt in America* (New York: Oxford University Press, 1978); Robert C. McMath Jr., *American Populism: A Social History, 1877–1898* (New York: Hill and Wang, 1993). For African Americans and land, see Steven Hahn, *A Nation under Our Feet: Black Political Struggles in the Rural South, from Slavery to the Great Migration* (Cambridge, MA: Belknap Press, 2003); Stephen Kantrowiz, *Ben Tillman and the Reconstruction of White Supremacy* (Chapel Hill: University of North Carolina Press, 2000); Nell Irvin Painter, *Exodusters: Black Migration to Kansas after Reconstruction* (New York: Knopf, 1977).

  17. The Repeal movement under Daniel O'Connell attempted to remove the Act of Union of 1800, which linked England, Scotland, and Ireland in the United Kingdom. Isaac Butt, a respected politician, faced increasing pressure from younger and more militant members of his party, including Charles Stewart Parnell, who argued for a more obstructionist policy in Parliament. Butt preferred a more gradual approach, believing that eventually British politicians would see the wisdom in granting Ireland home rule. Alan O'Day, *Charles Stewart Parnell* (Dundalk, Ireland: Dundalgan Press, 1998), 25–36; Alvin Jackson, *Home Rule: An Irish History, 1800–2000* (Oxford: Oxford University Press, 2003), 24–37.

  18. Though Young Ireland's efforts to remove British rule were unsuccessful, two of their main leaders and intellectuals, Thomas Davis and John Mitchel, influenced Irish and Irish-American nationalism. Niamh Lynch, "Live Ireland, Perish the Empire: Irish Nationalist Anti-Imperialism, c. 1840–1900" (PhD diss., Boston College, 2006). The Fenian movement was actually made up of two separate but complementary organizations in Ireland and the United States. Actively planning to spark a revolution against British rule in Ireland, the movement was put down quickly by British authorities. In the United States, the Fenians split; one faction launched two disastrous attacks on Canada and was apprehended by American government officials. For more on the Fenians in Ireland, see R. V. Comerford, *The Fenians in Context: Irish Politics and Society, 1848–82* (Dublin: Wolfhound Press, 1998); John Newsinger, *The Fenians in Mid-Victorian Britain* (London: Pluto Press, 1994); Owen McGee, *The IRB: The Irish Republican Brotherhood from the Land League to Sinn Féin* (Dublin: Four Courts Press, 2007), 15–37. On Fenianism in the United States, see William D'Arcy, *The Fenian Movement in the United States: 1858–1886* (Washington, DC: Catholic University of America Press, 1947); Mabel Gregory Walker,

The Fenian Movement (Colorado Springs, CO: R. Myles, 1969); Wilfried Neidhart, *Fenianism in North America* (University Park: Pennsylvania State University Press, 1975); Patrick Steward and Bryan McGovern, *The Fenians: Irish Rebellion in the North Atlantic World, 1858–1876* (Knoxville: University of Tennessee Press, 2013).

19. Terry Golway, *Irish Rebel: John Devoy and America's Fight for Ireland's Freedom* (New York: St. Martin's Press, 1998), 69–72.

20. Brown, *Irish-American Nationalism*, xiv.

21. Michael Glazier, ed., *The Encyclopedia of the Irish in America* (Notre Dame, IN: University of Notre Dame Press, 1999), 454.

22. See Dale Knobel, *Paddy and the Republic: Ethnicity and Nationality in Antebellum America* (Middletown, CT: Wesleyan University Press, 1986); Kerby Miller, *Emigrants and Exiles: Ireland and the Irish Exodus to North America* (New York: Oxford University Press, 1985); Brown, *Irish-American Nationalism*, 17–41.

23. Carla King, *Michael Davitt* (Dundalk: Dundalgan Press, 1999), 10–11.

24. T. W. Moody, *Davitt and Irish Revolution, 1846–82* (Oxford: Clarendon Press, 1981), 145. For more on Davitt's later career see Laurence Marley, *Michael Davitt: Freelance Radical and Frondeur* (Dublin: Four Courts Press, 2007); Laura McNeil, "Land, Labor, and Liberation: Michael Davitt and the Irish Question in the Age of British Democratic Reform, 1870–1906" (PhD diss., Boston College, 2002).

25. In his examination of the "New Departure," T. W. Moody argues that there were three distinct New Departures that took place in the 1870s. The first, in 1873, was marked by the support given by Fenians to Isaac Butt's home rule movement, the second in 1878 being Devoy's offering of an alliance with Parnell, and the third in 1879 after Michael Davitt's formation of the Land League. This is discussed further in Philip Bull, *Land, Politics, and Nationalism: A Study of the Irish Land Question* (Dublin: Gill and Macmillan, 1996), 86–87. For Devoy's interpretation of the terms of the New Departure, see a series of articles published by Devoy in *Gaelic American*, 9 June–3 November 1906. The author would like to thank Brandon Corcoran for sharing his work on the New Departure.

26. Bull, *Land, Politics, and Nationalism*, 95–100.

27. For a contemporary account of the Land League in Ireland, see Michael Davitt, *The Fall of Feudalism in Ireland, or the Story of the Land League Revolution* (Shannon, Ireland: Irish University Press, 1970). For general histories of the Land League in Ireland, see Samuel Clark, *Social Origins of the Irish Land War* (Princeton, NJ: Princeton University Press, 1979); Norman Dunbar Palmer, *The Irish Land League Crisis* (New Haven, CT: Yale University Press, 1940); Paul Bew, *Land and the National Question in Ireland, 1858–82* (Atlantic Highlands, NJ: Humanities Press, 1979); Margaret O'Callaghan, *British High Politics and a Nationalist Ireland: Criminality, Land, and the Law under Forster and Balfour* (Cork: Cork University Press, 1994); James S. Donnelly, Jr., *The Land and the People of Nineteenth-Century Cork: The Rural Economy and the Land Question* (London: Routledge and Kegan Paul, 1975), 251–307. For local studies, see Donald E. Jordan, *Land and Popular Politics in Ireland: County Mayo from the Plantation to the Land War* (Cambridge: Cambridge University Press, 1994); J. W. H. Carter, *The Land War and Its Leaders in Queen's County, 1879–82* (Portlaoise, Ireland: Leinster Express Newspapers, 1994).

Chapter 1. The "Uncrowned King of Ireland"

1. Brown, *Irish-American Nationalism*, 103. For more on Parnell's tour, see Michael Hazel, "First Link: Parnell's American Tour, 1880," *Éire-Ireland* 15, no. 1 (1980): 6–24. See also Alan O'Day, "Media and Power: Charles Stewart Parnell's 1880 Mission to North America," in *Information, Media, and Power through the Ages*, ed. Hiram Morgan (Dublin: University College Dublin Press, 2001), 202–21; Louis A. Parnell, "Charles Stewart Parnell's Land League Mission to America, January to March 1880" (MA thesis, Butler University, 1971), 1–111; Virgilius, *Parnell; or Ireland and America* (New York: Printed for the Publisher, 1880), 1–104; Michael Davitt, *Fall of Feudalism*, 193–210; F. S. L. Lyons, *Charles Stewart Parnell* (London: Collins, 1977), 106–15. For regional studies of Parnell's tour, see John R. O'Connor, "Parnell Visits 'The Ireland of America,'" *The Register of the Kentucky Historical Society*, 69 no. 2 (1971): 140–49; Kenneth E. Calton, "Parnell's Mission to Iowa," *Annals of Iowa* 15 (April 1940): 312–27; Robert Post, "Charles Stewart Parnell before Congress," *The Quarterly Journal of Speech* 51, no. 4 (December 1965): 419–25.

2. R. Barry O'Brien, *The Life of Charles Stewart Parnell*, vol. 1 (New York: Greenwood Press, 1969), 206.

3. The Penal Laws privileged members of the Church of Ireland and discriminated against all nonmembers, including the Catholic majority, placing restrictions on occupations, land ownership, and access to electoral politics and political office.

4. For the United Irishmen, see Kevin Whelan, *The Tree of Liberty: Radicalism, Catholicism, and the Construction of Irish Identity, 1760–1830* (Notre Dame, IN: University of Notre Dame Press, 1996); Marianne Elliott, *Wolfe Tone: Prophet of Irish Independence* (New Haven, CT: Yale University Press, 1989). For the United Irishmen and the United States, see David A. Wilson, *United Irishmen, United States: Immigrant Radicals in the Early Republic* (Ithaca, NY: Cornell University Press, 1998); David Brundage, "Matilda Tone in America: Exile, Gender, and Memory in the Making of Irish Republican Nationalism," *New Hibernia Review* 14, no. 1 (Spring 2010): 96–111.

5. Oliver MacDonagh, *The Emancipist: Daniel O'Connell, 1830–1847* (London: Weidenfeld and Nicolson, 1989), 84.

6. Thomas Bartlett, *Ireland: A History* (Cambridge: Cambridge University Press, 2010), 268–69.

7. Angela Murphy, *American Slavery, Irish Freedom: Abolition, Immigrant Citizenship, and the Transatlantic Movement for Irish Repeal* (Baton Rouge: Louisiana State University Press, 2010), 198–200.

8. Kevin Kenny, *The American Irish: A History* (Harlow, UK: Pearson Education, 2000), 91.

9. For the development of these views of the Irish within the British government and general British population, see Peter Gray, *Famine, Land, and Politics: British Government and Irish Society, 1843–1850* (Dublin: Irish Academic Press, 1999). See also James S. Donnelly, Jr., *The Great Irish Potato Famine* (Gloucestershire, England: Sutton Publishing, 2001); Cormac Ó Gráda, *Black '47 and Beyond: The Great Irish Famine in History, Economy, and Memory* (Princeton, NJ: Princeton University Press, 1999).

10. For the Fenians in Ireland, see Comerford, *Fenians in Context*; McGee, *IRB*; Fearghal McGarry and James McConnel, eds., *The Black Hand of Republicanism: Fenianism in Modern Ireland* (Dublin: Irish Academic Press, 2009). For the Fenians in the United States, see D'Arcy, *Fenian Movement*; Steward and McGovern, *Fenians*.

11. Comerford, *Fenians in Context*, 111.

12. Bartlett, *Ireland: A History*, 301.

13. Alvin Jackson, *Ireland, 1798-1998: Politics and War* (Oxford: Blackwell, 1999), 103.

14. Robert Kee, *The Green Flag: A History of Irish Nationalism* (London: Penguin Books, 2000), 345.

15. There remained, though, a sustained backlash against Fenians and Irish nationalism among the British public. Part of this is explained by the use of a bomb in London in December 1867 during an attempt to free a Fenian leader held in Clerkenwell prison. When the bomb exploded, it resulted in 12 civilian deaths and injuries to 120 more. This led to widespread anger and fear throughout English society. For more on the Clerkenwell bombing and the Skirmishing Campaign of the 1870s, see Niall Whelehan, *The Dynamiters: Irish Nationalism and Political Violence in the Wider World, 1867-1900* (Cambridge: Cambridge University Press, 2013), 71-75.

16. Jackson, *Home Rule*, 28.

17. David Thornley, *Isaac Butt and Home Rule* (London: Macgibbon and Kee, 1964), 100-101.

18. Ibid., 380.

19. Jackson, *Home Rule*, 32; Thornley, *Isaac Butt and Home Rule*, 216-19.

20. Ibid., 33.

21. Michael F. Funchion, ed., *Irish American Voluntary Organizations* (Westport, CT: Greenwood Press, 1983), 74-75.

22. Quoted in John Devoy, *Michael Davitt*, ed. Carla King and W. J. McCormack (Dublin: University College Dublin Press, 2008), 2.

23. T. W. Moody, "The New Departure in Irish Politics, 1878-9," in *Essays in British and Irish History in Honour of James Eadie Todd*, ed. H. A. Cronne, T. W. Moody, and D. B. Quinn (London: Frederick Muller, 1949), 321. Devoy had published this telegram because he believed in error that Parnell had finally broken with Butt. Davitt, who had been on tour when the telegram was published, thought that the publication of the telegram had been a mistake. In January 1879, the IRB Supreme Council rejected the terms of the New Departure because of a fear that involvement in political movements would undermine the purity of the movement, although they allowed for individual IRB members to follow their own consciences in deciding whether to support these activities. See McGee, *IRB*, 61.

24. Samuel Clark, *Social Origins of the Irish Land War* (Princeton, NJ: Princeton University Press, 1979), 107.

25. Donal McCarthy, "Parnell, Davitt, and the Land Question," in *Famine, Land, and Culture in Ireland*, ed. Carla King (Dublin: University College Dublin Press, 2000), 71.

26. Ibid.

27. Barbara Lewis Solow, *The Land Question and the Irish Economy, 1870–1903* (Cambridge, MA: Harvard University Press, 1971), 122.

28. McCarthy, "Parnell, Davitt, and the Land Question," 71.

29. Miller, *Emigrants and Exiles*, 399. Kerby Miller notes that deaths directly attributable to malnutrition remained low because of the large sums of donations for relief coming from Irish-American and British sources and the availability in many areas of imported cornmeal.

30. Ibid. For the decline of the Irish agricultural economy, see also Donnelly, *Land and the People of Nineteenth-Century Cork*, 251–57.

31. Anne Kane, *Constructing Irish National Identity: Discourse and Ritual during the Land War, 1879–1882* (London: Palgrave Macmillan, 2011), 58.

32. Solow, *The Land Question and the Irish Economy*, 127–28.

33. Miller, *Emigrants and Exiles*, 388.

34. James Fintan Lalor, *"The Faith of a Felon" and Other Writings*, edited by Marta Ramón (Dublin: University College Dublin Press, 2012), 17–21. There has been a debate among historians on just how influential Lalor was on the Land League. In *Fall of Feudalism* Davitt called Lalor "the prophet of Irish revolutionary land reform." But Davitt's biographer, T. W. Moody, claims that Davitt did not read Lalor's writings until 1880. Moody does believe that Lalor's ideas were known to John Devoy, and he may have helped transfer them into the New Departure. See Moody, *Davitt and Irish Revolution*, 36–37.

35. Quoted in Moody, *Davitt and Irish Revolution*, 36.

36. John Rodden, "'The lever must be applied in Ireland': Marx, Engels, and the Irish Question," *The Review of Politics* 70 (2008): 609–40. See also Fintan Lane, *The Origins of Modern Irish Socialism, 1881–1896* (Cork: Cork University Press, 1997), 19–27; Karl Marx and Frederick Engels, *Ireland and the Irish Question: A Collection of Writings by Karl Marx and Frederick Engels* (New York: International Publishers, 1972); Richard English, *Irish Freedom: The History of Nationalism in Ireland* (London: Pan Books, 2006), 172–77.

37. Moody, "New Departure in Irish Politics," 329.

38. See introduction for further discussion of the New Departure.

39. McGee, *IRB*, 61–62.

40. For more on the formation of the Mayo Land League, see Moody, *Davitt and Irish Revolution*, 316–20; Jordan, *Land and Popular Politics in Ireland*, 244–45.

41. Moody, "New Departure in Irish Politics," 332.

42. *Irish-American*, 1 November 1879, 1.

43. Golway, *Irish Rebel*, 125.

44. *New York Herald*, 10 November 1879, 5.

45. For more on Irish-American remittances to Ireland, see Robert A. Doan, "Green Gold to Emerald Shores: Irish Immigration to the United States and Transatlantic Monetary Aid, 1854–1923" (PhD diss., Temple University, 1999).

46. William O'Brien and Desmond Ryan, eds., *Devoy's Post Bag, 1871–1928*, vol. 1 (Dublin: C. J. Fallon, 1948), 457.

47. Mulligan, "Forgotten 'Greater Ireland,'" 226.

48. W. O'Brien and Ryan, *Devoy's Post Bag*, 1:456 (emphasis in original).

49. For more on Charles Stewart, see Claude G. Berube and John A. Rodgaard, *A Call to the Sea: Captain Charles Stewart of the USS Constitution* (Washington, DC: Potomac Books, 2005).

50. For a further discussion of Parnell's activities during this first visit, see John D. Gair and Cordelia C. Humphrey, "The Alabama Dimension to the Political Thought of Charles Stewart Parnell," *Alabama Review* 52, no. 1 (1999): 21–50. John Howard Parnell, Parnell's brother who owned a peach farm in Alabama, noticed the strange coincidence that the woman who jilted his brother, Mary Woods, shared the same maiden name as the great love of Charles Stewart Parnell, Katherine O'Shea (née Woods). Gair and Humphrey argue that Parnell's 1870s experiences in America played a substantial role in forming his later political thought. Their argument, however, is weakened by their reliance primarily on John Howard Parnell's memoirs, published in 1914, and various scholars disagree on this memoir's veracity.

51. *Irish-American*, 3 January 1880, 1.

52. Dennis Clark, *Hibernia America: The Irish and Regional Cultures* (New York: Greenwood Press, 1986), 58.

53. Ibid., 59.

54. Interview reprinted in *Freeman's Journal* (Dublin), 13 January 1880, 4. For a list of cities visited by Parnell during his tour, see appendix.

55. Ibid.

56. Ibid.

57. Ibid.

58. Ibid.

59. Lyons, *Charles Stewart Parnell*, 105.

60. Philip Bagenal, *The American Irish and Their Influence on Irish Politics* (London: Kegan, Paul, Trench, and Co., 1882), 202.

61. "Captain Moonlight" was a term used to describe anonymous agrarian violence in Ireland.

62. *Irish-American*, 17 January 1880, 1.

63. Ibid. Money given to the Land League was usually spent per the wishes of donors.

64. Ibid.

65. Ibid.

66. Ibid.

67. Ibid.

68. *Catholic Union*, 15 January 1880, 4.

69. Under pressure from the British government, Drexel Morgan and Company removed themselves as the receiver of Land League funds. The fund was then taken up by the Maverick National Bank of Boston.

70. Davitt, *Fall of Feudalism*, 209.

71. Ibid., 207.

72. *Missouri Republican*, 5 March 1880, 1.

73. Robert M. Post, "A Rhetorical Criticism of the Speeches Delivered by Charles Stewart Parnell during His 1880 American Tour" (PhD diss., Ohio State University, 1961), 169.

74. Miller, *Emigrants and Exiles*, 495.

75. O'Day, "Media and Power," 203.

76. *New York Herald*, 21 January 1880, 6.

77. Boston *Globe*, 13 January 1880, 1.

78. Quoted in the *Cincinnati Daily Enquirer*, 21 February 1880.

79. William Grace, *The Irish in America* (Chicago: McDannell Bros., 1886), 26.

80. Michael J. F. McCarthy, *The Irish Revolution*, vol. 1, *The Murdering Time, from the Land League to the First Home Rule Bill* (Edinburgh: William Blackwood and Sons, 1912), 94.

81. J. J. Lee, "Millennial Reflections on Irish-American History," *Radharc* 1 (November 2000): 36.

82. *Pilot*, 13 March 1880, 4. Parnell and Healy were in Canada for a few days near the very end of Parnell's tour. Their reception in Canada was as positive as in America.

83. *Catholic Universe*, 29 January 1880, 1.

84. John Mitchel, *The Last Conquest of Ireland (Perhaps)* (Dublin: University College Dublin Press, 2005), 219. For an excellent discussion of the construction of the memory of the famine, see Donnelly, *Great Irish Potato Famine*, 209–45; Miller, *Emigrants and Exiles*, 281–344.

85. *Chicago Tribune*, 24 February 1880, 8.

86. *Irish World*, 6 March 1880, 8. Two newspapers in Cincinnati use different language in their transcriptions of the speech. See Pat Power, transcriber, *Charles Stewart Parnell in Cincinnati, Ohio: An Account of a Visit by the Irish Patriot to the City of Cincinnati, February 20, 1880* (Cincinnati Historical Society, 2002).

87. For an extensive discussion of Parnell's speech in Cincinnati, see Lyons, *Charles Stewart Parnell*, 111–13.

88. *Pilot*, 20 March 1880, 4.

89. *Cleveland Universe*, 29 January 1880, 1. Patrick Sarsfield was an Irish Jacobite and esteemed Irish military leader who later exiled himself to France as part of the famous "Flight of the Wild Geese."

90. *Missouri Republican*, 5 March 1880, 2.

91. Florence Gibson, *The Attitudes of the New York Irish Toward State and National Affairs, 1848–1892* (New York: Columbia University Press, 1951), 332–33; *Irish World*, 6 March 1880, 5.

92. *Irish World*, 6 March 1880, 5. See also Post, "Charles Stewart Parnell before Congress," 419–25.

93. *Pilot*, 20 March 1880, 4.

94. Description based on a meeting in Chicago found in Post, "Rhetorical Criticism," 427. See also James Hunter, *For the People's Cause: From the Writings of John Murdoch—Highland and Irish Land Reformer* (Edinburgh: Crofters Commission, 1986), 183; Dennis Clark, *The Irish Relations: Trials of an Immigrant Tradition* (Rutherford, NJ: Associated University Press, 1982), 69.

95. *Missouri Republican*, 5 March 1880, 1.

96. *Redpath's Illustrated Weekly*, 9 November 1882, 7.

97. Megan Harrigan Joyce, "Elizabeth Gurley Flynn" (MA thesis, Wright State University, 1995), 24, 29. Elizabeth Gurley Flynn was a prominent orator and organizer for several twentieth-century radical movements including the Industrial Workers of the World, American Civil Liberties Union, and the United States Communist Party.

98. Hunter, *For the People's Cause*, 184; Michael J. Boyle Diary, Michael J. Boyle Papers, Diaries Box 1, Volume 5 (1880), Minnesota Historical Society. John Murdoch, the Scottish reformer, was in America during the time of Parnell's tour and shared the stage with him on several occasions, though Parnell and Dillon kept Murdoch at arm's length. For more on Murdoch in America, see also McNeil, "Land, Labor, and Liberation," 47–54.

99. William O'Brien, *Recollections* (New York: The Macmillan Company, 1905), 239.

100. *Catholic Union*, 29 January 1880, 4.

101. Alexander Sullivan, "Parnell as a Leader," *North American Review* 144, no. 6 (June 1887): 612–13.

102. Boston *Globe*, 13 January 1880, 1.

103. Ibid.

104. Ibid., 4.

105. Ralph Korngold, *Two Friends of Man: The Story of William Lloyd Garrison and Wendell Phillips and Their Relationship with Abraham Lincoln* (Boston: Little, Brown, and Company, 1950), 389.

106. Author's personal correspondence with Debby Applegate. The *Irish World* denounced the inclusion of Beecher in the Brooklyn demonstration because of his recent involvement in a prominent sex scandal. See *Irish World*, 10 January 1880, 2. For more on Beecher, see Debby Applegate, *The Most Famous Man in America: The Biography of Henry Ward Beecher* (New York: Doubleday, 2006).

107. *Brooklyn Daily Eagle*, 9 January 1880, 4. For more on Wendell Phillips, see James Brewer Stewart, *Wendell Phillips: Liberty's Hero* (Baton Rouge: Louisiana State University Press, 1986).

108. Ibid.

109. Charles Horner, *The Life of James Redpath and the Development of the Modern Lyceum* (New York: Barse and Hopkins, 1926), 254. Redpath's letters from Ireland were reprinted widely in American and Irish-American newspapers.

110. John Krieg, *Whitman and the Irish* (Iowa City: University of Iowa Press, 2000), 135. Unfortunately, it is unclear what Whitman's personal feelings on the Irish land question were. He was also close to John Boyle O'Reilly.

111. *Chicago Tribune*, 10 May 1880, 3.

112. *Catholic Union*, 2 September 1880, 6; Doan, "Green Gold to Emerald Shores," 101; *Irish-American*, 17 July 1880, 4.

113. *Irish-American*, 17 July 1880, 4.

114. *New York Herald*, 3 January 1880, 4.

115. *Pilot*, 12 June 1880, 4.

116. *Pilot*, 20 March 1880, 1.

117. *Pilot*, 13 March 1880, 4.

118. For an example of the conflict found between the Catholic Church and other Irish-American nationalist organizations, see Kevin Kenny, "The Molly Maguires and the Catholic Church," *Labor History* 36 (Summer 1995): 345–76.

119. For the anti-Irish bias of the *New York Times*, see Michael Gordon, *The Orange Riots: Irish Political Violence in New York City, 1870 and 1871* (Ithaca, NY: Cornell University Press, 1993), 165–67.

120. *New York Times*, 5 January 1880, 4.

121. *New York Herald*, 10 November 1879, 6.

122. *New York Herald*, 30 November 1879, 6.

123. *New York Herald*, 5 December 1879, 4.

124. *New York Herald*, 3 December 1879, 6.

125. Lyons, *Charles Stewart Parnell*, 107. Bennett was known for staging publicity stunts (he had organized Morton Stanley's mission to find Dr. David Livingston in Africa), and he probably hoped that his philanthropic efforts in Ireland would bring him and his paper great acclaim.

126. *New York Herald*, 3 December 1879, 6.

127. Ibid.

128. L. Perry Curtis, *Apes and Angels: The Irishman in Victorian Caricature* (Washington, DC: Smithsonian Institution Press, 1997), 65. See also, Leroy V. Eid, "*Puck* and the Irish: 'The One American Idea,'" *Éire Ireland* 11 (1976): 18–35.

129. *New York Herald*, 11 November 1880, 1.

130. *Puck* (New York), 31 December 1879, 696 (emphasis in original).

131. *Puck*, 19 October 1881. See also *Puck*'s cartoon on O'Donovan Rossa titled "Gorilla Warfare Under the Protection of the American Flag," *Puck*, 19 March 1884. For a fuller discussion of depictions of the Irish in editorial cartoons, specifically English-based newspapers, see R. F. Foster, *Paddy and Mr. Punch: Connections in Irish and English History* (London: A. Lane, 1993); and Michael De Nie, *The Eternal Paddy: Irish Identity and the English Press, 1798–1882* (Madison: University of Wisconsin Press, 2004).

132. *Catholic Universe*, 29 January 1880, 4.

133. Ibid.

134. *Harper's Weekly*, 7 February 1880, 8. *Harper's Weekly*, and especially its star cartoonist, Thomas Nast, saw the Irish in America as a drain on the Republic and little more than pawns of the Democratic Party. See also Virgilius, *Parnell*, 8.

135. Boston *Globe*, 12 January 1880, 2.

136. *Daily Morning Call* (San Francisco), 15 February 1880, 2.

137. For more on the American press reaction to Parnell, see Post, "Rhetorical Criticism," 165–68.

138. *ICBU Journal*, February 1880, 1.

139. Côté, *Fanny and Anna Parnell*, 119–21.

140. *Irish-American*, 13 March 1880, 5. Robert McWade claims that the first Land League branch in America was formed in Cleveland in 1879. However, an examination

of the Cleveland newspapers does not support this. St. Louis and Rochester, New York, claim to be the first branches as well. See William Hyde and Howard Conrad, eds., *Encyclopedia of the History of St. Louis*, vol. 2 (St. Louis: Southern History Company, 1899), 1222; *Daily Union and Advertiser* (Rochester, NY), 2 February 1880, 2.

141. *Daily Union and Advertiser*, 2 February 1880, 2.

142. Circular from Charles Stewart Parnell and John Dillon on behalf of the Irish National Land League, St. Louis, March 4, 1880, Reel 2, Terence V. Powderly Papers, The American Catholic History Research Center and University Archives, Catholic University of America, Washington, DC.

143. John Devoy, *The Land of Eire: The Irish Land League, Its Origins and Consequences* (Boston: Patterson and Neilson, 1882), 67.

144. Ibid.

145. *Catholic Union and Times*, 15 April 1880, 3.

146. Ibid.

147. W. O'Brien and Ryan, *Devoy's Post Bag*, 1:484.

148. Ibid., 500.

149. Quoted in Frank Callahan, *T. M. Healy* (Cork: Cork University Press, 1996), 35.

150. T. M. Healy, *Letters and Leaders of My Day*, vol. 1 (New York: Frederick A. Stokes Company, 1929), 85.

Chapter 2. "An Agitator of the Best Kind"

1. W. O'Brien and Ryan, *Devoy's Post Bag*, 1:510.

2. Moody, *Davitt and Irish Revolution*, 376.

3. Conor Cruise O'Brien, *Parnell and His Party, 1880–1890* (Oxford: Oxford University Press, 1974), 26. Parnell ultimately decided to represent Cork.

4. J. E. Devlin to Patrick Collins, 27 April 1880, Patrick Collins Papers, Box 1, Folder 9, John J. Burns Library, Boston College, Chestnut Hill, MA (hereafter BC).

5. Moody, *Davitt and Irish Revolution*, 376.

6. *Pilot*, 17 July 1880, 4.

7. King, *Michael Davitt*, 22.

8. Peasant proprietorship meant the conversion of tenants into owner-occupiers.

9. Diaries and Records of Tours and Other Special Occasions, 18 May to 19 December 1880, Michael Davitt Papers, Trinity College Dublin (hereafter TCD), MS 9533/27.

10. Moody, *Davitt and Irish Revolution*, 306.

11. W. O'Brien, *Recollections*, 216.

12. D. B. Cashman, *The Life of Michael Davitt* (Boston: Murphy and Murphy Publishers, 1881), 226.

13. John Pomfret, *The Struggle for Land in Ireland, 1880–1923* (Princeton, NJ: Princeton University Press, 1930), 147. Over the course of the next two years, Davitt's views on the land question would grow gradually more radical, leading him to eventually support a plan for land nationalization, as discussed in chapter 8.

14. McNeil, "Land, Labor, and Liberation," 42.

15. King, *Michael Davitt*, 24–25.

16. Michael Davitt to Matt Harris, W. G. Fallon Papers, National Library of Ireland, Dublin (hereafter NLI), MS 22704.

17. McNeil, "Land, Labor, and Liberation," 40–41.

18. Moody, *Davitt and Irish Revolution*, 545–46. Davitt would finally break with Parnell when Parnell's affair with Katharine O'Shea became public in 1890.

19. *Pilot*, 10 April 1880, 1.

20. Devoy, *Land of Eire*, 2.

21. *Pilot*, 10 April 1880, 1.

22. *Pilot*, 29 May 1880, 1.

23. Ibid.

24. Ibid.

25. Ibid.

26. Ibid.

27. Ibid., 6.

28. Ibid., 6.

29. *First Annual Convention of the Irish National Land League, held at Buffalo, New York, January 12th and 13th, 1881* (Richmond, VA: P. Keenan, 1881), 12.

30. *Pilot*, 29 May 1880, 1.

31. Ibid.

32. British Consulate General, New York, May 14, 1880, Fenian "A" Files 3/714, Box 5/A622, National Archives of Ireland (hereafter NAI), Dublin, Ireland.

33. *Pilot*, 29 May 1880, 6; Boston *Globe*, 13 January 1881, 1. Patrick Collins believed that the president and secretary of the League should come from the same city because of the close collaboration required between the two offices.

34. *Pilot*, 29 May 1880, 4.

35. *Irish-American*, 19 June 1880, 5.

36. Ibid.

37. Michael Davitt Papers, MS 9533/22, TCD.

38. *Irish-American*, 5 June 1880, 1.

39. Ibid.

40. *Irish World*, 27 November 1880, 8.

41. Anna Parnell to Michael Davitt, Michael Davitt Papers, MS 9378-1088, TCD.

42. McNeil, "Land, Labor, and Liberation," 68.

43. Patrick Ford publicly supported the nationalization of land in Ireland and the United States from the mid-1870s through the late 1880s. James Paul Rodechko, *Patrick Ford and His Search for America: A Case Study of Irish-American Journalism, 1870–1913* (New York: Arno Press, 1976), 71.

44. Davitt, *Fall of Feudalism*, 257–58. See also Philip A. Bagenal, *The American Irish and Their Influence on Irish Politics* (n.p.: Jerome S. Ozer, 1971), 220–29; Brown, *Irish-American Nationalism*, 104–11.

45. Michael Davitt to John Devoy, 17 June 1880, Devoy Papers, MS 18003/6, NLI.

46. Davitt, *Fall of Feudalism*, 257.

47. This thesis, first proposed by Thomas Brown, will be discussed in detail in chapter 4. Brown, *Irish-American Nationalism*, 24–25.

48. Ibid.

49. *Irish World*, 10 July 1880, 4.

50. *Pilot*, 26 June 1880, 1.

51. Moody, *Davitt and Irish Revolution*, 414.

52. Edward O'Donnell, "'Though Not an Irishman': Henry George and the American Irish," *American Journal of Economics and Sociology* 56, no. 4 (October 1997): 457.

53. Moody, *Davitt and Irish Revolution*, 414.

54. Michael Davitt to John Devoy, 17 June 1880, John Devoy Papers, MS 18003/6, NLI.

55. Two examples during his tour illustrate Davitt's modest demeanor. In Chicago, arriving late in the evening, he was unable to get a hotel room and was forced to attempt to sleep in a doorstep, until he was awoken by an Irish policeman and ordered to show identification. After learning his identity, the officer apologized profusely for Chicago's lack of hospitality and immediately found him lodging in a German hotel. The San Francisco *Monitor* wrote of his initial arrival in California that "the expression of mingled gratification and disappointment on the faces of the passengers was amusing to behold" as his fellow passengers only discovered Davitt's identity when the Reception Committee boarded the train. Davitt, *Fall of Feudalism*, 401; *Monitor*, 23 September 1880, 1.

56. For Davitt's complete itinerary see appendix.

57. Diaries and Records of Tours and Other Special Occasions, 18 May to 19 December 1880, Michael Davitt Papers, MS 9429–2526, TCD.

58. *Irish World*, 21 August 1880, 5.

59. The *ICBU Journal* was the journal of the Irish Catholic Benevolent Union. On Griffin, see Martin Griffin Papers, Box 8, Folder 3, Philadelphia Archdiocesan Historical Research Center, Wynnewood, PA. See also D. Clark, *Irish Relations*, 114–19.

60. *Pilot*, 29 May 1880, 1.

61. Ibid.

62. Davitt, *Fall of Feudalism*, 252.

63. *Irish World*, 4 September 1880, 5.

64. *Missouri Republican*, 23 August 1880, 4.

65. *Irish World*, 21 August 1880, 5.

66. Quoted in James Patrick Walsh, "Michael Mooney and the Leadville Irish: Respectability and Resistance at 10,200 Feet, 1875–1900" (PhD diss., University of Colorado, 2010), 208. Davitt made a similar argument in a speech in Cincinnati as well. See *Irish World*, 28 August 1880, 1.

67. Ibid.

68. Moody, *Davitt and Irish Revolution*, 404.

69. Ibid., 407.

70. *Monitor*, 23 September 1880, 4. San Francisco was the center of a large anti-Chinese nativist movement headed by the popular Irish-American orator Denis Kearney.

71. Ibid.

72. Ibid., 5.

73. Here 1867 refers to the failed Fenian uprisings in Ireland and attacks on Canada by Irish-American Fenians.

74. *Monitor*, 23 September 1880, 5.

75. *Irish World*, 16 October 1880, 5.

76. Moody, *Davitt and Irish Revolution*, 409.

77. Ibid.

78. *Catholic Sentinel*, 20 September 1880, 2. His friend Henry George held strong anti-Chinese views, but whether these had any influence over Davitt is unknown.

79. *Irish World*, "Land League Fund" totals, March–April 1880.

80. Michael Davitt, *Speech Delivered by Michael Davitt in Defence of the Land League* (London: Kegan, Paul, Trench, Trüber and Co., 1890), 77–78. See also *Irish World*, 6 November 1880, 5.

81. King, *Michael Davitt*, 22.

82. Moody, *Davitt and Irish Revolution*, 381.

83. Devoy, *Land of Eire*, 74.

84. Brown, *Irish-American Nationalism*, 110.

85. For the breakdown of Davitt and Devoy's friendship, see Moody, *Davitt and Irish Revolution*, 441–42.

86. Boston *Globe*, 7 November 1880, 8.

87. Boston *Globe*, 9 November 1880, 8.

88. The Ladies' Land League will be discussed in detail in chapter 6.

89. *Irish World*, 20 November 1880, 1; Moody, *Davitt and Irish Revolution*, 415.

90. *Monitor*, 19 August 1880, 1.

91. The Land League argued that rents should be based on the values ascribed in Griffith's valuation, which was a survey undertaken in Ireland from 1848 to 1864. The term "boycott" came from the actions taken by County Mayo Land League activists to publicly shame and isolate imported tenants brought in by Captain Charles Boycott, land agent of Lord Erne, to replace striking tenants.

92. F. S. L. Lyons, *John Dillon: A Biography* (Chicago: University of Chicago Press, 1968), 43. The charged leaders were Parnell, Joseph Biggar, Michael Boyton, Thomas Brennan, John Dillon, Patrick Egan, Patrick Gordon, Matt Harris, J. W. Nally, Michael O'Sullivan, Thomas Sexton, Francis Sheridan, T. D. Sullivan, and John W. Walshe.

93. Moody, *Davitt and Irish Revolution*, 455.

94. Being a parolee on ticket-of-leave meant that Davitt's release was conditional and could be revoked if he acted in a manner deemed by the British authorities to be out of order. The fact that the British government had allowed Davitt free rein since 1878 clearly demonstrates that his rearrest was a political measure intended to hamper the Land League agitation in Ireland.

95. McNeil, "Land, Labor, and Liberation," 71.

96. Bernhard O'Hara, *Davitt* (Castlebar: Mayo County Council, 2006), 59–60.

97. Ibid.

98. Funchion, *Irish American Voluntary Organizations*, 191; Brown, *Irish-American Nationalism*, 112.

99. Brown, *Irish-American Nationalism*, 112.

100. *Irish World*, 26 February 1881, 8.

101. *ICBU Journal*, February 1881, 4.

102. *ICBU Journal*, March 1881, 4.

103. British Consul General, 9 February 1881, Fenian "A" Files 3/715, Box 5/A639, NAI.

Chapter 3. From Plymouth Rock to the Golden Gate

1. *First Annual Convention of the Irish National Land League*, 16.

2. Ibid.

3. Devoy, *Land of Eire*, 78.

4. Brown, *Irish-American Nationalism*, 112.

5. *Irish-American*, 12 February 1881, 8. "Bael-fires" refer to an earlier Irish practice of lighting bonfires on hilltops to warn villages of oncoming invaders.

6. *Second Quarterly Report of the Irish National Land League United States for Quarter Ending July 10th, 1881* (n.p.: n.p., 1881), 1.

7. Grace McDonald, *History of the Irish in Wisconsin in the Nineteenth Century* (New York: Arno Press, 1976), 243–44.

8. *Irish-American*, 19 March 1881, 1.

9. *Second Quarterly Report of the Irish National Land League United States*, 1.

10. *Irish World*, 10 January 1880, 4.

11. It is impossible for the author to determine exactly how many and which branches of the Land League affiliated themselves with the American Land League established at Buffalo or the *Irish World* Land League. In this book, references to the "American Land League" will refer to both organizations. Any disagreements over tactics, principles, and ideologies among branches or individuals will be implicitly noted.

12. *Irish World*, 19 March 1881, 4.

13. *Pilot*, 1 January 1881, 4.

14. Editorial published in *First Annual Convention of the Irish National Land League*, 30.

15. Ibid.

16. Ibid., 17.

17. *Pilot*, 1 May 1880, 1.

18. *Catholic Union*, 24 March 1881, 6.

19. *Pilot*, 29 January 1881, 5.

20. *Irish Nation*, 15 April 1882, 2.

21. Doan, "Green Gold to the Emerald Shores," 116–18.

22. *Monitor*, 7 April 1881, 3.

23. Margaret Sullivan, *Ireland of To-Day: Causes and Aims of Irish Agitation* (Philadelphia: J. C. McCurdy and Co., 1881), 384. Sullivan's estimate included members of the Ladies' Land League.

24. Miller, *Emigrants and Exiles*, 540.

25. In 1860, according to Dennis Clark, there were 84,000 Irish-born people in the southern states, a total smaller than that found in several northern cities. These numbers also remained relatively static as Irish immigration to the South had slowed considerably. Clark, *Hibernia America*, 99.

26. *Irish World*, 5 February 1881, 5. Unfortunately, this examination of the Land League in the South must be only cursory. Catholic or Irish-American papers during this period in the 1880s in New Orleans and Memphis proved impossible to obtain. The experience of Irish Catholics in the South remains understudied. The most complete book on the topic, David T. Gleeson's *The Irish in the South* (Chapel Hill: University of North Carolina Press, 2001), ends in 1877.

27. *Atlanta Daily Constitution*, 2 February 1881, 4.

28. Mary Doline O'Connor, *The Life and Letters of M. P. O'Connor* (New York: Dempsey and Carroll, 1893), 193–95.

29. David T. Gleeson and Brendan J. Buttimer, "'We Are Irish Everywhere': Irish Immigrant Networks in Charleston, South Carolina, and Savannah, Georgia," *Immigrants & Minorities* 23, nos. 2–3 (July–November 2005): 196.

30. *Irish World*, 12 August 1882, 8.

31. John Ellis, *The Irish Question: A Speech Delivered Before the Land League of the 6th District of New Orleans, at St. Stephen's Hall, New Orleans, Louisiana, on the Evening of March 17th, 1882* (Washington, DC: R. O. Polkinhorn, 1882), 12.

32. *AOH Journal*, February 1881, 4. Ryan's poem "The Conquered Banner" was one of the key precursors to the rise of "Lost Cause" ideology and interpretation of post–American Civil War Reconstruction.

33. Avery Meriwether, *English Tyranny and Irish Suffering: Dedicated to the Irish Land League of Memphis* (Memphis: R. M. Mansford, 1881), 27.

34. *Monitor*, 9 November 1881, 4.

35. *Catholic Sentinel*, 21 July 1881, 5.

36. David Emmons, *Beyond the American Pale: The Irish in the West, 1845–1910* (Norman: University of Oklahoma Press, 2010), 296.

37. Emmons, *Butte Irish*, 53.

38. Alexander Saxton, *The Indispensable Enemy: Labor and the Anti-Chinese Movement in California* (Berkeley: University of California Press, 1971), 115–56.

39. Ibid., 152–56. See also Timothy Sarbaugh, "Exiles of Confidence: The Irish-American Community of San Francisco, 1880–1920," in *From Paddy to Studs: Irish-American Communities in the Turn of the Century Era, 1880 to 1920*, ed. Timothy Meagher (Westport, CT: Greenwood Press, 1986), 164–65. The author would like to thank Andy Urban for helping place the anti-Chinese movement in San Francisco in context.

40. The author would like to thank one of the anonymous readers of this manuscript for highlighting this important point.

41. Walsh, "'A Fanatic Heart,'" 189–90.

42. Ibid., 191.

43. *First Annual Convention of the Irish National Land League*, 39.

44. *Western Home Journal*, 22 January 1881, 4.

45. *Western Home Journal*, 12 March 1881, 5.

46. *Pilot*, 5 February 1881, 1; *Irish World*, 26 February 1881, 2; James J. Green, "American Catholics and the Irish Land League, 1879–1882," *Catholic Historical Review* 35 (April 1949): 30.

47. Green, "American Catholics and the Irish Land League," 33.

48. Alfred Isacsson, *The Determined Doctor: The Story of Edward McGlynn* (Tarrytown, NY: Vestigium Press, 1998), 77. McGlynn would soon become famous, or infamous, for his support of Henry George's 1886 New York mayoral campaign. His refusal to withdraw his support would lead to his excommunication from the Catholic Church.

49. *Catholic Union*, 3 November 1881, 4.

50. *Monitor*, 19 August 1880, 1.

51. For San Francisco, *Monitor*, 7 July 1881, 4; for Philadelphia, *ICBU Journal*, September 1882, 4; for Cleveland, *Catholic Universe*, 17 August 1882, 4.

52. Angela Murphy, "Daniel O'Connell and the 'American Eagle' in 1845: Slavery, Diplomacy, Nativism, and the Collapse of America's First Irish Nationalist Movement," *Journal of American Ethnic History* 26, no. 2 (2007): 3–26.

53. *Irish World*, 4 September 1880, 8.

54. *Irish National Land League of the United States Constitution, Adopted January 13th, 1881 at Buffalo, N.Y.* (Boston: M. H. Kennan Printer, 1881), 9.

55. *Chicago Tribune*, 6 March 1880, 2; Boston *Pilot*, 22 May 1880, 5.

56. *Irish-American*, 12 March 1881, 4.

57. *Chicago Tribune*, 3 April 1881, 7.

58. *ICBU Journal*, October 1882, 4.

59. *ICBU Journal*, 11 April 1881, 5; *Irish World*, 25 March 1882, 4.

60. M. Heanne d'Arc O'Hare, "The Public Career of Patrick Andrew Collins" (PhD diss., Boston College, 1959), 138; *Donahoe's Magazine* 8, no. 5 (November 1882): 457–58.

61. O'Hare, "Public Career of Patrick Andrew Collins," 122.

62. Michael F. Funchion, "Irish Nationalists and Chicago Politics in the 1880s," *Éire-Ireland* 10, no. 2 (1975): 10–11.

63. Michael F. Funchion, *Chicago's Irish Nationalists, 1881–1890* (New York: Arno Press, 1976), 44.

64. Ibid., 49.

65. Ibid.

66. O'Hare, "Public Career of Patrick Andrew Collins," 202.

67. Victor Walsh, "Irish Nationalism and Land Reform: The Role of the Irish in America," in *Irish Studies 4*, ed. P. J. Drudy (Cambridge: Cambridge University Press, 1986), 266.

68. *ICBU Journal*, March 1881, 5; Martin Griffin Papers, Box 8, Folder 3, Philadelphia Archdiocesan Historical Research Center, Wynnewood, PA; *Irish-American*, 8 May 1880, 1.

69. *ICBU Journal*, January 1881, 6; British Consulate General Philadelphia, April, 4, 1881, Fenian "A" Files 3/714, Box 5/A663, NAI.

70. Dale Light, "Class, Ethnicity, and the Urban Ecology in a Nineteenth Century City: Philadelphia's Irish, 1840–1890" (PhD diss., University of Pennsylvania, 1972), 204.

71. *ICBU Journal*, April 1881, 5.

72. *ICBU Journal*, March 1882, 6.

73. *AOH Journal*, June 1880, 2; *Irish-American*, 29 May 1880, 4; *Pilot*, 18 December 1880, 4.

74. *ICBU Journal*, September 1881, 7.

75. *Proceedings of the Twelfth Annual Convention of the Irish Catholic Benevolent Union, held at Wilmington, Del., September 22nd, 23rd, and 25th, 1880* (Philadelphia: Kildare's Printing House, 1880), 16.

76. *AOH Journal*, June 1881, 4; June 1880, 2.

77. Copy of a Report of the Executive Bureau of the UB to the Officers and Members, April 19, 1880, Fenian "A" Files 3/714, Box 4/A619, NAI.

78. T. H. Ronayne to John Devoy, September 21, 1881, John Devoy Papers, MS 18011/8, NLI.

79. Kenny, *American Irish*, 143–44. An earlier attempt at Catholic colonization had failed in the 1850s. See Michael F. Funchion, "Irish Catholic Society for the Promotion of Actual Settlements in North America," in Funchion, *Irish American Voluntary Organizations*, 161–64. Deirdre Moloney notes the irony for modern readers of the fact that Irish Catholics chose to label their efforts "colonization" after their use of the term to describe England's political and economic dominance in Ireland, but she notes that "the term 'colonization' at that time carried with it the benign connotation of developing new settlements in seventeenth- and eighteenth-century North America." Moloney, "Land League Activism in Transnational Perspective," *U.S. Catholic Historian* 22, no. 3 (Summer 2004): 67.

80. James P. Shannon, *Catholic Colonization on the Western Frontier* (New Haven, CT: Yale University Press, 1957), 67–68.

81. Gerard Moran, "'Shovelling Out the Poor:' Assisted Emigration from Ireland from the Great Famine to the Fall of Parnell," in *To and From Ireland: Planned Migration Schemes, c. 1600–2000*, ed. Patrick Duffy (Dublin: Geography Publications, 2004), 141–42.

82. *Irish World*, 14 August 1880, 6.

83. *ICBU Journal*, October 1880, 6.

84. *Irish Catholic Colonization Association of the United States: The Secretary's Second Annual Report* (Chicago: n.p., 1881), 8.

85. Quoted in *Redpath's Illustrated Weekly*, 2 September 1882, 7.

86. Moran, "Shovelling Out the Poor," 146–48. For more on the development of New York's immigration policy, see Hidetaka Hirota, "'The Great Entrepot for Mendicants': Foreign Poverty and Immigration Control in New York State to 1882," *Journal of American Ethnic History* 33, no. 32 (2014): 5–32.

87. *Harper's Weekly*, 23 June 1883, 387.

88. Alexander Sullivan, *Emigration vs. Enforced Emigration: Addresses to Chester A. Arthur, President of the United States* (Philadelphia: Convention of the Irish Race, 1883), 1–14. The Irish National League was the successor organization to the Land League.

89. *ICBU Journal*, June 1883, 7.

90. *Redpath's Illustrated Weekly*, 9 September 1882, 3.

91. Moran, "Shovelling Out the Poor," 148.

92. J. A. Anderson, *A Life and Memoirs of Rev. C. F. X. Goldsmith* (Milwaukee: Press of the Evening Wisconsin Company, 1895), 293–95.

93. *Redpath's Illustrated Weekly*, 2 September 1882, 7.

94. Moran, "Shovelling Out the Poor," 148.

95. *ICBU Journal*, January 1881, 1; *Proceedings of the Fourteenth Annual Convention of the Irish Catholic Benevolent Union, held at Philadelphia, September 27th and September 28th, 1882* (Philadelphia: Kildare's Printing House, 1882), 10–11.

96. Kenny, *American Irish*, 144. Three settlements, first organized in 1881, that remain today in Minnesota are Parnell in Polk County, Croke in Swift County, and Tara in Traverse County.

97. Shannon, *Catholic Colonization on the Western Frontier*, 254.

Chapter 4. "Ireland to Us Is Father and Mother and America Is the Wife"

1. My examination of conservative Irish-American nationalism owes much to Thomas N. Brown's interpretation of Irish-American nationalism. Brown argues that Irish-American nationalism was based on middle-class Irish-Americans' eagerness for upward mobility and American acceptance. See Brown, *Irish-American Nationalism*.

2. Davitt, *Speech Delivered by Michael Davitt*, 144–46, Funchion, *Chicago's Irish Nationalists*, 63–64. Number of delegates by State: NY (61), MA (23), CT (11), PA (10), NJ (2), VA (2), MD (1), RI (1), IA (2), MI (1), NH (1), IL (1), OH (1)—also representing Ireland and America, James Redpath.

3. Like the vice president of the United States (or at least until recently), the office of vice president of the Land League lacked any real responsibility or power.

4. *Irish National Land League of the United States Constitution*, 6.

5. *First Annual Convention of the Irish National Land League*, 14.

6. Ibid., 16.

7. *Catholic Union and Times*, 3 March 1881, 4.

8. Membership list with members' street addresses found in the *Catholic Union*, December 30, 1880, 3; United States Census (1880), Schedule 1 (Population) via ancestry .com. The category "White collar workers" includes clerks, bookkeepers, and two city comptrollers. "Skilled Workers" includes a harness maker, railroad engineers, shoemakers, a hammer maker, carpenter, painter, blacksmiths, stonemasons, butchers, etc. The ten "Others" occupations are three women listed as "keeping house," one biss shoveler, one patrolman, one ale peddler, one agent for the railroad, one coal retailer, one clerk in an elevator, and one female servant.

9. William Jenkins, "Deconstructing Diasporas: Networks and Identities among the Irish in Buffalo and Toronto, 1870–1910," *Immigrants & Minorities* 23, nos. 2–3 (July–November 2005): 377.

10. Ibid.

11. Eric Foner has rightly criticized Brown's thesis that working-class life should be seen as "a transitional stage on the road to bourgeois respectability." Instead, Foner

argues that workers' aspirations "could mean a merger not with the dominant culture and its values, but with a strong emergent oppositional working-class culture." E. Foner, "Class, Ethnicity, and Radicalism," 195. I argue throughout the book that Irish-American nationalism existed along a broad ideological spectrum, with class, gender, and individual experience playing a large role in determining how and why Irish-American men and women supported ethnic nationalism.

12. Kenny, *American Irish*, 149.

13. Stephan Thernstrom, *Poverty and Progress: Social Mobility in a Nineteenth-Century City* (Cambridge, MA: Harvard University Press, 1964), 184–185.

14. Kenny, *American Irish*, 150; David Noel Doyle, "The Irish and American Labor, 1880–1920," *Saothar: Journal of the Irish Labor History Society* 1 (1975): 50–51.

15. Diner, *Erin's Daughters*, 94. See also, Maureen Murphy, "Bridget and Biddy: Images of the Irish Servant Girl in Puck Cartoons, 1880–1890," in *New Perspectives on the Irish Diaspora*, ed. Charles Fanning (Carbondale, IL: Southern Illinois Press, 2000), 172.

16. O'Hare, "Public Career of Patrick Andrew Collins," 21.

17. Boston *Globe*, 15 September 1905, 1.

18. O'Hare, "Public Career of Patrick Andrew Collins," 22.

19. Thomas O'Connor, *The Boston Irish: A Political History* (Boston: Back Bay Books, 1995), 132.

20. Ibid., 38–63. To raise funds for their activities in the United States and Ireland the Fenians sold bonds to supporters for the establishment of an Irish republic.

21. *Irish-American*, 19 February 1881, 4.

22. M. P. Curran, *Life of Patrick A. Collins with Some of His Most Notable Public Addresses* (Norwood, MA: The Norwood Press, 1906), xi.

23. T. O'Connor, *Boston Irish*, 134.

24. Francis Walsh, "John Boyle O'Reilly, the Boston *Pilot*, and Irish-American Assimilation, 1870–1890," in *Massachusetts in the Gilded Age: Selected Essays*, ed. Jack Tager and John W. Ifkovic (Amherst: University of Massachusetts Press, 1985), 151.

25. Francis G. McManamin, *The American Years of John Boyle O'Reilly* (New York: Arno Press, 1976), 208–15.

26. E. Foner, "Class, Ethnicity, and Radicalism," 163.

27. Arthur Mann, *Yankee Reformers in the Urban Age: Social Reform in Boston, 1880–1900* (New York: Harper and Row Publishers, 1954), 50.

28. Kenny, *American Irish*, 150; Lawrence McCaffrey, *The Irish Diaspora in America* (Bloomington: Indiana University Press, 1976), 79; Miller, *Emigrants and Exiles*, 520–23; D. Clark, *Hibernia America*.

29. Lawrence McCaffrey, *Textures of Irish America* (Syracuse: Syracuse University Press, 1992), 31; Kenny, *American Irish*, 150.

30. Emmons, *Butte Irish*.

31. For the Irish in San Francisco, see Sarbaugh, "Exiles of Confidence," 161–79; see also James P. Walsh, "The Evolution of the Thesis: The Irish Experience in California Was Different," in *The Irish in the San Francisco Bay Area: Essays on Good Fortune*, ed. Donald Jordan and Timothy J. O'Keefe (San Francisco: The Executive Council of the Irish Literary and Historical Society, 2005), 273–92.

32. Emmons, *Beyond the American Pale*, 213–15.

33. David Brundage, "Irish Land and American Workers: Class and Ethnicity in Denver, Colorado," in *"Struggle a Hard Battle": Essays on Working-Class Immigrants*, ed. Dirk Hoerder (Dekalb: Northern Illinois University Press, 1986), 58–59.

34. Miller, *Emigrants and Exiles*, 545. In an article, Kerby Miller argues that the Irish American bourgeoisie was successful in asserting a "social and cultural hegemony over its own lower classes." While this may be true in later periods, during the Land League era, any attempts to assert such hegemony were seriously undermined because of the relative strength and ideological variety of different Irish-American groups at this time. For Miller's argument, see "Class, Culture, and Immigrant Group Identity in the United States: The Case of Irish-American Ethnicity," in *Immigration Reconsidered: History, Sociology, and Politics*, ed. Virginia Yans-McLaughlin (New York: Oxford University Press, 1990), 96–129.

35. *AOH Journal*, March 1881, 2.

36. D. Clark, *Irish Relations*, 115.

37. Ibid., 118.

38. Brown, *Irish-American Nationalism*, 21–22.

39. *Irish World*, 8 January 1881, 5.

40. *ICBU Journal*, March 1881, 4.

41. Devoy, *Land of Eire*, 63–65.

42. Moody, *Davitt and Irish Revolution*, 410.

43. See, for example, Kenny, "Molly Maguires," 345–76.

44. *Catholic Universe*, 6 November 1879, 4. John Murdoch, the Scottish reformer and editor of the *Highlander*, also joined Parnell and Dillon occasionally in the United States.

45. Green, "American Catholics and the Irish Land League," 19–22.

46. Frederick J. Zwierlein, *The Life and Letters of Bishop McQuaid*, vol. 2 (Rochester: Art Print Shop, 1926), 222–24.

47. Ibid., 227 (emphasis in original).

48. Quoted in James Jeremiah Green, "First Impact of the Henry George Agitation on Catholics in the United States" (MA thesis, University of Notre Dame, 1948), 146.

49. Ibid., 148.

50. Meagher, *Inventing Irish America*, 184.

51. *AOH Journal*, March 1881, 2.

52. *First Annual Convention of the Irish National Land League*, 30.

53. Ibid., 24.

54. Funchion, *Chicago's Irish Nationalists*, 40.

55. Eric L. Hirsch, *Urban Revolt: Ethnic Politics in the Nineteenth-Century Chicago Labor Movement* (Berkeley: University of California Press, 1990), 142.

56. *Pilot*, 5 February 1881, 1.

57. Davitt, *Fall of Feudalism*, 257; Brown, *Irish-American Nationalism*, 104.

58. Brown, *Irish-American Nationalism*, 22.

59. Ibid., 23.

60. *Pilot*, 4 May 1878, 4; *Catholic Union*, 6 October 1881, 4. The scene in question was a drunken wake scene.

61. Legally, Ireland was not a colony, having become a part of the United Kingdom in 1801, alongside England, Scotland, and Wales, as part of the Act of Union. Irish nationalists believed that despite this legal status Ireland was still treated as a colony by British officials. Among historians, whether Ireland was a colony after 1800 remains a heated question. For two of the best works on this question, see Stephen Howe, *Ireland and Empire: Colonial Legacies in Irish History and Culture* (New York: Oxford University Press, 2000); and Kevin Kenny, ed., *Ireland and the British Empire* (New York: Oxford University Press, 2004).

62. *Pilot*, 15 May 1880, 8.

63. *Pilot*, 13 March 1880, 1.

64. *Catholic Union and Times*, 14 April 1881, 5.

65. *Irish World*, 4 September 1880, 5.

66. *Harper's Weekly*, 12 May 1883, 290.

67. *Republic*, 1 July 1882.

68. *AOH Journal*, March 1880, 4.

69. *Daily Union and Advertiser*, 6 May 1882, 6.

70. Ibid.

71. For examples of Irish-American caricature in antebellum America, see Knobel, *Paddy and the Republic*; for Ireland, see Curtis, *Apes and Angels*, and Michael De Nie, *Eternal Paddy*. For an early case of the application of the pseudo-science of Social Darwinism to the Irish, see the anonymously authored *What Science Is Saying about Ireland* (London: Hamilton, Adams, and Co. 1881).

72. Kevin Kenny, "Diaspora and Comparison: The Global Irish as a Case Study," *Journal of American History* 90, no. 1 (June 2003): 155.

73. See Curtis, *Apes and Angels*, 58–67.

74. *Pilot*, 13 November 1880, 1. O'Reilly was a strong supporter of African Americans. For his views on African Americans, see, McManamin, *The American Years of John Boyle O'Reilly*, 212–15; and John R. Betts, "The Negro and the New England Conscience in the Days of John Boyle O'Reilly," *Journal of Negro History* 51, no. 4 (1965): 246–61.

75. *Brooklyn Daily Eagle*, 30 March 1882, 2.

76. Scrapbook No. 1, Martin Griffin Papers, Philadelphia Archdiocesan Historical Research Center, Wynnewood, PA.

77. *United Ireland*, 12 November 1881, 2.

78. *Monitor*, 24 March 1881, 4.

79. *Pilot*, 8 May 1880, 6.

Chapter 5. "Spreading the Light"

1. Quoted in Sean Wilentz, "Industrializing America and the Irish: Towards the New Departure," *Labor History* 19 (1979): 592. See also E. Foner, "Class, Ethnicity, and Radicalism," 194–95.

2. Kenny, *American Irish*, 149.

3. For a discussion of the dimensions of much of this ideology, which many historians have termed "labor republicanism," see David Montgomery, "Labor and the Republic in Industrial America: 1860–1920," *Le Mouvement social* 111 (April–June 1980): 201–15; Sean Wilentz, "Against Exceptionalism: Class Consciousness and the American Labor Movement 1790–1920," *International Labor and Working Class History* 26 (Fall 1984): 1–24; Leon Fink, *Workingmen's Democracy: The Knights of Labor and American Politics* (Urbana: University of Illinois Press, 1985), 11–15; Kim Voss, *The Making of American Exceptionalism: The Knights of Labor and Class Formation in the Nineteenth Century* (Ithaca, NY: Cornell University Press, 1993), 34–35, 85–88; Leon Fink, *In Search of the Working Class: Essays in American Labor History and Political Culture* (Urbana: University of Illinois Press, 1994), 89–105; Schneirov, *Labor and Urban Politics*, 6–10. For a critique, see Daniel T. Rodgers, "Republicanism: The Career of a Concept," *Journal of American History* 79, no. 1 (June 1992): 11–38.

4. Despite this exclusion, Irish-American women (as we will see in chapter 6) asserted their own right to participation in the movement, and many became strong advocates of the radical wing of the Land League. Historians have presented important critiques of "labor republicanism" and the historiography surrounding this concept by focusing on the importance of race and gender in nineteenth-century labor. See Kevin Kenny, *Making Sense of the Molly Maguires* (New York: Oxford University Press, 1998), 121–22; David Roediger, *The Wages of Whiteness: Race and the Making of the American Working Class* (New York: Verso, 1991); Ava Baron, ed., *Work Engendered: Toward a New History of American Labor* (Ithaca, NY: Cornell University Press, 1991); Joseph Gerteis, *Class and the Color Line: Interracial Class Coalition in the Knights of Labor and the Populist Movement* (Durham, NC: Duke University Press, 2007).

5. On this earlier agrarian tradition, see Reeve Huston, *Land and Freedom: Rural Society, Popular Protest, and Party Politics in Antebellum New York* (New York: Oxford University Press, 2000). See also Bronstein, *Land Reform and Working-Class Experience*.

6. E. Foner, "Class, Ethnicity, and Radicalism," 195.

7. Rodechko, *Patrick Ford*, 30–31. Unfortunately, Ford left very little personal correspondence and did not write a memoir, making historians focus mainly on his views and opinions expressed in the pages of the *Irish World*. See also Ford's obituary, *Irish World*, September 27, 1913, 1.

8. Rodechko, *Patrick Ford*, 71–74.

9. W. O'Brien, *Recollections*, 274–75.

10. James Paul Rodechko, "An Irish-American Journalist and Catholicism: Patrick Ford of the *Irish World*," *Church History* 39, no. 4 (December 1979): 525.

11. Subscription prices listed in Rodechko, *Patrick Ford*, 41. Rodechko notes that the paper did struggle financially throughout the 1880s because of lack of advertising revenue.

12. Ibid., 36.

13. *Irish World*, 5 June 1880, 4. For more on Ford's anti-imperialism, see Lynch, "Live Ireland, Perish the Empire." For an examination of the Land League and the

British Empire, see Paul A. Townend, "Between Two Worlds: Irish Nationalists and Imperial Crisis, 1878–1880," *Past and Present* 194 (2007): 139–74.

14. *Irish World*, 9 April 1881, 1.

15. *Irish World*, 20 November 1880, 4.

16. *Irish World*, 26 February 1881, 4; 17 January 1880, 4.

17. *Irish World*, 7 August 1880, 4. "Pittsburg [*sic*] riots" refers to the violent clashes between striking railroad strikers and state and federal troops brought in to break the strike in 1877.

18. *Irish World*, 20 November 1880, 4.

19. *Irish World*, 17 January 1880, 4.

20. *Irish World*, 10 July 1880, 4.

21. McNeil, "Land, Labor, and Liberation," 72–75. For more on the Land League in Great Britain, see Letter from Frank Byrne to Officers and Members of the Irish National Land League of Great Britain, Oct. 21, 1881, Box 1, Folder 1, Luke O'Connor Papers, American Irish Historical Society, New York.

22. *Irish World*, 14 May 1881, 4; 8 January 1881, 4. Ford's belief in a dangerous "British system" spreading to America was similar in many ways to the views of the mid-nineteenth-century Irish nationalist John Mitchel. Both men shared a hatred of British imperialism, but Ford would have found Mitchel's support of African-American slavery abhorrent. For Mitchel's views, see Niamh Lynch, "Defining Irish Nationalist Anti-Imperialism: Thomas Davis and John Mitchel," *Éire-Ireland* 42, nos. 1–2 (Spring/ Summer 2007): 94–103.

23. *Irish World*, 12 July 1879, 4. See also 11 June 1881, 4; 17 January 1880, 4.

24. *Irish World*, 11 June 1881, 4.

25. *Irish World*, 9 April 1881, 4.

26. *Irish World*, 17 April 1880, 4.

27. *Irish World*, 16 April 1881, 4. In the same editorial, Ford pointed to the politicization of the New York land reform movement and its subsequent disintegration after disagreements emerged among leaders.

28. *Irish World*, 8 January 1881, 4.

29. Ibid.

30. *Irish World*, 4 December 1880, 4.

31. Quoted in *Western Home Journal*, 3 April 1879, 4.

32. *Irish World*, 22 May 1880, 4. Ford also criticized the Irish Catholic hierarchy for their tepid support of the Land League in Ireland. Rodechko, *Patrick Ford*, 211. For more on the Catholic hierarchy's reaction to the Land League, see Emmet Larkin, *The Roman Catholic Church and the Creation of the Modern Irish State, 1878–1886* (Philadelphia: American Philosophical Society, 1975).

33. *Rerum Novarum* was an encyclical issued by Pope Leo XIII on 15 May 1891, which argued for a policy of accommodation between the government, business, labor, and the Catholic Church. While rejecting socialism, the encyclical attempted to redirect the church toward a more sympathetic view of the problems workers faced in a period of industrialization. The practical effect for American Catholics was that *Rerum Novarum*

supported workers' rights to join unions (particularly the Knights of Labor) and advocated the idea of a just wage and a more equitable relationship between labor and capital. For more, see John T. McGreevey, *Catholicism and American Freedom: A History* (New York: W. W. Norton and Company, 2003), 126–38.

34. *Irish World*, 22 May 1880, 4.

35. Robert Emmett Curran, "Prelude to 'Americanism': The New York Accademia and Clerical Radicalism in the Late Nineteenth Century," *Church History* 47, no. 1 (March 1978): 54–55. Members of the Accademia also defended the Fenian Brotherhood in the 1860s against New York Archbishop John McCloskey's condemnation of the movement.

36. McGlynn's participation in this controversy came to a head in 1886 when he supported Henry George's campaign for mayor of New York City, despite demands by his superiors to desist. When he was called before Rome to explain his actions, McGlynn refused to go, leading to his excommunication for several years. For more on the "Americanist" controversy, see Deirdre M. Moloney, *American Catholic Lay Groups and Transatlantic Social Reform in the Progressive Era* (Chapel Hill: University of North Carolina Press, 2002), 15–19.

37. *Pilot*, 15 May 1880, 4.

38. Sylvester Malone, *Dr. Edward McGlynn* (New York: Arno Press, 1978), 65.

39. *Irish World*, 19 March 1881, 4 (emphasis in original).

40. *Irish World*, 26 March 1881, 8.

41. *Irish World*, 19 March 1881, 4.

42. *Irish World*, 5 June 1880, 5.

43. *Irish World*, 28 August 1880, 5 (emphasis in original).

44. W. O'Brien, *Recollections*, 272.

45. Fenian "A" Files 3/714, Box 5/A624, NAI.

46. *Irish World*, 9 April 1881, 6; *Report of Rev. Lawrence Walsh, Central Treasurer of the Irish National Land League, U.S., from January 10, 1881, to April 10, 1881* (n.p.: n.p., 1881), 2.

47. *ICBU Journal*, 15 February 1884, 3.

48. Doan, "Green Gold to the Emerald Shores," 112. An additional $90,000 was sent direct to Ireland by branches in the Midwest and California, making the total $343,000 to $270,000 for the *Irish World* and other sources.

49. *Special Commission Act, 1888: Reprint of the shorthand notes of the speeches, proceedings, and evidence taken before the Commissioners appointed under the above-named act*, vol. 7 (London: Printed for her Majesty's Stationery Office by Eyre and Spottiswoode, 1890), 62. See also Patrick Egan to Patrick Collins, 7 March 1881, Box 1, Folder 24, Patrick Collins Papers, BC.

50. *Irish Nation*, 10 June 1882, 4.

51. E. Foner, "Class, Ethnicity, and Radicalism," 168. Thomas N. Brown and Foner believe that Irish Americans were drawn to the *Irish World*'s social message, while James Paul Rodechko and Robert Doan side with the notoriety element of seeing your name in print. For a local debate from the Parnell-Dillon Land League of St. Louis on the merits of the radical and conservative interpretations of the Land League, see *Missouri Republican*, 16 October 1882, 4.

52. *Irish World*, 7 May 1881, 2.

53. *Irish World*, 25 September 1880, 8; 5 February 1881, 8.

54. *Irish World*, 16 April 1881, 8; 30 April 1881, 8.

55. *New York Times*, 24 June 1881, 4.

56. Quoted in E. Foner, "Class, Ethnicity, and Radicalism," 169.

57. Doan, "Green Gold to the Emerald Shores," 233.

58. *Irish World*, 9 July 1881, 8.

59. E. Foner, "Class, Ethnicity, and Radicalism," 170. An incomplete list of contributors can be found in the *Irish World*, 24 September 1881, 8.

60. *Irish World*, 5 February 1881, 8.

61. *Irish World*, 15 January 1881, 5; P. McGlynn to John Devoy, 18 May 1883, MS 18007/29, John Devoy Papers, NLI.

62. Bagenal, *American Irish*, 72–73.

63. *Irish Nation*, 31 December 1881, 1.

64. *Irish World*, 8 January 1881, 4.

65. Ibid., 8.

66. Ibid., 5.

67. Fenian "A" Files 3/714, Box 5/A670, NAI.

68. David Montgomery, "The Irish and the American Labor Movement," in *America and Ireland, 1776–1976: The American Identity and the Irish Connection*, ed. David Noel Doyle and Owen Dudley Edwards (Westport, CT: Greenwood Press, 1980), 216.

69. *First Annual Convention of the Irish National Land League*, 26.

70. E. Foner, "Class, Ethnicity, and Radicalism," 151.

71. Mark Lause, *Young America: Land, Labor, and the Republican Community* (Urbana: University of Illinois Press, 2005), 3. See also Huston, *Land and Freedom*. The author would like to thank Professor Lause for his comments on the links between the Land League and earlier American agrarian movements.

72. Mark Lause, "Progress Impoverished: Origin of Henry George's Single Tax," *Historian* 52, no. 3 (May 1990): 397. Lause argues that many of Henry George's ideas had their origins in the writings and speeches of Evans and other National Reformers in the 1840s and 1850s. For *Irish World* editorials referencing land reform in the 1840s, see *Irish World*, 16 April 1881, 4; 23 April 1881, 4.

73. *Missouri Republican*, 16 May 1881, 5.

74. William Deverell, "To Loosen the Safety Valve: Eastern Workers and Western Lands," *Western Historical Quarterly* 19, no. 3 (August 1998): 282.

75. *Irish World*, 29 January 1881, 4.

76. E. Foner, "Class, Ethnicity, and Radicalism," 158; Reeve Huston, "Multiple Crossings: Thomas Ainge Devyr and Transatlantic Land Reform," in *Transatlantic Rebels: Agrarian Radicalism in Comparative Context*, ed. Thomas Summerhill (East Lansing: Michigan State University Press, 2004), 139–54; Rachael O'Higgins, "The Irish Influence in the Chartist Movement," *Past and Present* 20 (November 1961): 93; Montgomery, "Irish and the American Labor Movement," 216. For transatlantic connections within nineteenth-century British and American agrarian reform, see in particular Bronstein, *Land Reform and Working-Class Experience*.

77. Thomas Ainge Devyr, *The Odd Book of the Nineteenth Century* (New York: Garland Publishing, 1986), 198.

78. Ibid., 199.

79. McMath, *American Populism*, 136.

80. *Irish World*, 9 July 1881, 3.

81. Neil Foley, *The White Scourge: Mexicans, Blacks, and Poor Whites in Texas Cotton Culture* (Berkeley: California University Press, 1997), 97. Tom Hickey, one of the leaders of the Renters' Union, was an Irish immigrant. His acceptance of Mexican Americans in the movement was only partial (they were organized in segregated locals) and did not extend to African Americans, who were excluded entirely.

82. John L. Thomas, *Alternative America: Henry George, Edward Bellamy, Henry Demarest Lloyd and the Adversary Tradition* (Cambridge, MA: Harvard University Press, 1982), 10–13. For more on George's life, see Charles Albro Barker, *Henry George* (New York: Oxford University Press, 1955); Henry George Jr., *The Life of Henry George* (New York: Robert Schalkenbach Foundation, 1960); and Edward O'Donnell, "Henry George and the 'New Political Forces': Ethnic Nationalism, Labor Radicalism, and Politics in Gilded Age New York City" (PhD diss., Columbia University, 1995).

83. Barker, *Henry George*, 293.

84. *Irish World*, 4 December 1880, 3.

85. *Irish World*, 11 December 1880, 4.

86. *Irish World*, 1 January 1881, 2.

87. Edward O'Donnell, "'Though not an Irishman': Henry George and the American Irish," *American Journal of Economics and Sociology* 56, no. 4 (October 1997): 415.

88. Henry George, *The Irish Land Question* (n.p.: Elbrion Classics, 2005), 10.

89. Ibid., 3.

90. Ibid., 11.

91. Ibid., 6.

92. Ibid., 15.

93. Ibid., 31 (emphasis in original).

94. Ibid., 35.

95. Quoted in E. Foner, "Class, Ethnicity, and Radicalism," 191.

96. *Irish Nation*, 17 December 1881, 4.

97. *Irish World*, 16 April 1881, 4.

98. E. Foner, "Class, Ethnicity, and Radicalism," 185.

99. *Irish World*, 14 May 1881, 8.

100. *Irish World*, 2 July 1881, 8.

101. Fink, *Workingmen's Democracy*, 9. For more on the Knights of Labor, see Henry J. Browne, *The Catholic Church and the Knights of Labor* (Washington, DC: Catholic University of America Press, 1949); Voss, *Making of American Exceptionalism*; Robert E. Weir, *Knights Unhorsed: Internal Conflict in a Gilded Age Social Movement* (Detroit: Wayne State University Press, 2000).

102. E. Foner, "Class, Ethnicity, and Radicalism," 173. For more on Powderly, see Craig Phelan, *Grand Master Workman: Terence Powderly and the Knights of Labor* (Westport,

CT: Greenwood Press, 2000); Terence V. Powderly, *The Path I Trod: The Autobiography of Terence V. Powderly*, ed. Harry J. Carman, Henry David, and Paul N. Guthrie (New York: Ams Press, 1968).

103. Quoted in Montgomery, "Irish and the American Labor Movement," 216.

104. Terence Powderly to John J. Joyce, 13 May 1882, Terence V. Powderly Papers, American Catholic History Research Center and University Archives, Catholic University, Washington, DC; E. Foner, "Class, Ethnicity, and Radicalism," 175.

105. Paul Buhle, *From the Knights of Labor to the New World Order: Essays on Labor and Culture* (New York: Garland Publishing Inc., 1997), 23.

106. Schneirov, *Labor and Urban Politics*, 122.

107. See Brundage, *Making of Western Labor Radicalism*, and "Irish Land and American Workers," 46–67.

108. Ibid., 58.

109. Quoted in O'Donnell, "'Though Not an Irishman,'" 415.

110. *Truth*, 18 January 1881, 2; 19 January 1881, 2.

111. *Missouri Republican*, May 16, 1881, 5. McGuire was also a member of the Knights of Labor. He relocated to New York in 1882, continuing his participation in the Land League and working-class organization.

112. Quoted in *Monitor*, 23 September 1880, 1.

113. Schneirov, *Labor and Urban Politics*, 119.

114. Michael A. Gordon, "The Labor Boycott in New York City, 1880–1886," *Labor History* 16 (Spring 1975): 186–87 (emphasis in original).

115. *Irish World*, 9 April 1882, 2.

116. Paul Krause, *The Battle for Homestead, 1880–1892: Politics, Culture and Steel* (Pittsburgh: University of Pittsburgh Press, 1992), 182.

117. *Irish World*, 18 February 1882, 3.

118. *Irish Nation*, 4 February 1882, 1. On New York German-American support for the Land League, see also *Irish Nation*, 31 December 1881, 1.

Chapter 6. "Let Us Rise to Action"

1. Hasia Diner writes of Irish-American women's nationalist participation: "Beyond a few scattered cases in which Irish women banded together to form a short-lived Ladies' Land League or a Fenian Sisterhood to collect money to help the brotherhood, few Irish-American women participated in the effort to rid the Emerald Isle of the hated British oppressors." Diner, *Erin's Daughters*, 128. See also V. Walsh, "Irish Nationalism and Land Reform," 259–60. For Irish-American women's contributions as domestic servants and teachers, see Diner, *Erin's Daughters*; Diane M. Hotten-Summers, "Relinquishing and Reclaiming Independence: Irish Domestic Servants, American Middle-Class Mistresses, and Assimilation, 1850–1890," in *New Directions in Irish-American History*, ed. Kevin Kenny (Madison: University of Wisconsin Press, 2003), 227–42; Janet Nolan, *Servants of the Poor: Teachers and Mobility in Ireland and Irish America* (Notre Dame, IN: University of Notre Dame Press, 2004). Both E. Foner and Brown in their examinations of the American Land League deal very little with the Ladies' Land League. Some works

that deal briefly (but very well) with the Ladies' Land League in the United States are Meagher, *Inventing Irish America*, 178–95; Brundage, *Making of Western Labor Radicalism*, 43–45; Deirdre M. Moloney, "Land League Activism in Transnational Perspective," *U.S. Catholic Historian* 22, no. 3 (Summer 2004): 61–74. A chapter on the Ladies' Land League in the United States and Canada can also be found in Côté, *Fanny and Anna Parnell*, 130–47.

2. Linda Kerber, "Separate Spheres, Female Worlds, Woman's Place: The Rhetoric of Women's History," *Journal of American History* 75, no. 1 (June 1988): 21.

3. Barbara Welter, "The Cult of True Womanhood: 1820–1860," *American Quarterly* 18, no. 2 (Summer 1966): 152. For a critique of separate sphere ideology and historians use of the concept, see Kerber, "Separate Spheres, Female Worlds, Woman's Place," 9–39.

4. Quoted in Karen Kennelly, "Ideals of American Catholic Womanhood," in *American Catholic Women: A Historical Exploration*, ed. Karen Kennelly (New York: Macmillan, 1989), 4. For further discussion of Catholic True Womanhood and separate spheres ideology, see James Kenneally, "Eve, Mary, and the Historians: American Catholicism and Women," *Horizons* 3, no. 2 (1976): 189–95; Colleen McDannell, "Catholic Domesticity, 1860–1960," in *American Catholic Women: A Historical Explanation*, ed. Karen Kennelly (New York: Macmillan, 1989), 49–54; Kathleen Sprows Cummings, "'Not the New Woman?' Irish-American Women and the Creation of a Usable Past, 1890–1900," *U.S. Catholic Historian* 19, no. 1 (Winter 2001): 37–52.

5. Diner, *Erin's Daughters*, xiv.

6. Ardis Cameron, *Radicals of the Worst Sort: Laboring Women in Lawrence, Massachusetts, 1860–1912* (Urbana: University of Illinois Press, 1995), 29. See also Carole Turbin, *Working Women of Collar City: Gender, Class, and Community in Troy, New York, 1864–86* (Urbana: University of Illinois Press, 1992), 34–42.

7. Susan Levine, "Labor's True Woman: Domesticity and Equal Rights in the Knights of Labor," *Journal of American History* 70, no. 2 (September 1983): 325. The Irish-born Elizabeth Rodgers of Chicago was the first female Master Workman in the Knights of Labor. For more on Rodgers, see Levine, "Labor's True Woman," 331–332; James J. Kenneally, *The History of American Catholic Women* (New York: Crossroad, 1990), 116.

8. Diner, *Erin's Daughters*, 71, 93–96.

9. On Irish-American domestic servants, see Diner, *Erin's Daughters*; Hotten-Somers, "Relinquishing and Reclaiming Independence," 227–42; Kenny, *American Irish*, 153–54.

10. Hotten-Somers, "Relinquishing and Reclaiming Independence," 247.

11. Deirdre Moloney, "Combating 'Whiskey's Work': The Catholic Temperance Movement in Late Nineteenth Century America," *US Catholic Historian* 16, no. 3 (Summer 1998): 5–9.

12. For a further discussion of the differences between Protestant and Catholic reform efforts, see Moloney, *American Catholic Lay*, 13–68.

13. Hasia Diner notes the high rates of alcoholism that also plagued Irish-American women. Diner, *Erin's Daughters*, 113.

14. Murphy, *American Slavery, Irish Freedom*, 63–65.

15. Unfortunately, very little is known of the Fenian Sisterhood. The most detailed account of their activity is found in Patrick Steward and Bryan McGovern, *The Fenians: Irish Rebellion in the North Atlantic World, 1858–1876* (Knoxville: University of Tennessee Press, 2013), 102–3. For general references see Diner, *Erin's Daughters*, 128. For more information on the Fenian Sisterhood in New York City, see Mary C. Kelly, *The Shamrock and the Lily: The New York Irish and the Creation of a Transatlantic Identity, 1845–1921* (New York: Peter Lang, 2005), 57–59.

16. Diner, *Erin's Daughters*, 103.

17. For the CTAU, see Sister Joan Bland, *Hibernian Crusade: The Story of the Catholic Total Abstinence Union of America* (Washington, DC: Catholic University of America Press, 1951), 98, 100, 144; Joseph Gibbs, *History of the Catholic Total Abstinence Union of America* (Philadelphia: n.p., 1907), 59. On the AOH, see Funchion, *Irish American Voluntary Organizations*, 57.

18. By his retirement, Charles Stewart had achieved the rank of Rear Admiral and in 1815, acquired a 225-acre estate in Bordentown, New Jersey, which he dubbed "Ironsides."

19. Côté, *Fanny and Anna Parnell*, 131–37.

20. *Pilot*, 6 September 1879, 6.

21. Jane Côté and Dana Hearne, "Anna Parnell," in *Women, Power, and Consciousness in 19th Century Ireland: Eight Biographical Studies*, ed. Mary Cullen and Maria Luddy (Dublin: Attic Press, 1995), 167–68.

22. Justin McCarthy, ed., *Irish Literature*, vol. 7 (Philadelphia: J. D. Morris and Co., 1904), 2871.

23. Davitt, *Fall of Feudalism*, 292.

24. *Irish World*, 21 August 1880, 5. See also J. J. Prendergast's letter calling for women to participate in the Land League, *Irish World*, 11 September 1880, 8.

25. *Redpath's Illustrated Weekly*, 5 August 1882, 5. For American and Irish-American newspapers reporting on the founding of the Ladies' Land League, see *Irish World*, 30 October 1880, 8; *Pilot*, 23 October 1880, 5; *Catholic Union*, 16 December 1880, 8; *Western Home Journal*, 27 November 1880, 1.

26. On the establishment of Ladies' Land Leagues in San Francisco and St. Louis, see *Daily Morning Call*, 16 December 1880, 2; William Hyde and Howard Conrad, eds., *Encyclopedia of the History of St. Louis*, vol. 2 (New York: Southern History Co., 1899), 1210; *Missouri Republican*, 20 December 1880, 3.

27. *Irish World*, 15 January 1881, 5.

28. Compiled from the *Irish World*, October 1880 to December 1882.

29. This estimate is reached by giving each of the 203 branches identified an average membership of 60, which yields a total of 12,180.

30. For Philadelphia branches, see *Irish World*, 28 May 1881, 8; for Hartford, *Irish World*, 5 March 1881, 5; for Woonsocket, *Irish World*, 8 January 1881, 4.

31. Kenny, *American Irish*, 142. See also Emmons, *Beyond the American Pale*, 216.

32. *Irish World*, 18 December 1880, 5.

33. Unfortunately, very little is known about Quinn's life before or after her participation in the Land League. For information on Alice May Quinn, see *AOH Journal*, August 1878, 1; March 1879, 3, August 1881, 2; *Irish World*, 11 September 1880, 5. On Margaret Sullivan, see Kenneally, *History of American Catholic Women*, 108–9; Katherine E. Conway, "Margaret F. Sullivan, Journalist and Author," *Donahoe's Magazine* 51 (March 1904): 220–23. Margaret Sullivan was married to the Irish-American leader Alexander Sullivan. Alexander Sullivan was elected president of the Irish National League in 1883, the successor organization to the Land League.

34. *Western Home Journal*, 29 November 1883, 1. Sadly, it seems that the proposed book was never published.

35. Doan, "Green Gold to the Emerald Shores," 294.

36. Ibid.

37. Colleen McDannell, "Going to the Ladies' Fair: Irish Catholics in New York City, 1870–1900," in *The New York Irish*, ed. Ronald Bayor and Timothy Meagher (Baltimore: Johns Hopkins University Press, 1996), 237–38.

38. *Irish World*, 31 January 1881 to 31 October 1882, Donations to Land League Fund.

39. *Irish-American*, 19 February 1881, 8.

40. *Irish World*, 19 March 1881, 8.

41. Davitt, *Fall of Feudalism*, 299.

42. Katharine Tynan, *Twenty-Five Years: Reminiscences* (London: Smith, Elder and Co., 1913), 82, 96.

43. Ibid., 83.

44. For information on the Ladies' Land League in Ireland, see Ward, *Unmanageable Revolutionaries*, 4–39; Côté, *Fanny and Anna Parnell*, 156–219; Janet Tebrake, "Irish Peasant Women in Revolt: The Land League Years," *Irish Historical Studies* 33, no. 109 (May 1992): 63–80; Cynthia Hyatt Walker, "Banshees, Dogooders, or Undervalued Radicals? Anna Parnell and the Ladies' Land League" (MA thesis, Villanova University, 1993); Parnell, *Tale of a Great Sham*.

45. Davitt, *Speech Delivered by Michael Davitt*, 265.

46. *Irish-American*, 11 December 1880, 5.

47. *Irish World*, 25 September 1880, 8.

48. *Catholic Union and Advertiser*, 23 February 1882; Scrapbook Number 29, Volume 21, John Ireland Papers, Minnesota Historical Society, St. Paul, MN.

49. Quoted in Kenneally, "Eve, Mary, and the Historians," 190.

50. *Irish World*, 21 May 1881, 8.

51. *Irish World*, 25 December 1880, 5.

52. Ibid.

53. Ibid.

54. *Irish World*, 25 September 1880, 8.

55. *Irish World*, 25 December 1880, 5.

56. *Irish World*, 11 December, 1880, 5.

57. Quote from *Catholic Universe* (Cleveland), 7 July 1881, 1.

58. See M. Murphy, "Bridget and Biddy," 152–75, for a wide-ranging discussion of

these stereotypes. In Ireland, Katharine Tynan of the Irish Ladies' Land League once asked in a meeting, "Why not Women's Land League?" and was told she was being "too democratic." Tynan, *Twenty-Five Years*, 75.

59. Miller, "Class, Culture, and Immigrant Group Identity," 111.

60. *Irish American*, 25 December 1880, 4.

61. Colleen McDannell, "'True men as we need them': Catholicism and the Irish-American Male," *American Studies* 27, no. 2 (1986): 29.

62. *Irish World*, 5 March 1881, 7.

63. *Brooklyn Daily Eagle*, 10 February 1881, 2.

64. *Pilot*, 29 January 1881, 4.

65. *Irish World*, 28 May 1881, 2.

66. *Irish World*, 16 April 1881, 8.

67. *Northwestern-Chronicle*, 26 March 1881, 1. In Ireland, Archbishop Edward McCabe of Dublin attacked the Ladies' Land League of Ireland, claiming that women were being "asked to forget womanhood." As in the United States, the archbishop's statement was repudiated by several male members of the Land League and his request for women to not join the movement ignored.

68. *St. Paul Globe*, 19 March 1881; Scrapbook Number 29, Volume 21, John Ireland Papers, Minnesota Historical Society, St. Paul, MN.

69. *Irish World*, 25 September 1880, 8.

70. For the origins of the American belief in the exalted role of mothers in shaping the citizenry of the Republic, see Linda Kerber, *Women of the Republic: Intellect and Ideology in Revolutionary America* (Chapel Hill: University of North Carolina Press, 1980).

71. Timothy Meagher, "'Sweet Mothers and Young Women Out in the World': The Roles of Irish American Women in Late Nineteenth and Early Twentieth Century Worcester, Massachusetts," *US Catholic Historian* 5, nos. 3–4 (1986): 343.

72. *Irish World*, 30 April 1881, 8.

73. *Catholic Union*, 30 December 1880, 4.

74. *Irish World*, 5 February 1881, 2.

75. Fanny Parnell, "Nationalization of the Land vs. Peasant Proprietary," *Donohoe's Magazine* 8, no. 3 (September 1882): 195–202.

76. Ibid., 202.

77. *Irish World*, 4 September 1880, 8; 11 September 1880, 8. For more on the Workingwomen's Union of Chicago, see Meredith Tax, *The Rising of the Women* (New York: Monthly Review Press, 1980), 41–43, 45–49; Philip S. Foner, *Women and the American Labor Movement: From Colonial Times to the Eve of World War I* (New York: The Free Press, 1979), 181–82; Lizzie Swank, "Women Workers of Chicago," *American Federationist* 12 (August 1905): 507–10.

78. *Irish World*, 11 September 1880, 8. The truck system, also known as the company store system, was a wage system where workers, usually in isolated or company-dominated areas, were paid in credit that was only good in company-owned stores. The prices in these stores were oftentimes overpriced, forcing workers into a vicious cycle of debt.

79. Quoted in Phelan, *Grand Master Workman*, 154–55.

80. Ibid., 155.

81. *Irish World*, 5 March 1881, 7.

82. *Irish World*, 4 June 1881, 8.

83. *Irish World*, 28 May 1881, 8.

84. *Missouri Republican*, 20 June 1881, 5.

85. *Irish World*, 9 July 1881, 2.

86. E. Foner, "Class, Ethnicity, and Radicalism," 175.

87. Harvey Strum, "'Not Forgotten in their Affliction': Irish Famine Relief from Rhode Island, 1847," *Rhode Island History* 60, no. 1 (2002): 30–31.

88. Woonsocket Ladies' Land League membership list found in *Irish World*, 19 March 1881, 8. All 1880 census work was done using www.ancestry.com. Out of this group of 119, 53 women (44.54 percent) were employed in the cotton mills, 24 women (20.17 percent) were employed in the woolen mills, 6 women (5.04 percent) were employed in the rubber works, and 1 woman (0.84 percent) worked in a braid factory.

89. Meagher, *Inventing Irish America*, 185.

90. A list of the Worcester Ladies' Land League Executive Committee is found in the *Irish World*, December 4, 1880, 5; United States Census (1880), Schedule 1 (Population) via www.ancestry.com. The women's names are Maggie Geary, Mary E. Fitzgerald, Theresa Timon, Margaret Hickey, Margaret O'Grady, Lizzie O'Keefe, and Katie Simmons.

91. Quoted in Meagher, *Inventing Irish America*, 186; ibid., 186.

Chapter 7. "Ireland Is Fighting Humanity's Battle"

1. In Ireland there was a suspension of habeas corpus, and severe restrictions were placed on public gatherings and Irish newspapers.

2. *Irish-American*, 11 February 1882, 5.

3. Conor Cruise O'Brien, *Parnell and His Party, 1880–1890* (Oxford: Oxford University Press, 1974), 60–61; Lyons, *Charles Stewart Parnell*, 147; Davitt, *Fall of Feudalism*, 302; Brown, *Irish-American Nationalism*, 111.

4. C. C. O'Brien, *Parnell and His Party*, 62; Davitt, *Fall of Feudalism*, 305–6. O'Brien believes that it would have been impossible for Parnell to win over the majority of Irish Parliamentary Party members to a more radical policy. C. C. O'Brien, *Parnell and His Party*, 61.

5. Lyons, *Charles Stewart Parnell*, 148.

6. C. C. O'Brien, *Parnell and His Party*, 64–65.

7. Lyons, *Charles Stewart Parnell*, 143–44.

8. O'Callaghan, *British High Politics*, 78.

9. Quoted in R. B. O'Brien, *Life of Charles Stewart Parnell*, 1:257.

10. Brown, *Irish-American Nationalism*, 112.

11. Palmer, *Irish Land League Crisis*, 246.

12. O'Callaghan, *British High Politics*, 79.

13. Ibid. Also arrested under this act in Ireland was Michael Boyton, an Irish-American Land Leaguer who claimed American intervention against Britain owing to his American citizenship. Irish Americans hounded the American minister to the English Court, James Russell Lowell, to intervene in the Boyton case, but he refused. Eventually, it was determined that Boyton was not an American citizen but soon after other cases of proven American citizens being detained by the British occurred (including Henry George, though his arrest lasted only a few hours). Irish-American newspapers attempted to pressure President Chester A. Arthur to recall Lowell, but to no avail. Eventually, the matter was settled when the British government released the suspects in 1882 after conditions in Ireland had settled down. For more on this controversy see Joseph Patrick O'Grady, *Irish-Americans and Anglo-American Relations, 1880–1888* (New York: Arno Press, 1976), 139–67; Leslie Butler, *Critical Americans: Victorian Intellectuals and Transatlantic Liberal Reform* (Chapel Hill: University of North Carolina Press, 2007), 232–41.

14. Joseph Lee, *The Modernisation of Irish Society, 1848–1918* (Dublin: Gill and Macmillan, 1973), 84–85.

15. Solow, *Land Question and the Irish Economy*, 157; see also O'Callaghan, *British High Politics*, 89–90.

16. Donal McCarthy, "Parnell, Davitt, and the Land Question," in *Famine, Land, and Culture in Ireland*, ed. Carla King (Dublin: University College Dublin Press, 2000), 79.

17. W. O'Brien and Ryan, *Devoy's Post Bag*, 2:23.

18. C. C. O'Brien, *Parnell and His Party*, 66.

19. Ibid., 69–70; Palmer, *Irish Land League Crisis*, 284.

20. Palmer, *Irish Land League Crisis*, 286.

21. *Irish World*, 17 September 1881, 4.

22. Brown, *Irish-American Nationalism*, 115.

23. Lyons, *Charles Stewart Parnell*, 167–68.

24. Palmer, *Irish Land League Crisis*, 297.

25. Davitt, *Fall of Feudalism*, 337.

26. Fanny Parnell to Patrick Collins, 10 November 1881, Patrick Collins Papers, BC.

27. C. C. O'Brien, *Parnell and His Party*, 74–75. Parnell's support for the No Rent Manifesto seems to have been based on expediency. In a letter to John Dillon dated 13 October 1881, the day of his arrest, Parnell recommended "that the Test cases should be proceeded with, and that no means should be left untried to protect by mortgage the sale of the interests of the more substantial class of tenants. If we can do this, and if the government do not suppress the organization, we can, I am sure, maintain and strengthen the movement." One day later, Parnell informed Dillon that the government's arrest of most of the leadership of the Land League had made "it practically impossible for the resolutions of the Convention to be carried out as the absence of our Central Officials and the certain arrest of any who may take their place will render it impossible to work out the details of the policy recommended by the Convention. I am, therefore, with great reluctance driven to admit that there is no resource save the adoption of a Strike against all rent, and suggest you should announce the adoption of this

policy at the Meeting tonight and withdrawal of test cases." From these letters, Parnell's adoption of the No Rent policy as a temporary tactic is clear. MS6745–9, MS6745–10, John Dillon Papers, TCD.

28. *Irish World*, 29 October 1881, 1.

29. Ibid., 4.

30. Henry George to E. R. Taylor, 12 September 1881, Henry George Papers, Manuscripts and Archives Division, The New York Public Library, Astor, Lenox, and Tilden Foundations (hereafter NYPL).

31. Quoted in Brown, *Irish-American Nationalism*, 115. For earlier examples of Ford's support for a rent strike, see *Irish World*, 17 January 1880, 4; 28 May 1881, 4; 18 September 1880, 4.

32. *ICBU Journal*, December 1881, 4.

33. Quoted in Brown, *Irish-American Nationalism*, 120.

34. *Western Home Journal*, 12 November 1881, 4.

35. Ibid. For similar attacks on the *Irish World* see *Catholic Universe*, 3 November 1881, 7; *Irish Nation*, 17 December 1881, 4.

36. See telegrams from T. P. O'Connor and John F. Finerty to Patrick Collins, Box 2, Folder 2, Patrick Collins Papers, BC.

37. Patrick Collins to T. P. O'Connor, 16 November 1881, Box 2, Folder 6, Patrick Collins Papers, BC.

38. *ICBU Journal*, December 1881, 1.

39. Circular from *Irish World* to the "Officers and Members of the Auxiliary Land and Industrial Leagues of America," New York, 12 November 1881, Reel 3, Terence V. Powderly Papers, American Catholic History Research Center and University Archives, Catholic University, Washington, DC.

40. *Irish World*, 5 November 1881, 4.

41. Fanny Parnell to Patrick Collins, 25 September 1881, Box 1, Folder 54, Patrick Collins Papers, BC.

42. Ibid.

43. Funchion, *Chicago's Irish Nationalists*, 69. For more on Alexander Sullivan, see *Chicago Tribune*, 22 August 1913; Brown, *Irish-American Nationalism*, xvi.

44. Henri Le Caron, *Twenty-Five Years in the Secret Service: The Recollections of a Spy* (Boston: American Citizen Co., 1892), 150.

45. Funchion, *Chicago's Irish Nationalists*, 72.

46. Ibid.

47. Convention proceedings printed in the *ICBU Journal*, December 1881, 1.

48. Ibid.

49. Ibid.

50. Ibid.

51. Brown, *Irish-American Nationalism*, 121. The delegates were T. J. Morgan, a socialist leader, M. W. Ryan, and A. O. Johnson. The Chicago Fifth and Seventeenth Ward Land Leagues had elected them delegates. The chairman of credentials, a Mr. Agnew, stated that the Spread the Light Club had not been recognized as delegates

because it was the committee's opinion that the club they claimed to represent had a political nature and that there was "strong opposition from all quarters to their admission as socialists." See also *ICBU Journal*, December 1881, 1.

52. *ICBU Journal*, December 1881, 2.

53. By the first week of March 1882, $108,000 was sent to Patrick Egan in Paris. Brown, *Irish-American Nationalism*, 121.

54. Funchion, *Chicago's Irish Nationalists*, 73.

55. The members of the Irish National Executive Committee, also known as the "Committee of Seven," were Patrick Ford, Patrick Collins, Alexander Sullivan, Michael Boland of Louisville, Andrew Brown of St. Louis, Dr. William Wallace of New York, and Judge Birdsall of Connecticut. Four members of the committee were members of Clan na Gael (Sullivan, Boland, Brown, and Wallace). Funchion, *Chicago's Irish Nationalists*, 73; Brown, *Irish-American Nationalism*, 121. For disagreements within the "Committee of Seven," see A. F. Brown to Patrick Collins, Box 2, Folders 26, 28, 29, Patrick Collins Papers, BC.

56. *Western Home Journal*, 15 December 1881, 1.

57. *Catholic Universe*, 5 January 1882, 4.

58. *Monitor*, 8 March 1882, 1.

59. *Daily Union and Advertiser*, 19 December 1881, 2.

60. Ibid.

61. Zwierlein, *Life and Letters of Bishop McQuaid*, 2:269–70; *Irish Nation*, 14 January 1882, 2.

62. Richard Gilmour, *Lecture on the Land League by Rt. Rev. Richard Gilmour, Bishop of Cleveland, Delivered at the Tabernacle, Cleveland, Ohio, February 6, 1882* (Cleveland: J. B. Savage, 1882), 10. In contrast to Gilmour, in Chicago Archbishop Feehan looked very favorably on Clan na Gael activities, and his feelings were shared by several Chicago parish priests. Funchion, *Chicago's Irish Nationalists*, 40–41.

63. Gilmour, *Lecture on the Land League*, 15.

64. Ibid., 24.

65. John Boyle O'Reilly, "Ireland's Opportunity—Will It Be Lost?," *American Catholic Quarterly Review* 7 (1882): 116.

66. Ibid., 117.

67. Ibid., 118.

68. Golway, *Irish Rebel*, 142–43.

69. *Irish Nation*, 17 December 1881, 4.

70. Ibid.

71. *Irish World*, 11 March 1882, 3.

72. *Irish World*, 3 December 1881, 4.

73. Ibid.

74. *Irish World*, 31 December 1881, 6.

75. *Irish World*, 22 July 1882, 4.

76. *Irish World*, 28 January 1882, 4.

77. Ibid.

78. *Irish World*, 8 October 1881, 8.

79. This number is reached by combining the weekly totals of the Land League Fund in the *Irish World* from 18 October 1881 to 29 April 1882.

80. *Irish World*, 4 February to 25 March 1882.

81. *Irish World*, 6 May 1882, 5.

82. *Irish World*, 4 February 1882, 4.

83. *Irish World*, 18 February 1882, 7.

84. *Irish World*, 27 May 1882, 5.

85. *Irish World*, 18 February 1882, 5.

86. Isacsson, *Determined Doctor*, 76–81.

87. *Irish-American*, 18 February 1882, 1.

88. *Irish World*, 18 February 1882, 5.

89. *Irish Nation*, 7 January 1882, 6.

90. Brown, *Irish-American Nationalism*, 122.

91. *Irish World*, 27 May 1882, 5.

92. *Truth*, 22 October 1881, 1.

93. *Truth*, 24 October 1881, 1.

94. *Irish World*, 3 December 1881, 1.

95. Ibid.

96. O'Donnell, "Henry George," 269; Michael Gordon, "Studies in Irish and Irish-American Thought and Behavior in Gilded Age New York City" (PhD diss., University of Rochester, 1977), 463.

97. For a full list of the unions represented at the 30 January 1882 meeting, see O'Donnell, "Henry George," 271.

98. Ibid.

99. *Irish Nation*, 4 February 1882, 1.

100. Ibid.

101. Ibid. For more on German-American participation, see O'Donnell, "Henry George," 269–70.

102. Ibid., 272. The countries named in the declaration were England, Scotland, France, Germany, Russia, Austria, Italy, Spain, Portugal, Belgium, and Holland.

103. Ibid., 273.

104. The CLU platform is found in ibid., 681–86.

105. Gordon, "Studies in Irish and Irish-American Thought," 451; Edwin G. Burrows and Mike Wallace, *Gotham: A History of New York City to 1898* (Oxford: Oxford University Press, 1999), 1091.

Chapter 8. The Road from Kilmainham Jail

1. "Kilmainham Treaty" is the name given to the informal agreement between Parnell and Gladstone by contemporaries and historians. While Gladstone always denied that a *quid pro quo* settlement was ever made, the historical evidence seems to suggest otherwise.

2. Moody, *Davitt and Irish Revolution*, 497–98.

3. Lee, *Modernisation of Irish Society*, 88.

4. Jordan, *Land and Popular Politics in Ireland*, 312.

5. A. Parnell, *Tale of a Great Sham*, 55.

6. Paul Bew, *Enigma: A New Life of Charles Stewart Parnell* (Dublin: Gill and Macmillan, 2011), 90.

7. This law had survived on the statute books from Edward III's time. The statue empowered authorities to imprison "persons not of good fame" if these persons did not put up bail to prove their good behavior. Hannah Reynolds, a member of the Ladies' Land League arrested under this law, refused to pay the bail as she considered her help for evicted tenants the best example of good behavior. In all, thirteen women were arrested under this statute. When pressed in Parliament to explain this policy, Chief Secretary Forster replied that he was merely enforcing ordinary law and he could not interfere with local authority. Côté, *Fanny and Anna Parnell*, 207–8.

8. J. L. Hammond, *Gladstone and the Irish Nation* (London: Frank Cass and Co., 1964), 267.

9. See for example Lyons, *Charles Stewart Parnell*, 178–79; R. F. Foster, *Modern Ireland, 1600–1972* (New York: Penguin Press, 1988), 410; Moody, *Davitt and Irish Revolution*, 499. For a fuller discussion of this issue, see Walker, "Banshees, Dogooders, or Undervalued Radicals?," 37–44.

10. Côté, *Fanny and Anna Parnell*, 183–86.

11. Davitt, *Fall of Feudalism*, 348. Parnell was given his own fourteen-by-eight-foot cell in Kilmainham, was allowed multiple visitors, could play handball in the prison courtyard, and had the freedom to wake up and sleep when he desired. Lyons, *Charles Stewart Parnell*, 183.

12. Davitt, *Fall of Feudalism*, 349.

13. Lyons, *Charles Stewart Parnell*; 194; James S. Donnelly, Jr., "The Land Question in Nationalist Politics," in *Perspectives on Irish Nationalism*, ed. Thomas E. Hachey and Lawrence J. McCaffrey (Lexington: University Press of Kentucky, 1989), 92. Paul Bew has said since no rent was a failure, Parnell had nothing to lose. Bew, *Land and the National Question*, 215.

14. Hammond, *Gladstone and the Irish Nation*, 263–67; O'Callaghan, *British High Politics*, 90.

15. Davitt, *Fall of Feudalism*, 351; Hammond, *Gladstone and the Irish Nation*, 263–67, 275–79; Alan O'Day, *The English Face of Irish Nationalism: Parnellite Involvement in British Politics, 1880–86* (Dublin: Gill and Macmillan, 1977), 60.

16. Henry George to Patrick Ford, 28 February, 22 April 1882, Henry George Papers, NYPL.

17. *Irish World*, 25 March 1882, 6.

18. Quoted in Moody, *Davitt and Irish Revolution*, 532.

19. Ibid.

20. R. B. O'Brien, *Life of Charles Stewart Parnell*, 1:364.

21. Quoted in Marley, *Michael Davitt*, 48.

22. R. B. O'Brien, *Life of Charles Stewart Parnell*, 1:358.

23. Marley, *Michael Davitt*, 48.

24. *Times*, 8 May 1882, 7.

25. Quoted in James Jeffrey Roche, *John Boyle O'Reilly: His Life, Poems, and Speeches* (Philadelphia: John J. McVey, 1891), 216.

26. Ibid., 218.

27. *Irish World*, 20 May 1882, 4.

28. For several years, conservatives attempted to link Charles Stewart Parnell and the Land League to the murders. Even today, there is no complete understanding of the conspiracy to murder Cavendish and Burke. It is possible that the target had been Burke and that Cavendish was the victim of being in the wrong place at the wrong time. There is also circumstantial evidence that Patrick Egan, the Land League treasurer, may have been aware of the plot. In the end, five of the killers were captured, convicted, and hanged after the leader of the Invincibles, James Carey, turned state's evidence. Carey fled to South Africa but was recognized on the boat and killed by a fellow passenger and Irishman Patrick O'Donnell. O'Donnell was subsequently tried in London and hanged in late 1883. McGee, *IRB*, 99–102.

29. O'Callahan, *British High Politics*, 93.

30. Moody, *Davitt and Irish Revolution*, 539; Robert Kee, *The Laurel and the Ivy: The Story of Charles Stewart Parnell and Irish Nationalism* (London: Hamish Hamilton, 1993), 456–58; Lee, *Modernisation of Irish Society*, 86–88.

31. Davitt, *Fall of Feudalism*, 363.

32. O'Donnell, "Henry George," 280. The "Haymarket Bombing" refers to a bombing that occurred at a labor-organized May Day rally in 1886 in Chicago's Haymarket Square. As the meeting was dispersing, a bomb was thrown from the crowd at police, killing four policemen and wounding several others. Among historians there is still a dispute whether the bomb was thrown by a worker at the rally or by an agent provocateur. Despite this uncertainty, several local radicals and anarchists were rounded up and four executed despite their known innocence. The response to the bombing in the rest of the United States led to a general crackdown on labor and radical activism.

33. Lyons, *John Dillon*, 68.

34. Bull, *Land, Politics, and Nationalism*, 98.

35. For a discussion of Parnell's motivations for land reform, see McCarthy, "Parnell, Davitt, and the Land Question," 73–75.

36. During his time in prison, Davitt began writing notes for a planned book to be published on his release. In 1885 he published *Leaves of a Prison Diary*, which contained some of his prison notes. Carla King published the rest of Davitt's prison musings. Michael Davitt, *Jottings in Solitary*, ed. Carla King (Dublin: University College Dublin Press, 2004).

37. Moody, *Davitt and Irish Revolution*, 504–5.

38. Brown, *Irish-American Nationalism*, 125.

39. Quoted in *Irish World*, 17 June 1882, 1.

40. Shortly after his release, Davitt had requested that Land League funds be used

to print a cheap edition of *Progress and Poverty* to distribute in Great Britain. There were important distinctions between Davitt's ideas and George's theories. Davitt's plan differed from George's in offering compensation to landlords for their holdings. George also favored the land to be administered under private ownership as opposed to state ownership. Despite these variations, George and Ford supported Davitt's plan. See Henry George to Mr. Briggs, 9 June 1882, Henry George Papers, NYPL; *Irish World*, 8 July 1882, 8.

41. Moody, *Davitt and Irish Revolution*, 520; Michael Davitt, *Speech on Land Nationalization at Liverpool* (Liverpool: Universal Land Nationalization League, 1882), 1–12.

42. Lyons, *Charles Stewart Parnell*, 232–33.

43. *Dublin Review*, 8 (July–October 1882): 198.

44. Brown, *Irish-American Nationalism*, 126.

45. Henry George to Francis Shaw, 30 May 1882, Henry George Papers, NYPL.

46. Quoted in M. M. O'Hara, *Chief and Tribune: Parnell and Davitt* (Dublin: Maunsel and Co., 1919), 222.

47. Devoy, *Land of Eire*, 85; *Second Annual Convention of the Irish National Land League of the United States Held at Washington, D.C., April 12th and 13th, 1882* (Buffalo: Union and Time Print, 1882).

48. *Irish Nation*, 22 April 1882, 4.

49. *Irish World*, 8 April 1882, 4; 29 April 1882, 4.

50. *Irish World*, 17 June 1882, 4.

51. Ibid., 4 February 1882, 1.

52. *Redpath's Illustrated Weekly*, 22 July 1882, 2. This was a reference to Dennis Kearney and the Workingmen's Party of California who were responsible for leading the anti-Chinese agitation in the late 1870s in California. By 1882 many respectable reformers had come to see Kearney as a blustering demagogue.

53. *ICBU Journal*, July 1882, 4.

54. Quoted in the *Irish-American*, 24 June 1882, 5.

55. John Boyle O'Reilly to Michael Davitt, 12 June 1882, MS 9448–3607, Michael Davitt Papers, TCD.

56. *Irish World*, 29 July 1882, 1.

57. *Irish World*, 6 August 1881, 8.

58. *Irish World*, 11 February 1882, 8; 29 July 1882, 2.

59. *Irish World*, 22 July 1882, 8.

60. *Irish World*, 29 July 1882, 1.

61. *Irish Nation*, 8 July 1882, 1.

62. *Irish World*, 8 July 1882, 1.

63. Henry George to Patrick Ford, 3 August 1882, Henry George Papers, NYPL. This period was the beginning of a long friendship and partnership between McGlynn and George. Unknown to McGlynn, his speech attracted the negative attention of clerical authorities, who reported his activities to the *Propaganda Fide* in Rome. McGlynn would later be excommunicated for his support of George's 1886 mayoral campaign.

64. F. Parnell, "Nationalization of the Land," 195.

65. Fanny Parnell to T. D. Sullivan, 4 February 1881, MS 8237/4, T. D. Sullivan Papers, NLI.

66. *Irish Nation*, 1 July 1881, 5.

67. *Irish Nation*, 15 July 1882, 7.

68. *Irish Nation*, 1 July 1882, 2.

69. *Irish World*, 1 July 1882, 2.

70. Ibid.

71. Ibid., 7.

72. Brown, *Irish-American Nationalism*, 129.

73. Marley, *Michael Davitt*, 63–64.

74. Michael Davitt to John Dillon, 7 June 1882, MS 9403-1555, Michael Davitt Papers, TCD.

75. Tim Healy to Patrick Collins, 4 November 1882, Box 2, Folder 47, Patrick Collins Papers, BC. For the difference in temperament between Parnell and Davitt, see also M. M. O'Hara, *Chief and Tribune*, 67–71.

76. Michael Davitt to John Dillon, 21 June 1882, MS9403-1555a, Michael Davitt Papers, TCD.

77. *Truth*, 7 July 1882, 2.

78. O'Donnell, "Henry George," 299–300.

79. Quoted in *Irish Nation*, 8 July 1882, 8.

80. Quoted in McNeil, "Land, Labor, and Liberation, 106.

81. Davitt, *Fall of Feudalism*, 356.

82. Quoted in Margaret Ward, "The Ladies' Land League and the Irish Land War, 1881/1882: Defining the Relationship between Women and Nation," in *Gendered Nations: Nationalisms and Gender Order in the Long 19th Century*, ed. Ida Blom, Karen Hagemann, and Catherine Hall (Oxford: Berg, 2000), 240.

83. Côté and Hearne, "Anna Parnell," 284.

84. A. Parnell, *Tale of a Great Sham*, 155. Anna Parnell wrote this history of the Land League in 1907 but was unable to find a publisher in her lifetime. The manuscript was lost until 1959 and it was only first published in 1986 by a small feminist press.

85. Michael Davitt to John Dillon, 24 August 1882, MS 9403-1556, Michael Davitt Papers, TCD.

86. C. C. O'Brien, *Parnell and His Party*, 129.

87. Quoted in Paul Bew, *Ireland: The Politics of Enmity, 1789–2006* (Oxford: Oxford University Press, 2007), 340–41.

88. Ward, *Unmanageable Revolutionaries*, 36.

89. *Irish Nation*, 6 May 1882, 2.

90. Totals complied from weekly totals in the *Irish World* "Land League Fund."

91. Stephen Cleary to John Heffernan, 12 September 1882, MS 21904/3, John Heffernan Papers, NLI.

92. Brown, *Irish-American Nationalism*, 122.

93. *St. Joseph's Catholic Church, Petersburg, Virginia, Virginia I.N.L.L. of America Minute Book*, Reel 1281, Library of Virginia, Richmond, Virginia.

94. A. M. Sullivan to Michael Davitt, 21 September 1882, MS 9332–235, Michael Davitt Papers, TCD.

95. For Bishop Gilmour's collection for Parnell, see *Catholic Universe* (Cleveland), 6 November 1879, 4. For his speech denouncing the No-Rent Manifesto, see *Catholic Universe*, 9 February 1882, 8.

96. *Catholic Universe*, 25 May 1882, 4.

97. Ibid.

98. *Catholic Universe*, 1 June 1882, 4.

99. *Cleveland Leader*, 6 June 1882, 4.

100. Ibid. The Rev. Edward McGlynn, despite the bull of excommunication against the Cleveland women, spoke at their picnic, drawing the ire of Bishop Gilmour.

101. For Denver, see Brundage, *Making of Western Labor Radicalism*, 44–45; *Cleveland Leader*, 6 June 1882, 3; 19 June 1882, 1; 24 July 1882, 5; *Irish World*, 29 July 1882, 8.

102. *Western Watchman* (St. Louis), 8 July 1882, 8.

103. For an interesting discussion of the controversy over Fanny Parnell's body, see Paula Bernat Bennett, *Poets in the Public Sphere: The Emancipatory Project of America Women's Poetry, 1800–1900* (Princeton, NJ: Princeton University Press, 2003), 91–97.

104. *Catholic Sentinel for the Northwest* (Portland, OR), 7 September 1882, 4.

105. In St. Louis, Missouri, the Fanny Parnell branch of the Irish National League existed through 1886, though it seems to have become subsumed into the Emerald Literary and Debating Club, a group made up of young Irish Americans. *Western Watchman*, 13 November 1886. 4.

106. The Knights of Labor was perhaps the most inclusive labor movement of the nineteenth century but despite its successful attempts to mobilize workingwomen, the appointment of important women leaders, and the support for these policies from its Grand Master Workman Terence Powderly, women oftentimes faced an uphill battle in the organization. Phelan, *Grand Master Workman*, 154–56.

107. O'Donnell, "Henry George," 265.

108. Brundage, *Making of Western Labor Radicalism*, 52.

109. *Irish World*, 14 October 1882, 8 (emphasis in original).

110. Ibid. (emphasis in original).

111. Henry George to Terence V. Powderly, 25 July 1883, Reel 5, Terence V. Powderly Papers, American Catholic History Research Center and University Archives, Catholic University, Washington, DC.

112. David Brundage, "After the Land League: The Persistence of Irish-American Labor Radicalism in Denver, 1897–1905," *Journal of American Ethnic History* 2, no. 3 (1992): 6.

113. Montgomery, "Irish and the American Labor Movement," 211.

114. Gordon, "Labor Boycott in New York City," 206.

115. John R. McKivigan and Thomas J. Robertson, "The Irish American Worker in Transition, 1877–1914," in *The New York Irish*, ed. Ronald H. Bayor and Timothy J. Meagher (Baltimore: Johns Hopkins University Press, 1996), 305.

116. Schneirov, *Labor and Urban Politics*, 135.

117. T. P. O'Connor and Robert McWade, *Gladstone-Parnell and the Great Irish Struggle* (Boston: E. R. Curtis and Co., 1886), 556–61; *Third Annual Convention of the Irish National Land League and First Convention of the Irish National League of America, Held at Philadelphia, April 25th, 26th, and 27th, 1883* (Buffalo: Union and Times Print, 1883), 9, 35.

118. Funchion, *Chicago's Irish Nationalists*, 77.

119. *Third Annual Convention of the Irish National Land League*, 44–50.

120. Charles O'Reilly to John Devoy, 16 May 1883, MS 18010/10, John Devoy Papers, NLI.

121. Funchion, *Chicago's Irish Nationalists*, 84–85.

122. Michael F. Funchion, "Irish National League of America," in *Irish American Voluntary Organizations*, ed. Michael F. Funchion (Westport, CT: Greenwood Press, 1983), 195–96.

123. *ICBU Journal*, 15 October 1884, 2.

124. *Pilot*, 8 August 1885, 5.

Epilogue

1. Brown, *Irish-American Nationalism*, 171.

2. Funchion, "Irish Parliamentary Fund Association," 205.

3. Jackson, *Home Rule*, 75; Bew, *Ireland: The Politics of Enmity*, 359.

4. E. Foner, "Class, Ethnicity, and Radicalism," 198.

5. David Scobey, "Boycotting the Politics Factory: Labor Radicalism and the New York City Mayoral Election of 1884," [*sic*] *Radical History Review* 28–30 (1984): 293.

6. McKivigan and Robertson, "Irish American Worker," 306. For more on the adoption of the labor boycott in the United States, see Gordon, "Labor Boycott in New York City," 184–229.

7. Henry George to Patrick Ford, 17 May 1882, Henry George Papers, NYPL.

8. O'Donnell, "Henry George," 478–79.

9. Scobey, "Boycotting the Politics Factory," 285.

10. Quoted in Louis F. Post and Fred C. Leubuscher, *Henry George's 1886 Campaign: An Account of the George-Hewitt Campaign in the New York Municipal Election of 1886* (Westport, CT: Hyperion Press, 1976), 25.

11. Quoted in ibid., 72.

12. *Irish World*, 16 October 1882, 4.

13. Quoted in Post and Leubuscher, *Henry George's 1886 Campaign*, 129–30. McGlynn had been under orders from Archbishop Michael Corrigan to not participate publicly in the campaign, and he was subsequently suspended for two weeks from his duties.

14. Barker, *Henry George*, 471–72.

15. Arthur Nichols Young, *The Single Tax Movement in the United States* (Princeton, NJ: Princeton University Press, 1916), 248; Robert Emmet Curran, "The McGlynn Affair and the Shaping of the New Conservatism in American Catholicism, 1886–1894," *Catholic Historical Review* 66, no. 2 (April 1980): 191; David Brundage, "'In Time of Peace, Prepare for War': Key Themes in the Social Thought of New York's Irish Nationalists,

1890–1916," in *The New York Irish*, ed. Ronald H. Bayor and Timothy J. Meagher (Baltimore: John Hopkins University Press, 1997), 324; Samuel J. Thomas, "Portraits of a 'Rebel' Priest: Edward McGlynn in Caricature, 1886–1893," *Journal of American Culture* 7, no. 2 (1987): 23. See also the *Puck* political cartoon featuring McGlynn and his female supporters, *Puck*, 22 June 1887, 276–77.

16. Tara Monica McCarthy, "True Women, Trade Unionists, and the Lessons of Tammany Hall: Ethnic Identity, Social Reform, and the Political Culture of Irish Women in America, 1880–1923" (PhD diss., University of Rochester, 2005), 59–60.

17. McKivigan and Robertson, "Irish American Worker," 310. Archbishop Corrigan, increasingly unhappy with McGlynn's activities in favor of Henry George, suspended him, and McGlynn was summoned to Rome to explain his actions. McGlynn refused to go and was excommunicated. His sentence of excommunication continued until 1892.

18. *Worcester Evening Post*, 5 January 1909, 1. Her obituary also says that Dougherty was responsible for raising money for a graveside monument to McGlynn.

19. *Brooklyn Daily Eagle*, 24 September 1886, quoted in O'Donnell, "Henry George," 527.

20. Quoted in McKivigan and Robertson, "Irish American Worker," 308.

21. Post and Leubuscher, *Henry George's 1886 Campaign*, 168.

22. Quoted in Barker, *Henry George*, 479.

23. Burrows and Wallace, *Gotham*, 1106.

24. Ibid.

25. Barker, *Henry George*, 478.

26. Burrows and Wallace, *Gotham*, 1106.

27. Barker, *Henry George*, 484–85. In 1886 Catholic officials decided that it was acceptable for Catholics to join the Knights of Labor.

28. Rodechko, *Patrick Ford*, 98–104. In contrast to Rodechko, Sabina Taylor argues that it was merely Ford's tactics that changed and that his views in the 1890s and 1900s were consistent with his earlier beliefs. Sabina Taylor, "Patrick Ford and His Pursuit of Social Justice" (MA thesis, Saint Mary's University, 1993).

29. James Green, *Death in the Haymarket: A Story of Chicago, the First Labor Movement, and the Bombing that Divided Gilded Age America* (New York: Pantheon Books, 2006), 257–58.

Bibliography

Manuscript Sources, Republic of Ireland

Manuscript Division, Trinity College, Dublin
    John Dillon Papers
    Michael Davitt Papers
National Archives of Ireland, Dublin
    Fenian "A" Files
National Library of Ireland, Dublin
    John Devoy Papers
    John Heffernan Papers
    T. D. Sullivan Papers
    W. G. Fallon Papers

Manuscript Sources, United States

American Irish Historical Society, New York, NY
    Luke O'Connor Papers
Archdiocese of Chicago Joseph Cardinal Bernardin Archives and Record Center, Chicago, IL
    Madaj Collection
Catholic University of America, Washington, DC
    Terence V. Powderly Papers (Microfilm Edition)
Cincinnati Historical Society, Cincinnati, OH
    Charles Stewart Parnell in Cincinnati, Ohio: An Account of a visit by the Irish Patriot to the City of Cincinnati, February 20, 1880, transcribed by Pat Power
John J. Burns Library, Boston College, Chestnut Hill, MA
    George D. Cahill Papers
    Patrick Collins Papers
Library of Virginia, Richmond, VA

St. Joseph's Catholic Church, Petersburg, Virginia, I.N.L.L. of America Minute
      Book, Misc. Reel 1281.
Manuscripts and Archives Division, New York Public Library, New York, NY
      Henry George Papers
Minnesota Historical Society, St. Paul, MN
      Michael J. Boyle Papers
Philadelphia Archdiocesan Historical Research Center, Wynnewood, PA
      Martin Griffin Papers

Newspapers and Periodicals

AOH Journal (Richmond, VA)
Atlanta Daily Constitution
Brooklyn Daily Eagle
Catholic Mirror (Baltimore)
Catholic Sentinel for the Northwest (Portland, OR)
Catholic Union (Buffalo)
Catholic Universe (Cleveland)
Celtic World (Minneapolis)
Chicago Tribune
Cincinnati Daily Enquirer
Citizen (Chicago)
Cleveland Leader
Cleveland Universe
Daily Morning Call (San Francisco)
Daily Union and Advertiser (Rochester, NY)
Donahoe's Magazine (Boston)
Dublin Review
Freeman's Journal (Dublin)
Gaelic American
Globe (Boston)
Harper's Weekly (New York)
ICBU Journal (Philadelphia)
Irish-American (New York)
Irish Nation (New York)
Irish World and American Industrial Liberator (New York)
Leader (Cleveland)
Liberty
Los Angeles Times
Missouri Republican (St. Louis)
Monitor (San Francisco)
New York Herald
New York Tablet
New York Times

New York Tribune
Northwestern-Chronicle (St. Paul)
Pilot (Boston)
Pioneer Press (St. Paul)
Puck (New York)
Redpath's Illustrated Weekly (New York)
Republic (Boston)
St. Paul Globe
Truth (New York)
United Ireland (Dublin)
Western Home Journal (Detroit)
Western Watchman (St. Louis)
Worcester Evening Post

Published Diaries, Letters, and Memoirs

Anderson, J. A. *A Life and Memoirs of Rev. C. F. X. Goldsmith*. Milwaukee: Press of the Evening Wisconsin Company, 1895.

Bagenal, Philip A. *The American Irish and Their Influence on Irish Politics*. n.p.: Jerome S. Ozer, 1971.

Cashman, D. B. *The Life of Michael Davitt*. Boston: Murphy and Murphy Publishers, 1881.

Curran, M. P. *Life of Patrick A. Collins with Some of His Most Notable Public Addresses*. Norword, MA: The Norwood Press, 1906.

Davitt, Michael. *The Fall of Feudalism in Ireland, or the Story of the Land League Revolution*. Shannon, Ireland: Irish University Press, 1970.

————. *Jottings in Solitary*. Edited by Carla King. Dublin: University College Dublin Press, 2004.

Devoy, John. *The Land of Eire: The Irish Land League, Its Origins and Consequences*. Boston: Patterson and Neilson, 1882.

————. *Michael Davitt*. Edited by Carla King and W. J. McCormack. Dublin: University College Dublin Press, 2008.

Devyr, Thomas Ainge. *The Odd Book of the Nineteenth Century*. New York: Garland Publishing, 1986.

George, Henry. *The Irish Land Question*. N.p.: Elbrion Classics, 2005.

George, Henry, Jr. *The Life of Henry George*. New York: Robert Schalkenbach Foundation, 1960.

Healy, T. M. *Letters and Leaders of My Day*. Vol. 1. New York: Frederick A. Stokes Company, 1929.

Lalor, James Fintan. *"The Faith of a Felon" and Other Writings*. Edited by Marta Ramón. Dublin: University College Dublin Press, 2012.

Le Caron, Henri. *Twenty-Five Years in the Secret Service: The Recollections of a Spy*. Boston: American Citizen Co., 1892.

Marx, Karl, and Frederick Engels. *Ireland and the Irish Question: A Collection of Writings by Karl Marx and Frederick Engels*. New York: International Publishers, 1972.

McCarthy, Michael J. F. *The Irish Revolution*. Vol. 1, *The Murdering Time, from the Land League to the First Home Rule Bill*. Edinburgh and London: William Blackwood and Sons, 1912.

O'Brien, R. Barry. *The Life of Charles Stewart Parnell, 1846–1891*. 2 vols. New York: Greenwood Press Publishers, 1969.

O'Brien, William, and Desmond Ryan. *Devoy's Post Bag, 1871–1928*. 2 vols. Dublin: C. J. Fallon, 1953.

O'Brien, William. *Recollections*. New York: The Macmillan Company, 1905.

O'Connor, Mary Doline. *The Life and Letters of M. P. O'Connor*. New York: Dempsey and Carroll, 1893.

O'Connor, T. P., and Robert McWade. *Gladstone-Parnell and the Great Irish Struggle*. Boston: E. R. Curtis and Co., 1886.

Parnell, Anna. *Tale of a Great Sham*. Edited by Dana Hearne. Dublin: Arlen House, 1986.

Parnell, John Howard. *Charles Stewart Parnell: A Memoir*. London: Constable and Co., 1921.

Post, Louis F., and Fred C. Leubuscher. *Henry George's 1886 Campaign: An Account of the George-Hewitt Campaign in the New York Municipal Election of 1886*. Westport, CT: Hyperion Press, 1976.

Powderly, Terence V. *The Path I Trod: The Autobiography of Terence V. Powderly*. Edited by Harry J. Carman, Henry David, and Paul N. Guthrie. New York: Ams Press, 1968.

Roche, James Jeffrey. *John Boyle O'Reilly: His Life, Poems, and Speeches*. Philadelphia: John J. McVey, 1891.

Tynan, Katharine. *Twenty-Five Years: Reminiscences*. London: Smith, Elder and Co., 1913.

Zwierlein, Frederick. *The Life and Letters of Bishop McQuaid*. Vol. 2. Rochester: Art Print Shop, 1926.

Pamphlets, Speeches, and Works

Bagenal, Philip. *The American Irish and Their Influence on Irish Politics*. London: Kegan, Paul, Trench, and Co., 1882.

Conway, Katherine E. "Margaret F. Sullivan, Journalist and Author." *Donahoe's Magazine* 51 (March 1904): 220–23.

Davitt, Michael. *Speech Delivered by Michael Davitt in Defence of the Land League*. London: Kegan, Paul, Trench, Trüber and Co., 1890.

———. *Speech on Land Nationalization at Liverpool*. Liverpool: Universal Land Nationalization League, 1882.

Ellis, John. *The Irish Question: A Speech Delivered Before the Land League of the 6th District of New Orleans, at St. Stephen's Hall, New Orleans, Louisiana, on the Evening of March 17th, 1882*. Washington, DC: R. O. Polkinhorn, 1882.

First Annual Convention of the Irish National Land League, held at Buffalo, New York, January 12th and 13th, 1881. Richmond, VA: P. Keenan, 1881.

Fox, R. M. *Parnell's Land League Songster*. New York: Richard K. Fox, 1880.

George, Henry. *The Irish Land Question*. N.p.: Elbrion Classics, 2005.

Gilmour, Richard. *Lecture on the Land League by Rt. Rev. Richard Gilmour, Bishop of Cleveland, Delivered at the Tabernacle, Cleveland, Ohio, February 6, 1882.* Cleveland: J. B. Savage, 1882.

Grace, William. *The Irish in America.* Chicago: McDannell Bros., 1886.

Irish Catholic Colonization Association of the United States: The Secretary's Second Annual Report. Chicago: n.p., 1881.

Irish National Land League of the United States Constitution, Adopted January 13th, 1881 at Buffalo, N.Y. Boston: M. H. Kennan Printer, 1881.

Meriwether, Avery. *English Tyranny and Irish Suffering: Dedicated to the Irish Land League of Memphis.* Memphis: R. M. Mansford, 1881.

O'Reilly, John Boyle. "Ireland's Opportunity—Will It Be Lost?" *American Catholic Quarterly Review* 7 (1882): 114–20.

Parnell, Fanny. "Nationalization of the Land vs. Peasant Proprietary." *Donohoe's Magazine* 8, no. 3 (September 1882): 195–202.

Proceedings of the Fourteenth Annual Convention of the Irish Catholic Benevolent Union, held at Philadelphia, September 27th and September 28th, 1882. Philadelphia: Kildare's Printing House, 1882.

Proceedings of the Twelfth Annual Convention of the Irish Catholic Benevolent Union, held at Wilmington, Del., September 22nd, 23rd, and 25th, 1880. Philadelphia: Kildare's Printing House, 1880.

Redpath, James. *Talks about Ireland.* New York: P. J. Kennedy, 1881.

Report of Rev. Lawrence Walsh, Central Treasurer of the Irish National Land League, U.S., from January 10, 1881, to April 10, 1881. N.p.: n.p., 1881.

Second Annual Convention of the Irish National Land League of the United States Held at Washington, D.C., April 12th and 13th, 1882. Buffalo: Union and Time Print, 1882.

Second Quarterly Report of the Irish National Land League United States for Quarter Ending July 10th, 1881. N.p.: n.p., 1881.

Special Commission Act, 1888: Reprint of the shorthand notes of the speeches, proceedings, and evidence taken before the Commissioners appointed under the above-named act. Vols. 1–11. London: Printed for her Majesty's Stationery Office by Eyre and Spottiswoode, 1890.

Sullivan, Alexander. *Emigration vs. Enforced Emigration: Addresses to Chester A. Arthur, President of the United States.* Philadelphia: Convention of the Irish Race, 1883.

———. "Parnell as a Leader." *North American Review* 144, no. 6 (June 1887): 609–24.

Sullivan, Margaret. *Ireland of To-Day: Causes and Aims of Irish Agitation.* Philadelphia: J. C. McCurdy and Co., 1881.

Swank, Lizzie. "Women Workers of Chicago." *American Federationist* 12 (August 1905): 507–10.

Third Annual Convention of the Irish National Land League and First Convention of the Irish National League of America, Held at Philadelphia, April 25th, 26th, and 27th, 1883. Buffalo: Union and Times Print, 1883.

Virgilius. *Parnell; or Ireland and America.* New York: Printed for the Publisher, 1880.

What Science Is Saying about Ireland. London: Hamilton, Adams, and Co. 1881.

Published Document Collections

McCarthy, Justin, ed. *Irish Literature*. Vol. 7. Philadelphia: J. D. Morris and Co., 1904.

Tucker, Benjamin. *Individual Liberty: Selections from the Writings of Benjamin R. Tucker*. Edited by C. L. S. New York: Vanguard Press, 1926.

Secondary Sources

Anderson, J. A. *A Life and Memoirs of Rev. C. F. X. Goldsmith*. Milwaukee: Press of the Evening Wisconsin Company, 1895.

Applegate, Debby. *The Most Famous Man in America: The Biography of Henry Ward Beecher*. New York: Doubleday, 2006.

Barker, Charles Albro. *Henry George*. New York: Oxford University Press, 1955.

Baron, Ava, ed. *Work Engendered: Toward a New History of American Labor*. Ithaca, NY: Cornell University Press, 1991.

Bartlett, Thomas. *Ireland: A History*. Cambridge: Cambridge University Press, 2010.

Bender, Thomas, ed. *Rethinking American History in a Global Age*. Berkeley: University of California Press, 2002.

Bennett, Paula Bernat. *Poets in the Public Sphere: The Emancipatory Project of American Women's Poetry, 1800–1900*. Princeton, NJ: Princeton University Press, 2003.

Berube, Claude G., and John A. Rodgaard. *A Call to the Sea: Captain Charles Stewart of the USS Constitution*. Washington, DC: Potomac Books, 2005.

Betts, John R. "The Negro and the New England Conscience in the Days of John Boyle O'Reilly." *Journal of Negro History* 51, no. 4 (1965): 246–61.

Bew, Paul. *C. S. Parnell*. Dublin: Gill and Macmillan, 1980.

———. *Enigma: A New Life of Charles Stewart Parnell*. Dublin: Gill and Macmillan, 2011.

———. *Ireland: The Politics of Enmity, 1789–2006*. Oxford: Oxford University Press, 2007.

———. *Land and the National Question in Ireland, 1858–82*. Atlantic Highlands, NJ: Humanities Press, 1979.

Bland, Sister Joan. *Hibernian Crusade: The Story of the Catholic Total Abstinence Union of America*. Washington, DC: Catholic University of America Press, 1951.

Bronstein, Jamie. *Land Reform and Working-Class Experience in Britain and the United States, 1800–1862*. Stanford, CA: Stanford University Press, 1990.

Brooks, Frank H., ed. *The Individualist Anarchists: An Anthology of Liberty, 1881–1908*. New Brunswick, NJ: Transaction Publishers, 1994.

Brown, Thomas N. *Irish-American Nationalism, 1870–1879*. Philadelphia: J. B. Lippincott, 1966.

Browne, Henry J. *The Catholic Church and the Knights of Labor*. Washington, DC: Catholic University of America Press, 1949.

Brundage, David. "After the Land League: The Persistence of Irish-American Labor Radicalism in Denver, 1897–1905." *Journal of American Ethnic History* 2, no. 3 (1992): 3–26.

———. "'In Time of Peace, Prepare for War': Key Themes in the Social Thought of New York's Irish Nationalists, 1890–1916." In *The New York Irish*, edited by Ronald

H. Bayor and Timothy J. Meagher, 321–34. Baltimore: Johns Hopkins University
Press, 1997.

———. "Irish Land and American Workers: Class and Ethnicity in Denver, Colorado."
In *"Struggle a Hard Battle": Essays on Working-Class Immigrants*, edited by Dirk Hoerder,
46–67. Dekalb: Northern Illinois University Press, 1986.

———. *The Making of Western Labor Radicalism: Denver's Organized Workers, 1878–1905*.
Urbana: University of Illinois Press, 1994.

———. "Matilda Tone in America: Exile, Gender, and Memory in the Making of
Irish Republican Nationalism." *New Hibernia Review* 14, no. 1 (Spring 2010): 96–111.

Buhle, Paul. *From the Knights of Labor to the New World Order: Essays on Labor and Culture*.
New York: Garland Publishing, 1997.

Bull, Philip. *Land, Politics, and Nationalism: A Study of the Irish Land Question*. Dublin: Gill
and Macmillan, 1996.

Burrows, Edwin G., and Mike Wallace. *Gotham: A History of New York City to 1898*. Oxford:
Oxford University Press, 1999.

Butler, Leslie. *Critical Americans: Victorian Intellectuals and Transatlantic Liberal Reform*.
Chapel Hill: University of North Carolina Press, 2007.

Callahan, Frank. *T. M. Healy*. Cork: Cork University Press, 1996.

Calton, Kenneth E. "Parnell's Mission to Iowa." *Annals of Iowa* 22 (April 1940): 312–27.

Cameron, Ardis. *Radicals of the Worst Sort: Laboring Women in Lawrence, Massachusetts, 1860–
1912*. Urbana: University of Illinois Press, 1995.

Carter, J. W. H. *The Land War and Its Leaders in Queen's County, 1879–82*. Portlaoise, Ireland:
Leinster Express Newspapers, 1994.

Clark, Dennis. *Hibernia America: The Irish and Regional Cultures*. New York: Greenwood
Press, 1986.

———. *The Irish Relations: Trials of an Immigrant Tradition*. Rutherford, NJ: Associated
University Press, 1982.

Clark, Samuel. *Social Origins of the Irish Land War*. Princeton, NJ: Princeton University
Press, 1979.

Clarke, Brian P. *Piety and Nationalism: Lay Voluntary Associations and the Creation of an Irish-
Catholic Community in Toronto, 1850–1895*. Montreal: McGill-Queen's University
Press, 1993.

Comerford, R. V. *The Fenians in Context: Irish Politics and Society, 1848–82*. Dublin: Wolfhound Press, 1998.

Corcoran, Brandon Shane. "The New Departure in Irish-American Nationalism,
1878–1880." MA thesis, University College Cork, 2007.

Côté, Jane. *Fanny and Anna Parnell: Ireland's Patriot Sisters*. London: Macmillan, 1991.

Côté, Jane, and Dana Hearne. "Anna Parnell." In *Women, Power and Consciousness in
19th-Century Ireland: Eight Biographical Studies*, edited by Mary Cullen and Maria
Luddy, 263–293. Dublin: Attic Press, 1995.

Cummings, Kathleen Sprows. "'Not the New Woman?' Irish-American Women and
the Creation of a Usable Past, 1890–1900." *U.S. Catholic Historian* 19, no. 1 (Winter
2001): 37–52.

Curran, Robert Emmett. "The McGlynn Affair and the Shaping of the New Conserva-
    tism in American Catholicism, 1886–1894." *Catholic Historical Review* 66, no. 2 (April
    1980): 184–204.

———. "Prelude to 'Americanism': The New York Accademia and Clerical Radicalism
    in the Late Nineteenth Century." *Church History* 47, no. 1 (March 1978): 48–65.

Curtis, L. Perry. *Apes and Angels: The Irishman in Victorian Caricature*. Washington, DC:
    Smithsonian Institution Press, 1997.

D'Arcy, William. *The Fenian Movement in the United States: 1858–1886*. Washington, DC:
    Catholic University of America Press, 1947.

De Nie, Michael. *The Eternal Paddy: Irish Identity and the English Press, 1798–1882*. Madison:
    University of Wisconsin Press, 2004.

Deverell, William. "To Loosen the Safety Valve: Eastern Workers and Western Lands."
    Western Historical Quarterly 19, no. 3 (August 1998): 269–85.

Diner, Hasia. *Erin's Daughters in America: Irish Immigrant Women in the Nineteenth Century*.
    Baltimore: Johns Hopkins University Press, 1983.

Doan, Robert A. "Green Gold to Emerald Shores: Irish Immigration to the United
    States and Transatlantic Monetary Aid, 1854–1923." PhD diss., Temple University,
    1999.

Donnelly, James S., Jr. *The Great Irish Potato Famine*. Gloucestershire, England: Sutton
    Publishing, 2001.

———. *The Land and the People of Nineteenth-Century Cork: The Rural Economy and the Land
    Question*. London: Routledge and Kegan Paul, 1975.

———. "The Land Question in Nationalist Politics." In *Perspectives on Irish Nationalism*,
    edited by Thomas E. Hachey and Lawrence J. McCaffrey, 79–98. Lexington: Uni-
    versity Press of Kentucky, 1989.

Doyle, David Noel. "The Irish and American Labor, 1880–1920." *Saothar: Journal of the
    Irish Labor History Society* 1 (1975): 42–53.

Edwards, Rebecca. *New Spirits: Americans in the Gilded Age, 1865–1905*. New York: Oxford
    University Press, 2006.

Eid, Leroy V. "*Puck* and the Irish: 'The One American Idea.'" *Éire Ireland* 11 (1976):
    18–35.

Elliott, Marianne. *Wolfe Tone: Prophet of Irish Independence*. New Haven, CT: Yale University
    Press, 1989.

Emmons, David. *Beyond the American Pale: The Irish in the West, 1845–1910*. Norman: Uni-
    versity of Oklahoma Press, 2010.

———. *The Butte Irish: Class and Ethnicity in an American Mining Town, 1875–1925*. Urbana:
    University of Illinois Press, 1990.

English, Richard. *Irish Freedom: The History of Nationalism in Ireland*. London: Pan Books,
    2006.

Fink, Leon. *In Search of the Working Class: Essays in American Labor History and Political Culture*.
    Urbana: University of Illinois Press, 1994.

———. *Workingmen's Democracy: The Knights of Labor and American Politics*. Urbana: Uni-
    versity of Illinois Press, 1993.

Foley, Neil. *The White Scourge: Mexicans, Blacks, and Poor Whites in Texas Cotton Culture.* Berkeley: California University Press, 1997.

Foner, Eric. "Class, Ethnicity, and Radicalism in the Gilded Age: The Land League and Irish-America." In *Politics and Ideology in the Age of the Civil War*, 150–200. Oxford: Oxford University Press, 1980.

Foner, Philip S. *Women and the American Labor Movement: From Colonial Times to the Eve of World War I.* New York: The Free Press, 1979.

Foster, R. F. *Modern Ireland, 1600–1972.* New York: Penguin Press, 1988.

————. *Paddy and Mr. Punch: Connections in Irish and English History.* London: A. Lane, 1993.

Funchion, Michael F. *Chicago's Irish Nationalists, 1881–1890.* New York: Arno Press, 1976.

————, ed. *Irish American Voluntary Organizations.* Westport, CT: Greenwood Press, 1983.

————. "Irish Catholic Society for the Promotion of Actual Settlements in North America." In *Irish American Voluntary Organizations*, edited by Michael F. Funchion, 161–64. Westport, CT: Greenwood Press, 1983.

————. "Irish National League of America." In *Irish American Voluntary Organizations*, edited by Michael F. Funchion, 189–93. Westport, CT: Greenwood Press, 1983.

————. "Irish Nationalists and Chicago Politics in the 1880s." *Éire-Ireland* 10, no. 2 (1975): 3–18.

————. "Irish Parliamentary Fund Association." In *Irish American Voluntary Organizations*, edited by Michael F. Funchion, 204–6. Westport, CT: Greenwood Press, 1983.

Gair, John D., and Cordelia C. Humphrey. "The Alabama Dimension to the Political Thought of Charles Stewart Parnell." *Alabama Review* 52, no. 1 (1999): 21–50.

Gerteis, Joseph. *Class and the Color Line: Interracial Class Coalition in the Knights of Labor and the Populist Movement.* Durham, NC: Duke University Press, 2007.

Gibbs, Joseph. *History of the Catholic Total Abstinence Union of America.* Philadelphia: n.p., 1907.

Gibson, Florence. *The Attitudes of the New York Irish Toward State and National Affairs, 1848–1892.* New York: Columbia University Press, 1951.

Gleeson, David. *The Irish in the South, 1815–1877.* Chapel Hill: University of North Carolina Press, 2001.

Gleeson, David T., and Brendan J. Buttimer. "'We are Irish Everywhere': Irish Immigrant Networks in Charleston, South Carolina, and Savannah, Georgia." *Immigrants & Minorities* 23, nos. 2–3 (July–November 2005): 183–205.

Golway, Terry. *Irish Rebel: John Devoy and America's Fight for Ireland's Freedom.* New York: St. Martin's Press, 1998.

Goodwyn, Lawrence. *The Populist Moment: A Short History of the Agrarian Revolt in America.* New York: Oxford University Press, 1978.

Gordon, Michael A. "The Labor Boycott in New York City, 1880–1886." *Labor History* 16 (Spring 1975): 184–229.

————. *The Orange Riots: Irish Political Violence in New York City, 1870 and 1871.* Ithaca, NY: Cornell University Press, 1993.

————. "Studies in Irish and Irish-American Thought and Behavior in Gilded Age New York City." PhD diss., University of Rochester, 1977.

Gray, Peter. *Famine, Land, and Politics: British Government and Irish Society, 1843–1850*. Dublin: Irish Academic Press, 1999.

Green, James. *Death in the Haymarket: A Story of Chicago, the First Labor Movement, and the Bombing that Divided Gilded Age America*. New York: Pantheon Books, 2006.

Green, James J. "American Catholics and the Irish Land League, 1879–1882." *Catholic Historical Review* 35 (1949): 19–42.

————. "First Impact of the Henry George Agitation on Catholics in the United States." MA thesis, University of Notre Dame, 1948.

Grew, Raymond. "The Comparative Weakness of American History." *Journal of Interdisciplinary History* 16 (Summer 1985): 87–101.

Hahn, Steven. *A Nation under Our Feet: Black Political Struggles in the Rural South, from Slavery to the Great Migration*. Cambridge, MA: Belknap Press, 2003.

————. *The Roots of Southern Populism: Yeoman Farmers and the Transformation of the Georgia Upcountry, 1850–1890*. New York: Oxford University Press, 1983.

Hammond, J. L. *Gladstone and the Irish Nation*. London: Frank Cass and Co., 1964.

Hazel, Michael. "First Link: Parnell's American Tour, 1880." *Éire-Ireland* 15, no. 1 (1980): 6–24.

Hearne, Dana. "Rewriting History: Anna Parnell's *The Tale of a Great Sham*." In *Woman in Irish Legend, Life, and Literature*, edited by S. F. Gallagher, 138–49. Totowa: Barnes and Noble Books, 1983.

Hirota, Hidetaka. "'The Great Entrepot for Medicants': Foreign Poverty and Immigration Control in New York State to 1882." *Journal of American Ethnic History* 33, no. 32 (2014): 5–32.

Hirsch, Eric L. *Urban Revolt: Ethnic Politics in the Nineteenth-Century Chicago Labor Movement*. Berkeley: University of California Press, 1990.

Horner, Charles. *The Life of James Redpath and the Development of the Modern Lyceum*. New York: Barse and Hopkins, 1926.

Hotten-Summers, Diane M. "Relinquishing and Reclaiming Independence: Irish Domestic Servants, American Middle-Class Mistresses, and Assimilation, 1850–1890." In *New Directions in Irish-American History*, edited by Kevin Kenny, 227–42. Madison: University of Wisconsin Press, 2003.

Howe, Stephen. *Ireland and Empire: Colonial Legacies in Irish History and Culture*. New York: Oxford University Press, 2000.

Hunter, James. *For the People's Cause: From the Writings of John Murdoch—Highland and Irish Land Reformer*. Edinburgh: Crofters Commission, 1986.

Huston, Reeve. *Land and Freedom: Rural Society, Popular Protest, and Party Politics in Antebellum New York*. New York: Oxford University Press, 2000.

————. "Multiple Crossings: Thomas Ainge Devyr and Transatlantic Land Reform." In *Transatlantic Rebels: Agrarian Radicalism in Comparative Context*, edited by Thomas Summerhill, 137–66. East Lansing: Michigan State University Press, 2004.

Hyde, William, and Howard Conrad, eds. *Encyclopedia of the History of St. Louis*. Vol. 2. St. Louis: Southern History Company, 1899.

Isacsson, Alfred. *The Determined Doctor: The Story of Edward McGlynn.* Tarrytown, NY: Vestigium Press, 1998.

Jackson, Alvin. *Home Rule: An Irish History, 1800–2000.* Oxford: Oxford University Press, 2003.

———. *Ireland, 1798–1998: Politics and War.* Oxford: Blackwell, 1999.

Jacobson, Matthew Frye. *Special Sorrows: The Diasporic Imagination of Irish, Polish, and Jewish Immigrants in the United States.* Cambridge: Cambridge University Press, 1995.

Jenkins, William. "Deconstructing Diasporas: Networks and Identities among the Irish in Buffalo and Toronto, 1870–1910." *Immigrants & Minorities* 23, nos. 2–3 (July–November 2005): 359–398.

Jordan, Donald E. *Land and Popular Politics in Ireland: County Mayo from the Plantation to the Land War.* Cambridge: Cambridge University Press, 1994.

Joyce, Megan Harrigan. "Elizabeth Gurley Flynn." MA thesis, Wright State University, 1995.

Kane, Anne. *Constructing Irish National Identity: Discourse and Ritual during the Land War, 1879–1882.* London: Palgrave Macmillan, 2011.

Kantrowiz, Stephen. *Ben Tillman and the Reconstruction of White Supremacy.* Chapel Hill: University of North Carolina Press, 2000.

Kee, Robert. *The Green Flag: A History of Irish Nationalism.* London: Penguin Books, 2000.

———. *The Laurel and the Ivy: The Story of Charles Stewart Parnell and Irish Nationalism.* London: Hamish Hamilton, 1993.

Kelly, Mary C. *The Shamrock and the Lily: The New York Irish and the Creation of a Transatlantic Identity, 1845–1921.* New York: Peter Lang, 2005.

Kenneally, James J. "Eve, Mary, and the Historians: American Catholicism and Women." *Horizons* 3, no. 2 (1976): 187–202.

———. *The History of American Catholic Women.* New York: Crossroad, 1990.

Kennelly, Karen. "Ideals of American Catholic Womanhood." In *American Catholic Women: A Historical Exploration*, edited by Karen Kennelly, 1–16. New York: Macmillan, 1989.

Kenny, Kevin. *The American Irish: A History.* Harlow, UK: Pearson Education, 2000.

———. "Diaspora and Comparison: The Global Irish as a Case Study." *Journal of American History* 90, no. 1 (June 2003): 134–62.

———, ed. *Ireland and the British Empire.* New York: Oxford University Press, 2004.

———. *Making Sense of the Molly Maguires.* New York: Oxford University Press, 1998.

———. "The Molly Maguires and the Catholic Church." *Labor History* 36 (Summer 1995): 345–76.

Kerber, Linda. "Separate Spheres, Female Worlds, Woman's Place: The Rhetoric of Women's History." *Journal of American History* 75, no. 1 (June 1988): 9–39.

———. *Women of the Republic: Intellect and Ideology in Revolutionary America.* Chapel Hill: University of North Carolina Press, 1980.

Kinealy, Christine. *The Great Irish Famine: Impact, Ideology, and Rebellion.* New York: Palgrave, 2002.

———. *A New History of Ireland.* New York: Sutton Publishing, 2008.

King, Carla. *Michael Davitt.* Dundalk, Ireland: Dundalgan Press, 1999.

Knobel, Dale. *Paddy and the Republic: Ethnicity and Nationality in Antebellum America.* Middle-town, CT: Wesleyan University Press, 1986.

Korngold, Ralph. *Two Friends of Man: The Story of William Lloyd Garrison and Wendell Phillips and Their Relationship with Abraham Lincoln.* Boston: Little, Brown, and Company, 1950.

Krause, Paul. *The Battle for Homestead, 1880–1892: Politics, Culture and Steel.* Pittsburgh: University of Pittsburgh Press, 1992.

Krieg, John. *Whitman and the Irish.* Iowa City: University of Iowa Press, 2000.

Lane, Fintan. *The Origins of Modern Irish Socialism, 1881–1896.* Cork: Cork University Press, 1997.

Larkin, Emmet. *The Roman Catholic Church and the Creation of the Modern Irish State, 1878–1886.* Philadelphia: American Philosophical Society, 1975.

Lause, Mark. "Progress Impoverished: Origin of Henry George's Single Tax." *Historian* 52, no. 3 (1990): 394–410.

———. *Young America: Land, Labor, and the Republican Community.* Urbana: University of Illinois Press, 2005.

Lee, Joseph. "Millennial Reflections on Irish-American History." *Radharc* 1 (November 2000): 5–64.

———. *The Modernisation of Irish Society, 1848–1918.* Dublin: Gill and Macmillan, 1973.

Levine, Susan. "Labor's True Woman: Domesticity and Equal Rights in the Knights of Labor." *Journal of American History* 70, no. 2 (September 1983): 323–39.

Light, Dale. "Class, Ethnicity, and the Urban Ecology in a Nineteenth Century City: Philadelphia's Irish, 1840–1890." PhD diss., University of Pennsylvania, 1972.

Lynch, Niamh. "Defining Irish Nationalist Anti-Imperialism: Thomas Davis and John Mitchel." *Éire-Ireland* 42, nos. 1 and 2 (Spring/Summer 2007): 82–107.

———. "Live Ireland, Perish the Empire: Irish Nationalist Anti-Imperialism, c. 1840–1910." PhD diss., Boston College, 2006.

Lyons, F. S. L. *Charles Stewart Parnell.* London: Collins, 1977.

———. *John Dillon: A Biography.* Chicago: University of Chicago Press, 1968.

MacDonagh, Oliver. *The Emancipist: Daniel O'Connell, 1830–1847.* London: Weidenfeld and Nicolson, 1989.

Malone, Sylvester. *Dr. Edward McGlynn.* New York: Arno Press, 1978.

Mann, Arthur. *Yankee Reformers in the Urban Age: Social Reform in Boston, 1880–1900.* New York: Harper and Row Publishers, 1954.

Marley, Laurence. *Michael Davitt: Freelance Radical and Frondeur.* Dublin: Four Court Press, 2007.

McCaffrey, Lawrence. *The Irish Diaspora in America.* Bloomington: Indiana University Press, 1976.

———. *Textures of Irish America.* Syracuse: Syracuse University Press, 1992.

McCarthy, Donal. "Parnell, Davitt, and the Land Question." In *Famine, Land, and Culture in Ireland*, edited by Carla King, 71–82. Dublin: University College Dublin Press, 2000.

McCarthy, Tara Monica. "True Women, Trade Unionists, and the Lessons of Tammany Hall: Ethnic Identity, Social Reform, and the Political Culture of Irish Women in America, 1880–1923." PhD diss., University of Rochester, 2005.

McDannell, Colleen. "Catholic Domesticity, 1860–1960." In *American Catholic Women: A Historical Explanation*, edited by Karen Kennelly, 48–80. New York: Macmillan, 1989.

———. "Going to the Ladies' Fair: Irish Catholics in New York City, 1870–1900." In *The New York Irish*, edited by Ronald Bayor and Timothy Meagher, 234–51. Baltimore: Johns Hopkins University Press, 1996.

———. "'True men as we need them': Catholicism and the Irish-American Male." *American Studies* 27, no. 2 (1986): 19–36.

McDonald, Grace. *History of the Irish in Wisconsin in the Nineteenth Century*. New York: Arno Press, 1976.

McElroy, Wendy. "Benjamin Tucker, Individualism, and Liberty: Not the Daughter but the Mother of Order." *Literature of Liberty* 4, no. 3 (Autumn 1991): 7–39.

McGarry, Fearghal, and James McConnel, eds. *The Black Hand of Republicanism: Fenianism in Modern Ireland*. Dublin: Irish Academic Press, 2009.

McGee, Owen. *The IRB: The Irish Republican Brotherhood from the Land League to Sinn Féin*. Dublin: Four Courts Press, 2007.

McGreevey, John T. *Catholicism and American Freedom: A History*. New York: W. W. Norton and Company, 2003.

McKivigan, John R. and Thomas J. Robertson. "The Irish American Worker in Transition, 1877–1914." In *The New York Irish*, edited by Ronald H. Bayor and Timothy J. Meagher, 301–20. Baltimore: John Hopkins University Press, 1996.

McManamin, Francis G. *The American Years of John Boyle O'Reilly*. New York: Arno Press, 1976.

McMath, Robert C., Jr. *American Populism: A Social History, 1877–1898*. New York: Hill and Wang, 1993.

McNeil, Laura. "Land, Labor, and Liberation: Michael Davitt and the Irish Question in the Age of British Democratic Reform, 1878–1906." PhD diss., Boston College, 2002.

Meagher, Timothy. *Inventing Irish America: Generation, Class, and Ethnic Identity in a New England City, 1880–1928*. Notre Dame, IN: University of Notre Dame Press, 2001.

———. "'Sweet Mothers and Young Women Out in the World': The Roles of Irish American Women in Late Nineteenth and Early Twentieth Century Worcester, Massachusetts." *US Catholic Historian* 5, nos. 3–4 (1986): 325–44.

Miller, Kerby. "Class, Culture, and Immigrant Group Identity in the United States: The Case of Irish-American Ethnicity." In *Immigration Reconsidered: History, Sociology, and Politics*, edited by Virginia Yans-McLaughlin, 96–129. Oxford: Oxford University Press, 1990.

———. *Emigrants and Exiles: Ireland and the Irish Exodus to North America*. New York: Oxford University Press, 1985.

Mitchel, John. *The Last Conquest of Ireland (Perhaps)*. Dublin: University College Dublin Press, 2005.

Moloney, Deirdre M. *American Catholic Lay Groups and Transatlantic Social Reform in the Progressive Era*. Chapel Hill: University of North Carolina Press, 2002.

———. "Combating 'Whiskey's Work': The Catholic Temperance Movement in Late Nineteenth Century America." *US Catholic Historian* 16, no. 3 (Summer 1998): 1–23.

———. "Land League Activism in Transnational Perspective." *U.S. Catholic Historian* 22, no. 3 (Summer 2004): 61–74.

Montgomery, David. "The Irish and the American Labor Movement." In *America and Ireland, 1776–1976: The American Identity and the Irish Connection*, edited by David Noel Doyle and Owen Dudley Edwards, 205–18. Westport, CT: Greenwood Press, 1980.

———. "Labor and the Republic in Industrial America: 1860–1920." *Le Mouvement social* 111 (April–June 1980): 201–15.

Moody, T. W. *Davitt and Irish Revolution 1846–82*. Oxford: Clarendon Press, 1981.

———. "The New Departure in Irish Politics, 1878–9." In *Essays in British and Irish History in Honour of James Eadie Todd*, edited by H. A. Cronne, T. W. Moody, and D. B. Quinn, 303–33. London: Frederick Muller, 1949.

Moran, Gerard. "'Shovelling Out the Poor': Assisted Emigration from Ireland from the Great Famine to the Fall of Parnell." In *To and From Ireland: Planned Migration Schemes, c. 1600–2000*, edited by Patrick Duffy, 137–54. Dublin: Geography Publications, 2004.

Mulligan, Adrian N. "A Forgotten 'Greater Ireland': The Transatlantic Development of Irish Nationalism." *Scottish Geographical Journal* 118, no. 3 (2002): 219–34.

Murphy, Angela. *American Slavery, Irish Freedom: Abolition, Immigrant Citizenship, and the Transatlantic Movement for Irish Repeal*. Baton Rouge: Louisiana State University Press, 2010.

———. "Daniel O'Connell and the 'American Eagle' in 1845: Slavery, Diplomacy, Nativism, and the Collapse of America's First Irish Nationalist Movement." *Journal of American Ethnic History* 26, no. 2 (2007): 3–26.

Murphy, Maureen. "Bridget and Biddy: Images of the Irish Servant Girl in *Puck* Cartoons, 1880–1890." In *New Perspectives on the Irish Diaspora*, edited by Charles Fanning, 152–75. Carbondale, IL: Southern Illinois Press, 2000.

Neidhart, Wilfried. *Fenianism in North America*. University Park: Pennsylvania State University Press, 1975.

Newsinger, John. *The Fenians in Mid-Victorian Britain*. London: Pluto Press, 1994.

Nolan, Janet. *Servants of the Poor: Teachers and Mobility in Ireland and Irish America*. Notre Dame, IN: University of Notre Dame Press, 2004.

O'Brien, Conor Cruise. *Parnell and His Party, 1880–1890*. Oxford: Oxford University Press, 1974.

———. *States of Ireland*. New York: Vintage Books, 1973.

O'Callaghan, Margaret. *British High Politics and a Nationalist Ireland: Criminality, Land, and the Law under Forster and Balfour*. Cork: Cork University Press, 1994.

O'Connor, John R. "Parnell Visits 'The Ireland of America.'" *The Register of the Kentucky Historical Society* 69, no. 2 (1971): 140–49.

O'Connor, Thomas. *The Boston Irish: A Political History*. Boston: Back Bay Books, 1995.

O'Day, Alan. *Charles Stewart Parnell*. Dundalk, Ireland: Dundalgan Press, 1998.

———. *The English Face of Irish Nationalism: Parnellite Involvement in British Politics, 1880–86*. Dublin: Gill and Macmillan, 1977.

———. "Media and Power: Charles Stewart Parnell's 1880 Mission to North America."

In *Information, Media, and Power through the Ages*, edited by Hiram Morgan, 202–21. Dublin: University College Dublin Press, 2001.

O'Donnell, Edward. "Henry George and the 'New Political Forces': Ethnic Nationalism, Labor Radicalism, and Politics in Gilded Age New York." PhD diss., Columbia University, 1995.

———. "'Though Not an Irishman': Henry George and the American Irish." *American Journal of Economics and Sociology* 56, no. 4 (October 1997): 407–19.

O'Farrell, Patrick. *The Irish in Australia*. Sydney: University of New South Wales Press, 2000.

Ó Gráda, Cormac. *Black '47 and Beyond: The Great Irish Famine in History, Economy, and Memory*. Princeton, NJ: Princeton University Press, 1999.

O'Grady, Joseph Patrick. *Irish-Americans and Anglo-American Relations, 1880–1888*. New York: Arno Press, 1976.

O'Hara, Bernhard. *Davitt*. Castlebar: Mayo County Council, 2006.

O'Hara, M. M. *Chief and Tribune: Parnell and Davitt*. Dublin: Maunsel and Co., 1919.

O'Hare, M. Heanne d'Arc. "The Public Career of Patrick Andrew Collins." PhD diss., Boston College, 1959.

O'Higgins, Rachael. "The Irish Influence in the Chartist Movement." *Past and Present* 20 (November 1961): 83–96.

Painter, Nell Irvin. *Exodusters: Black Migration to Kansas after Reconstruction*. New York: Knopf, 1977.

———. *Standing at Armageddon: The United States, 1877–1919*. New York: W. W. Norton and Company, 1989.

Palmer, Norman Dunbar. *The Irish Land League Crisis*. New Haven, CT: Yale University Press, 1940.

Parnell, Louis A. "Charles Stewart Parnell's Land League Mission to America, January to March 1880." MA thesis, Butler University, 1971.

Phelan, Craig. *Grand Master Workman: Terence Powderly and the Knights of Labor*. Westport, CT: Greenwood Press, 2000.

Pomfret, John. *The Struggle for Land in Ireland 1880–1923*. Princeton, NJ: Princeton University Press, 1930.

Post, Robert. "Charles Stewart Parnell before Congress." *The Quarterly Journal of Speech* 51, no. 4 (December 1965): 419–25.

———. "A Rhetorical Criticism of the Speeches Delivered by Charles Stewart Parnell during his 1880 American Tour." PhD diss., Ohio University, 1961.

Richardson, Heather Cox. *West from Appomattox: The Reconstruction of America after the Civil War*. New Haven, CT: Yale University Press, 2007.

Rodden, John. "'The lever must be applied in Ireland': Marx, Engels, and the Irish Question." *The Review of Politics* 70 (2008): 609–40.

Rodechko, James Paul. "An Irish-American Journalist and Catholicism: Patrick Ford of the Irish World." *Church History* 39, no. 4 (December 1979): 524–40.

———. *Patrick Ford and His Search for America: A Case Study of Irish-American Journalism 1870–1913*. New York: Arno Press, 1976.

Rodgers, Daniel T. *Atlantic Crossings: Social Politics in a Progressive Age.* Cambridge, MA: Belknap Press of Harvard University Press, 1998.

———. "Republicanism: The Career of a Concept." *Journal of American History* 79, no. 1 (June 1992): 11–38.

Roediger, David. *The Wages of Whiteness: Race and the Making of the American Working Class.* New York: Verso, 1991.

Sarbaugh, Timothy. "Exiles of Confidence: The Irish-American Community of San Francisco, 1880–1920." In *From Paddy to Studs: Irish-American Communities in the Turn of the Century Era, 1880 to 1920,* edited by Timothy Meagher, 161–79. Westport, CT: Greenwood Press, 1986.

Saxton, Alexander. *The Indispensable Enemy: Labor and the Anti-Chinese Movement in California.* Berkeley: University of California Press, 1971.

Schneirov, Richard. *Labor and Urban Politics: Class Conflict and the Origins of Modern Liberalism in Chicago, 1864–97.* Urbana: University of Illinois Press, 1998.

Schneller, Beverly. *Anna Parnell's Political Journalism: Contexts and Texts.* Bethesda, MD: Academia Press, 2005.

Scobey, David. "Boycotting the Politics Factory: Labor Radicalism and the New York City Mayoral Election of 1884." [*sic*] *Radical History Review* 28–30 (1984): 280–325.

Shannon, James P. *Catholic Colonization on the Western Frontier.* New Haven, CT: Yale University Press, 1957.

Solow, Barbara Lewis. *The Land Question and the Irish Economy, 1870–1903.* Cambridge, MA: Harvard University Press, 1971.

Steward, Patrick, and Bryan McGovern. *The Fenians: Irish Rebellion in the North Atlantic World, 1858–1876.* Knoxville: University of Tennessee Press, 2013.

Stewart, James Brewer. *Wendell Phillips: Liberty's Hero.* Baton Rouge: Louisiana State University Press, 1986.

Strum, Harvey. "'Not Forgotten in their Affliction': Irish Famine Relief from Rhode Island, 1847." *Rhode Island History* 60, no. 1 (2002): 26–36.

Tax, Meredith. *The Rising of the Women.* New York: Monthly Review Press, 1980.

Taylor, Sabina. "Patrick Ford and His Pursuit of Social Justice." MA thesis, Saint Mary's University, 1993.

Tebrake, Janet. "Irish Peasant Women in Revolt: The Land League Years." *Irish Historical Studies* 33, no. 109 (May 1992): 63–80.

Thernstrom, Stephan. *Poverty and Progress: Social Mobility in a Nineteenth-Century City.* Cambridge, MA: Harvard University Press, 1964.

Thomas, John L. *Alternative America: Henry George, Edward Bellamy, Henry Demarest Lloyd and the Adversary Tradition.* Cambridge, MA: Harvard University Press, 1982.

Thomas, Samuel J. "Portraits of a 'Rebel' Priest: Edward McGlynn in Caricature, 1886–1893." *Journal of American Culture* 7, no. 2 (1987): 19–32.

Thornley, David. *Isaac Butt and Home Rule.* London: Macgibbon and Kee, 1964.

Townend, Paul A. "Between Two Worlds: Irish Nationalists and Imperial Crisis, 1878–1880." *Past and Present* 194 (2007): 139–74.

Turbin, Carole. *Working Women of Collar City: Gender, Class, and Community in Troy, New York, 1864–86.* Urbana: University of Illinois Press, 1992.

Tyrell, Ian. "American Exceptionalism in an Age of International History." *American Historical Review* 96 (October 1991): 1031–51.

Voss, Kim. *The Making of American Exceptionalism: The Knights of Labor and Class Formation in the Nineteenth Century*. Ithaca, NY: Cornell University Press, 1993.

Walker, Cynthia Hyatt. "Banshees, Dogooders, or Undervalued Radicals? Anna Parnell and the Ladies' Land League." MA thesis, Villanova University, 1993.

Walker, Mabel Gregory. *The Fenian Movement*. Colorado Springs, CO: R. Myles, 1969.

Walsh, Francis. "John Boyle O'Reilly, the Boston *Pilot*, and Irish-American Assimilation, 1870–1890." In *Massachusetts in the Gilded Age: Selected Essays*, edited by Jack Tager and John W. Ifkovic, 148–63. Amherst: University of Massachusetts Press, 1985.

Walsh, James P. "The Evolution of the Thesis: The Irish Experience in California Was Different." In *The Irish in the San Francisco Bay Area: Essays on Good Fortune*, edited by Donald Jordan and Timothy J. O'Keefe, 273–92. San Francisco: The Executive Council of the Irish Literary and Historical Society, 2005.

Walsh, James Patrick. "Michael Mooney and the Leadville Irish: Respectability and Resistance at 10,200 Feet, 1875–1900." PhD diss., University of Colorado, 2010.

Walsh, Victor A. "'A Fanatic Heart': The Cause of Irish-American Nationalism in Pittsburgh during the Gilded Age." *Journal of Social History* 15, no. 2 (Winter 1981): 187–204.

———. "Irish Nationalism and Land Reform: The Role of the Irish in America." In *The Irish in America: Emigration, Assimilation, and Impact*, edited by P. J. Drudy, 253–69. Cambridge, MA: Cambridge University Press, 1986.

Ward, Margaret. "The Ladies' Land League and the Irish Land War, 1881/1882: Defining the Relationship between Women and Nation." In *Gendered Nations: Nationalisms and Gender Order in the Long 19th Century*, edited by Ida Blom, Karen Hagemann, and Catherine Hall, 229–47. Oxford: Berg, 2000.

———. *Unmanageable Revolutionaries: Women and Irish Nationalism*. London: Pluto Press, 1995.

Weir, Robert E. *Knights Unhorsed: Internal Conflict in a Gilded Age Social Movement*. Detroit: Wayne State University Press, 2000.

Welter, Barbara. "The Cult of True Womanhood: 1820–1860." *American Quarterly* 18, no. 2 (Summer 1966): 151–74.

Whelan, Kevin. *The Tree of Liberty: Radicalism, Catholicism, and the Construction of Irish Identity, 1760–1830*. Notre Dame, IN: University of Notre Dame Press, 1996.

Whelehan, Niall. *The Dynamiters: Irish Nationalism and Political Violence in the Wider World, 1867–1900*. Cambridge: Cambridge University Press, 2013.

Wilentz, Sean. "Against Exceptionalism: Class Consciousness and the American Labor Movement, 1790–1920." *International Labor and Working Class History* 26 (Fall 1984): 1–24.

———. "Industrializing America and the Irish: Towards the New Departure." *Labor History* 19 (1979): 579–95.

Wilson, David. *United Irishmen, United States: Immigrant Radicals in the Early Republic*. Ithaca, NY: Cornell University Press, 1998.

Yarros, Victor S. "Philosophical Anarchism: Its Rise, Decline, and Eclipse." *American Journal of Sociology* 41, no. 4 (January 1936): 470–83.

Young, Arthur Nichols. *The Single Tax Movement in the United States*. Princeton, NJ: Princeton University Press, 1916.

Index

Page numbers in italics indicate illustrations. The letter "t" following a page number denotes a table.

History of Ireland and the Irish Diaspora